Total Manufacturing Management

Management

Production Organization for the 1990s

Total Manufacturing Management

Production Organization for the 1990s

GIORGIO MERLI

Foreword by Ryuji Fukuda

Productivity Press

Cambridge, Massachusetts and Norwalk, Connecticut

Originally published as *Total Manufacturing Management* © 1987 by ISEDI.

English translation © 1990 Productivity Press.

Productivity Press
P.O. Box 3007
Cambridge, Massachusetts 02140
United States of America
(617) 497-5146 (telephone)
(617) 868-3524 (telefax)

Cover design by Joyce C. Weston
Typeset by Rudra Press
Printed and bound by Arcata Graphics Halliday
Printed in the United States of America
Printed on acid-free paper

Library of Congress Cataloging-in-Publication Data

Merli, Giorgio
    Total manufacturing management. English
    Total manufacturing management: production organization for the 1990s/
        Giorgio Merli; foreword by Ryuji Fukuda.
    Translation of the original Italian with the same title. Includes bibliographical
    reference and index.
    ISBN 0-915299-76-3
    1. Production management. 2. Just-in-time systems.
I. Title.
TS155.M39713 1990   89-43700
658.5 – dc20   CIP

90 91 92 10 9 8 7 6 5 4 3 2 1

Contents

Publisher's Foreword

The 1990s have arrived accompanied by the emergence of three primary world markets: North America, the European Community (EC), and the Pacific Rim. The competitiveness of any company that does not have a stronghold in each of these critical marketplaces will be challenged. Though North America is still the largest of the world markets it cannot afford to stand still. The Pacific Rim has the fastest growth rate of the three. By the year 2000, Naisbitt and Aburdene predict in their *Megatrends 2000* that the GNP of the Pacific Rim will equal North America and surpass the EC. This is largely because the countries of the Pacific Rim have mastered the principles of total manufacturing management, and they are not complacent.

As the EC becomes the new trade Mecca for world class companies, European business managers are beginning to recognize what it will take to compete in a world market — total manufacturing management. The integrated TMM approach described by Giorgio Merli in this book includes the strategic objectives of total quality and continuous improvement and the production organization commitment to just-in-time and stockless production. He mentions as well the integral innovations of participatory management, management by policy, and total cost management.

European corporations have been the last to acknowledge the need for world class manufacturing methods, but they are catching up quickly. The emergence of their domestic marketplace as the second largest in the world has stimulated a tremendous surge of learning and change within business and manufacturing sectors. Merli has been one of the leaders to bring the new methods to European companies. He has benefitted from the American experiments in total quality and just-in-time implementation and from the long-term effectiveness of mature Japanese companies leading the way in quality production methods.

Consultant for the Italian firm Galgano & Associates in affiliation with the Coopers & Lybrand Group, Merli has worked extensively with businesses who understand the importance of total quality manufacturing and continuous improvement. He takes lessons from both Japanese and American innovations in production management. Merli integrates eastern and western perspectives into a competitive strategy and management plan for implementing company-wide quality control and total integrated manufacturing.

Much of the resistance in the West to Japanese manufacturing improvement methods has been based on assumptions of cultural differences. Merli addresses these concerns straightforwardly. He offers a thorough comparison of Western and Japanese management approaches and cultural distinctions. Strategic, organizational, cultural, and managerial revolutions have all taken place in Japanese corporations. They are the reason for impending Pacific Rim leadership in the world marketplace. Merli suggests that their strategic and organizational perspectives are the critical ones for the West to understand. He clarifies for Western managers the methodologies to pay attention to in developing strategies and designing changes in their companies' production organization. The strategic commitment to company-wide quality control and continuous improvement is assumed. Merli spends the first section of the book summarizing the fascinating evolution of management and production systems that have made such a commitment essential.

The second section describes his model for production organization. This is the primary purpose of the book. In the third section he thoroughly delineates and integrates the tools and methods that support this manufacturing model. He lays out the principles and steps for just-in-time, and the tools for effective production organization, including cells, kanban, synchronized and stockless production, total industrial engineering, and total productive maintenance. He also discusses process control, product development, production to order, and supplier relationships.

For ten years Productivity Press has been publishing in-depth books on the tools and methods surveyed in this book. This is the first time we have offered a book that puts them all together. Merli offers a powerfully integrated strategy and implementation plan. Upper managers of manufacturing companies must have the understanding offered by Merli to make sense of the manufacturing revolution that will make or break companies in the emerging world markets.

Any company committed to continuous improvement and total quality and organized for just-in-time and stockless production has the necessary tools for long-term competitive growth. Merli cuts through the cultural alibis and brings to Western managers the critical understanding for competing effectively in the fast changing and challenging global business environment.

We are honored to publish Mr. Merli's book and to be associated with him. Our gratitude extends also to those who helped produce this book: Diane Asay, Marie Cantlon, and Christine Carvajal who shared editorial responsibility; Katie Sweeney in our production department and the people at Rudra Press who, as usual, pulled together a beautiful book; and thanks once again to Joyce Weston for another great cover design.

Norman Bodek
President

Foreword

This book is a text on management written by my friend Giorgio Merli. I met Merli in 1983, as a result of my work. When I think of respect and trust between individuals, I can say that my years of working with him allowed me to understand that, with respect to Italy and Japan, nationality, ethnic distinctions, and distance pose no barriers to friendship. He is a deeply respected friend.

Inasmuch as management techniques constitute "the science of achievement," they should be regarded as reference models, and they should contribute ideas and practical guidelines that promote effective implementation. Insofar as a text on management can reflect these objectives, Giorgio Merli's book, in my opinion, is one of the best. It is admirably suited to this purpose because the book's rationale is based on the author's vast experience. Merli possesses not only an exceptional talent for expressing his ideas, but a keen awareness of how companies should be managed.

If managers and companies are to pursue "evolution" effectively, every participant must understand the proper method of achieving this goal. Evolution can be defined as a situation in which a manager can say yes whenever he asks himself, "Is there anything about my work that has improved since yesterday?"

This book emphasizes both the strategy and organization that are required to effectively ensure evolution, and it offers scientific methods for pursuing this objective. Merli examines the just-in-time principle in relation to the basic strategy of total quality control before he undertakes a more extensive scrutiny of such fundamental concepts as production management, supplier relationships, management scheduling, and balanced planning. Lastly, he explains the principal techniques that are needed for achieving just-in-time production. These techniques consist essentially of appropriate industrial engineering knowledge for preventing waste, reducing set-up time, and, within the domain of plant management, introducing a total productive maintenance system.

Merli also describes in this text a highly innovative technique called *quality function deployment*, which has been developed for defining the crucial elements of product quality, so as to allow subsequent planning and management of an entire quality control system.

The perspective adopted within this text defines values according to total costs, allowing adequate evaluation of ongoing needs for improvement as well as assessment of results.

I am convinced that all these concepts will serve as extremely useful guidelines for managers. As I noted at the beginning of my remarks, books about management present reference models. We define *implementation* as the steps a manager takes to apply these models — to adapt them to specific problems within a company. I encourage readers to approach their own problems with this text at hand. I am convinced that it will be useful not only for Western managers, but for their Japanese counterparts, because sound logic is applicable everywhere.

Ryuji Fukuda
Japan Management Association

Ryuji Fukuda is one of the world's most highly qualified experts in the fields of industrial engineering, stockless production, and quality improvement. After a brilliant career with leading Japanese firms, he is now serving as a consultant to the Japan Management Association and to major firms in Japan and in the West (such as Fiat, Michelin, Philips, Volvo, and SKF).

In 1978, Ryuji Fukuda was honored with the prestigious Japanese award known as the Deming Prize for his contributions in the field of productivity and quality improvement. He is the author of numerous publications pertaining to production management. These works include the book Managerial Engineering, *which has been highly successful in the United States. Ryuji Fukuda also teaches courses in quality assurance at the University of Kobe.*

Preface

Books and articles about Just-In-Time (JIT) methods are extremely numerous today, and their abundance seems to indicate the level of interest in this topic. In my opinion, however, this interest is not yet accompanied by sufficiently practical application. How can this be true, since we are continuing to discuss these methods so extensively?

My own answer is that many managers understand the significant impact of these techniques, so they wish to learn and read about them, but they fail to grasp their essence clearly. This situation probably arises from a fundamental misconception: just-in-time is often regarded as just another way of planning production (scheduling and dispatching). Responsibility for understanding it thoroughly has been entrusted to specialists in production planning and materials management. They have performed their duties well, by interpreting, describing, and comparing these new techniques with familiar ones, but they obviously have confined the just-in-time techniques to the domain of inventory control problems.

Extrapolating broad managerial perspectives from these technical descriptions is not an easy task. This is one of the reasons it has been difficult to move such topics to a more appropriate level of discussion — the realm of industrial strategy. Although just-in-time can be defined as merely a production management system if only its technical aspects are considered, its underlying rationale arises from a new vision of corporate strategy — time-based strategy in which direct linkage of production to markets is regarded as one of the most important factors in business.

Among the strong points of this strategy are the possibilities for obtaining sharp reductions (as much as 90 percent) in the time required to fill orders, eliminating the need for warehouses, increasing manufacturing productivity by 20 to 30 percent, increasing manufacturing flexibility by more than 50 percent, and even allowing inexpensive production of small lots. It is worth remembering that, at Toyota, this system was introduced with an extremely precise strategic objective: to enable the company to produce limited quantities of many different automobile models inexpensively.

With regard to the last of the advantages listed, I find it particularly unfortunate that many Western managers believe that just-in-time systems are suitable for very repetitive production, but not for "made-to-order," or custom-order, production (specific products for specific clients). Although this opinion may be correct with regard to the number of just-in-time techniques that can be applied to custom-order runs, the benefits that can be obtained by applying some of them (for example, curves for manufacturing costs) are, in my experience, even greater for custom production than those for mass production.

The purpose of this book is to correct these fundamental misconceptions by explaining just-in-time techniques in relation to industrial strategy and total organizational models, with examples of their applicability even to production categories that have received relatively little emphasis thus far.

The title *Total Manufacturing Management* is actually intended to summarize the following message: "The just-in-time concept is merely a technical aspect of a far more complex organizational model in which production management is perceived as a comprehensive, integrated activity, unlike the fragmentary and mechanistic concepts embodied in earlier models, which were oriented solely toward efficiency in production."

I wish to point out that the concepts presented in this book are derived from the research and experience of the entire team of experts affiliated with Alberto Galgano & Associati, a management consulting firm in which I am one of the partners. I have also relied extensively upon significant "lessons" imparted by Ryuji Fukuda, with whom I have worked on many occasions, and by Ichiro Miyauchi of the Japanese Union of Scientists and Engineers (JUSE), who has provided assistance to Galgano in the field of companywide quality control for several years.

Many of the examples cited in the book pertain to projects that have been completed or are being completed for Galgano client companies. I want to thank the boards of directors of these companies for allowing me to publish data pertaining to their firms. With respect to the American edition, I wish to express special appreciation to Robert Hall (who persuaded me to pursue this endeavor), and to William Wheeler and Patrick McHugh of Coopers & Lybrand, who provided me with basic know-how for the chapter on total business integration.

Introduction

Changes Occurring in the World of Manufacturing

The 1980s will be remembered as a period of major changes in Western manufacturing. Some might even call these changes a manufacturing revolution. Certain principles that have been fundamental to industrial management since its inception now appear to be wholly out of favor, and companies are transforming their strategic priorities.

Some eminent victims have been sacrificed on the altar of this revolution. Even *profits,* which have long been a strategic priority, and *efficiency* in production, which has been an operational priority, are increasingly regarded as derivative rather than primary priorities for companies. These modifications in priorities are consequences of extensive changes in the economic and social context within which firms must operate. As Theodore Levitt of the Harvard Business School has stated, "The term *profits,* when it is used to indicate the objective of a company, is devoid of meaning. If it is not actually possible to rely upon a sufficient number of stable clients, there is no company, nor do profits exist."

Manpower efficiency as an operational priority has suffered a similar fate. Its importance has even become marginal in many instances. In most manufacturing firms, costs for directly supervised labor at "assigned" times currently represent less than ten percent of total operating costs. These changes appear to be very significant when we realize that our managerial culture has been accustomed to regarding short-term profits as the most important objective for companies, and efficient use of operating resources has been perceived as the most important operational factor.

A more comprehensive analysis suggests that the revolution taking place is actually composed of four "subrevolutions":

- A revolution in *strategy*
- A revolution in *organization*
- A *cultural* revolution
- A revolution in *management*

Certain terms generated by this revolution are already being widely used in management publications, and they serve as helpful reference points in the effort to express relatively complex concepts. *Companywide quality control* and *time-based strategy* are often used in relation to the revolution in strategy. For the revolution in organization, *just-in-time* and *stockless production* are often invoked, while *participatory management* and *management by policy* are frequently associated with the cultural revolution. *Total cost management* is often used in relation to the revolution in management.

One of the objectives of this book is to explore the content of the so-called revolution in organization. Its links to the other revolutions will not be overlooked, however, because all of them belong to the same matrix and because their origin is the same.

With respect to the "total quality" revolution in strategy, the introductory summary that follows presents certain principles that are indispensable for understanding concepts discussed in subsequent sections of the book. In-depth explanations of these principles are provided in Chapter 1 ("The Strategic Approach") and in Chapter 6 ("Emerging Strategies").

The Total Quality Revolution

The dramatic changes taking place in industrial strategy throughout the world have a clearly definable source: the successes achieved by the Japanese. However, it was not until the reason that had long been invoked to explain these successes — low labor costs — began to appear less convincing that the Western world was able to see that one of the strengths of Japanese industry was a different concept of corporate strategy. This difference pertains not only to priorities, but to the horizon established for managing a company.

The operational priority in Japanese corporate strategy is *quality*, instead of efficiency, and the operating horizon encompasses a period longer than the three to five years typically envisioned by conventional Western companies. The fundamental entrepreneurial principle in the Japanese strategy is *survival* (in other words, consolidated occupational levels), instead of maximizing profits.

This revolutionary outlook is inspired more by social considerations and by the goal of long-term gains than by speculative considerations, or short-term profit. Although the entrepreneurial need for profits is fundamental, profits are regarded as a reward for a firm's success, instead of being a high-priority objective.

This orientation toward values that are more profound than mere economic and financial objectives is derived from an ethical view of the company that maintains, in contrast to prevailing concepts in the West, that a company whose perspectives allow exploitation of fellow human beings cannot achieve long-term success. According to a Taylorist outlook, the success of manufacturing firms was derived from the "inevitable" exploitation of others, who serve in one of three roles:

- The client, who must be exploited if a company is to earn profits
- The supplier, who must be "squeezed" as much as possible
- The employee, who must be "used" to the allowable limit

The new strategy depends on opposite assumptions, each of which serves as a fulcrum that provides leverage for implementing other important principles, including the following:

- Clients must be satisfied to the greatest possible extent, in order to ensure survival of the firm and a chance to earn profits.
- Suppliers are esteemed partners who are essential for the firm's success. They must be treated as such, rather than as adversaries.
- Employees are not merely suppliers of labor according to contracts whose basis is entirely economic. Employees *are* the company.

This strategic approach is known as companywide quality control (CWQC). Motivated by considerations linked to timeliness, economic appropriateness, and actual conditions, as distinguished from ethical considerations, Western industry is quickly adopting CWQC as a strategy. After the first "conversions" during the period from 1975 to 1978 in manufacturing sectors that were the first to experience the impact of Japanese competition (initially the electronics industry, and then the automobile industry), the transformation or revolution in strategy spread rapidly, and today it is affecting the entire manufacturing sector in Western nations.

The emergence of survival and socio-occupational goals as priorities for the wealthy in the West has decisively influenced this conversion. Ronald Reagan's October 1984 appeal for "quality months," which was intended to promote adoption of a quality strategy by American firms, along with a similar appeal by Margaret Thatcher in May 1983, and the "Quality Train" that was organized in June 1985 to promote this strategy in France can be considered symptomatic. For many Western firms, strategic reorientation has become official with the introduction of corporate policy concepts that specifically embody a philosophy of quality.

This phenomenon is expanding vigorously and is transcending the limits and meanings associated with the business world. Quality will become the key factor for the 1990s and will dominate industry during its mature phase, just as efficiency characterized its developmental phase. Our maxim for the years ahead may be "...from a civilization based on quantity and efficiency to a civilization based on quality — in products, services, and life."

The Revolution in Organization

The content of the organizational revolution in manufacturing is the main topic of this book, and we will therefore be studying it closely. In this introductory section, we consider some results that have been obtained by using these techniques in industry.

Since Japanese industry introduced this new organization model, the results obtained in Japan have been astonishing, and new advances are being cited in the press daily. Recall some of the successes that produced the most striking impressions several years ago:

- *Toyota*: just two hours of "inventory" between departments; just five days for filling orders
- *Suzuki*: a 144-cycle annual turnover for manufacturing inventory
- *Construction materials industry*: production time reduced to one-half the Western industry average
- *Electronic components*: level of manufacturing defects measured in i.p.t. (items per trillion components produced)

What was happening in Western industry in the meantime? Until the end of the 1970s, many Western managers believed that matching Japan's productivity would be practically impossible. Many also believed that just-in-time techniques could not even be applied in Western companies. These opinions arose from yet another misconception: that Japanese industry's high productivity was almost entirely dependent on favorable conditions that were neither available nor reproducible in Western nations, namely:

- Low labor costs
- High number of working hours per employee
- Favorable attitudes among workers
- Reliable and punctual suppliers

For a certain period of time, these four factors constituted "alibis" for Western management, which considered it unnecessary to gain thorough knowledge of Japanese organization models. The superficiality and tenacity of this outlook is demonstrated by the belief of some executives even today, for example, that Japanese labor costs less than Western labor. Now that these alibis are being wholly or partially refuted by facts and data, we can see clearly that superficial notions and arrogance were the true reasons for the "organization gap" that emerged in relation to the Japanese.

As Lee Iacocca observed with respect to the automobile industry in the United States, "Arrogance on the part of the leading firms caused us to be short-sighted about the Japanese phenomenon." The prevailing opinion was that "It will come to an end for them, too," as soon as a state of well-being emerged. This outcome did not materialize, however. After ameliorating their harsh working conditions, attaining higher salaries, and improving their living standards, the Japanese continue to be more productive than we are. Facts have demolished all of the alibis:

- For leading Japanese firms (contracts are adopted by individual companies, instead of on a nationwide basis), labor costs are higher than for Italian firms (in 1984, the ratio for salaries was already 14 to 9).
- Salaries of Japanese office managers are at least 50 percent higher than for their Italian counterparts.
- By 1986, per capita income in Japan had already reached $17,000, the same level as in the United States — in contrast to $8,880 in Italy (*Economist*, 25 October, 1986).

- For Japanese workers, between 5 and 10 percent of work time is allocated to training. Thus, in relation to Western nations, the actual difference in the average number of working hours is considerably less than official data may indicate.

With regard to the "cultural" alibi — attitudes among the labor force — many clues suggest that differences are more attributable to style (the methods that managers employ to motivate employees) than to workers' attitudes. Encouragement of employee participation "in the Japanese way" has been shown to be highly reproducible in Western firms where more participatory management methods have been introduced.

The experiences of Quasar (Motorola) have attracted considerable attention because this firm was one of the first to implement the Japanese model. In 1976, the firm's Chicago plant, which manufactured televisions, was purchased by the Japanese firm Matsushita. Within two years, and with the same full-time work force, Matsushita succeeded in doubling output, while achieving a 20-fold increase in product quality and a 16-fold reduction in costs for warranty service. The qualitative results were all the more astounding because they were so closely linked to the human factor. During this same period, the average defect rate for television manufacturing operations among Western firms approached 160 percent (160 defects to be remedied during the manufacturing process, for an output of 100 television sets). With its 20-fold reduction (to 8 percent), Quasar had attained quality levels comparable to those of Japanese firms, thereby demonstrating that it is possible to develop positive attitudes among Western workers. (In this particular instance, the workers were women.)

By now, situations of this kind have become relatively common. For example, the Toyota-General Motors plant in Fremont, which is managed according to Japanese methods and is not highly automated, is twice as productive as other General Motors plants, and the level of product quality is decisively higher.

The feasibility of constructive participation by workers, even in the context of Western manufacturing, has now been demonstrated by the proliferation of quality circles in every Western nation.

With regard to the fourth alibi — relationships with suppliers — experiences in both Japan and numerous Western nations have demonstrated that the existing "culture" is largely a consequence of the system in use. Many Western firms have discovered, for example, that "marriage with the supplier is beautiful"; they have been able to obtain just-in-time service (delivery in small lots, only when goods are needed, with guaranteed quality, etc.), and this has enabled them to sharply reduce the number of regular suppliers.

Western industry has understood the Japanese lesson, and it is making vigorous efforts to close the productivity and quality gaps. It has launched its own revolution in organization, and the first significant results are being obtained. The United States was the first nation to respond to the Japanese challenge, because American industry was the first to be directly confronted by the productivity and quality levels achieved by Japanese industry. The following results of adopting Japanese industrial practices in the United States were announced in the September-October 1985 issue of the *Harvard Business Review*:

- General Motors, which has been using kanban since 1980, has cut annual inventory costs from $8 million to $2 million. At the firm's pilot plant, the annual inventory turnover rate increased from 22 cycles (1982) to nearly 100.
- With kanban, Alfa-Laval (Sweden) has been able to reduce throughput time from 40 weeks to 8 weeks.
- American Motors has reduced average inventory levels from six days to less than one day, and Chrysler has obtained similar results.
- General Electric, Westinghouse, and RCA have reported similar or better results.

A survey conducted in the United States and published in the October 1984 *Forbes* found that American firms that had applied Japanese just-in-time methods had typically obtained the following results:

- 90 percent reduction in lead time ("throughput" time)
- 90 percent reduction in work-in-process (production delays)
- 10 to 30 percent reduction in manufacturing costs
- 75 percent reduction in setup time (time required for changes in production)
- 50 percent reduction in space requirements for manufacturing

The Computer System division of Hewlett-Packard provides some particularly interesting U.S. results, which are summarized in

Figure A. They are of special interest because, although Hewlett-Packard is a leader in use of electronic data-processing systems, the firm chose to adopt simple Japanese visual control systems for manufacturing operations. Harley-Davidson and AT&T have obtained the results shown in Figures B and C, respectively.

Improved Features	From	To	% Improvement
Printed circuits	$675,000	$190,000	72%
Increase in productivity (Standard hours)	87 hours	39 hours	55%
Level of defects:			
• Welding defects	5,000 ppm	100 ppm	98%
• Rejected items	$80,000	$5,000	94%
Required space for production	1,030 square meters	696 square meters	33%
Production time (lead time)	15 days	1.5 days	90%

Figure A. **Hewlett-Packard's Results (Computer Systems Division) after Introducing Total Quality Control and Just-In-Time (1984)**

- 49 percent overall productivity increases
- 75 percent overall setup reduction
- Inventory turns up from 5 to 20
- 60 percent reduction in WIP and raw material
- 65 percent decrease in scrap and rework
- 35 percent decrease in warranty costs
- 35 percent reduction in warehouse space
- 26 percent reduction in plant space
- 50 percent fewer suppliers

*Source: Target Magazine, AME, Spring 1989

Figure B. JIT Results at Harley-Davidson*

	1986	1988
Annual inventory turns	3	80
Shipping performance	44%	94%
Quality assurance (% defects)	2%	0.44%
Cost of quality	9%	2%
Yield — first test	80%	96%
Output versus Investment:	% of factory output	% of factory investment
JIT I Line	15%	1%
JIT III Line	29%	2%

*Source: Target Magazine, AME, Spring 1989

Figure C. Results of the AT&T JIT Journey*

Elettroconduttore, a manufacturer of electrical switches in Milan, was one of the first firms in Europe to apply a JIT system in the context of participatory management, with the following results:

• Reduction of manufacturing lead time from 40 work days to three work days
• Elimination of the warehouse for standard finished products
• Reduction of work-in-process from days to hours
• Reduction of inexpensive lots from tens of thousands of items to tens

Another interesting situation, one that does not involve mass production, is the example offered by AGIE in Lausanne, Switzerland. This firm manufactures equipment for spark machining. In this particular instance, it was possible to obtain the following results after introducing JIT on a trial basis for one product line for just six months:

• Throughput time reduced by 80 percent
• Work-in-process reduced by 55 percent
• Productivity increased by 20 percent
• Required time for return on investments is seven to eight months

At the present time, one can cite significant experiences within practically every sector in Europe. Some examples of interesting results include:

- Olivetti (typewriter production): throughput time reduced from 20 days to three days
- Michelin (steel cord): setup time reduced by 90 percent
- Uno a Erre (world leader in gold jewelry): production lead time reduced by 90 percent
- Fiat Aviazione (parts for aircraft engines): lead time reduced by 50 percent
- Farmitalia Carlo Erba (pharmaceuticals): WIP reduced by 60 percent
- Lever Industriale (detergents): working capital reduced by 50 percent
- Innocenti S. Eustachio (manufacturing equipment): lead time reduced by 30 percent
- Europa Metalli (a world leader in non-ferrous metals): setup reduced by 70 percent

JIT techniques are therefore being applied to certain areas of production formerly considered unlikely to benefit from these innovations, such as production "to order" (a specific product for a specific client) and processing industries (chemicals, pharmaceuticals, metals, paper, etc.). Throughout this book, one will encounter some of the interesting opportunities that JIT offers in these areas of production.

It is significant that, in Japan, JIT did not originate in mass production. It developed within the shipbuilding industry, where production by order is typical and where it is necessary to achieve cooperation with suppliers — such as iron and steel producers — who are considered relatively difficult when it comes to persuading them to adopt JIT methods.

Total Manufacturing Management

Production Organization for the 1990s

Part I

Lessons From Japan

1

The Strategic Approach

The model that is being adopted in the ongoing revolution has been described as being largely of Japanese origin. Upon discovering that it must start adopting the strategic and structural modifications discussed in the Introduction, Western industry began to promote various means of educating itself about the Japanese organization model. Between 1975 and 1980, universities, certain leading research institutions, and management experts in the United States allocated substantial resources to acceleration of the learning process. Westerners paid many visits to Japanese firms during that period.

These efforts have provided some reasonably detailed snapshots of the current situation in Japan. The information provided by these brief exposures to the Japanese model encouraged development of the Western organization model, which will be presented in the second section of this book.

In the following pages, we will provide a portrait of the Japanese manufacturing system, highlighting the principal differences between the Japanese and the Western models, using a qualitative approach (principles and models). Only a comprehensive "helicopter overview" of this kind can provide enough information to enable managers to effectively interpret the Japanese model.

The Cultural and Organizational Context

Before proceeding with analysis of the organization strategy for Japanese firms, it is appropriate to describe the context in which this model developed, with particular emphasis on the principal differences between the Japanese and the Western contexts. These differences are partially derived from Japan's cultural and social foundations, but they are partially the consequence of the organization models that

3

Cultural Characteristics	
Western World	***Japan***
— Continuous confrontation with the external environment	— Continuous adaptation to the external environment
— Christianity, based upon moral values and redemption of the soul	— Buddhism and Shintoism, which are based upon how to avoid worries and anxiety
— Orientation toward the future and the abstract	— Orientation toward the present and the tangible
— People seek a "reason" for living	— People wonder "how" to live
— Companies are based upon legally prescribed relationships	— Companies are based upon direct personal relationships
— Orientations are individual	— Orientations are collective
— Behavior is controlled by rules	— Behavior is controlled by groups and by a sense of duty
— A person's social level provides identification	— A person's company provides identification
— Weak hierarchical structures and contractual relationships	— Strong hierarchical structures and personal relationships
— Relationships in industry are based upon rights and duties	— Relationships in industry are based upon mutual respect and interdependence
— Education is oriented toward personal growth and independence	— Education is oriented toward cooperation and dependence
— The most cherished value: personal freedom	— The most cherished value: security

Management	
— Frequent changing of top managers	— Infrequent changes at the top
— Individual success, measured on a short-term basis	— Group success, measured on a long-term basis
— Authoritarianism and control	— Paternalism and obligation
— Individual decisions	— Group decisions
— *Top-down* communication without detours	— *Top-down* and *bottom-up* communication with detours
— Conflictive relationships between superiors and subordinates	— Cooperation between superiors and subordinates
— Obvious differences in *"look"* according to levels	— No differences in *"look"*

Personnel	
— Clear separation between work and private life	— Life is strongly company-centered
— Company training without examinations	— Company training with examinations
— Limited rotation of positions	— Frequent rotation of positions
— Passive attitudes	— Active attitudes
— Competition among individuals	— Competition among groups
— Temporary relationships	— "Marriage" for life

Organization	
— Precise boundaries for functions	— Boundaries not precisely delineated
— Job descriptions and levels	— No job descriptions or levels
— Emphasis upon functions	— Emphasis upon roles
— Sharp demarcation between line and staff	— Substantial cohesion between line and staff
— Strong staff	— Weak staff
— Orientation toward limited problems in terms of functions	— Orientation toward multiple interfunctional problems
— Employees supply labor	— Employees are the company
— Management by rules	— Management by consensus

Rewards	
— Results attributed to individuals	— Results attributed to groups
— Age and duration of employment are of limited significance	— Age and duration of employment are criteria for remuneration and promotions
— Remuneration is not heavily dependent upon company performance	— Remuneration (bonuses) is heavily dependent upon company performance

Business Philsophy	
— Immediate (short-term) profits	— Continuity (long-term)
— Short-term dividends	— Long-term investments
— Orientation toward "inventions"	— Orientation toward continuous innovation
— Independence from suppliers	— Cooperation with suppliers
— Emphasis upon results	— Emphasis upon efforts

Industrial Culture	
— Limited orientation toward manufacturing development *(invention oriented)*	— Favorable orientation toward manufacturing development *(process innovation oriented)*
— Great leaps	— Incremental improvements
— "Product out"	— "Market in"
— Inspection oriented	— Process control oriented
— *"Milk-cow"* attitude	— Cost cutting attitude
— Brief decision-making periods	— Protracted decision-making periods
— Protracted implementation periods	— Brief implementation periods
— High-risk projects	— Low-risk projects
— High development costs	— High manufacturing development costs
— Orientation toward unit margins	— Orientation toward high volume
— Implementation according to "directions"	— Implementation according to consensus

Figure 1-1. Comparison of Western and Japanese Cultural and Business Characteristics

have arisen. Awareness of these factors can enhance our understanding of both models. Figure 1-1 summarizes some of these cultural and managerial differences.

Companywide Quality Control

In order to understand the differences between Japanese and Western organization strategies, we need an overview of the entrepreneurial logic that has enabled Japanese industry to develop the strategy known as *Companywide Quality Control* (CWQC). This logic consists of ten major premises.

Quality Strategy

1. The *customer*, without whom companies cannot exist, constitutes a firm's highest priority. In other words, the customer is the essential condition for ensuring *survival* of a company.
2. The most important type of customer is a *reliable customer*, namely, a customer who buys repeatedly from the same company. Sales volume obtained from repeat customers is much more dependable (in terms of survival) than sales volume obtained from occasional customers.
3. A customer becomes reliable — buys again — if he or she is satisfied with prior purchases. Thus, *customer satisfaction* must be the firm's highest operational priority.
4. Sales volume is an indicator of customer satisfaction, and *profits are the reward.*
5. Customer satisfaction is obtained by providing *high quality* goods and services. The quality of the items that have been purchased in the past influences a customer most strongly when the next purchase is to be made. (Price is an important factor for winning new customers, however.)
6. In order to ensure customer loyalty, customer satisfaction must be renewed with each successive purchase. This cannot be achieved by merely providing high quality and keeping it at a constant level for an extended period. Satisfaction presupposes *improvement*. *Continuous improvement* of

goods and services is the only way to ensure a high level of customer satisfaction, so as to influence the customer favorably for the next purchase.

7. The quality of the goods and services being supplied is entirely the result of processes initiated by a company in order to produce these goods and services. *Product quality is the result of process quality.*

8. Continuous improvement of products requires *continuous improvement of company processes.* Hoping to obtain qualitative improvement of products by means of closer control is a method that is not entrepreneurially valid, because it is in conflict with cost control. "Higher quality = higher costs" was actually a postulate of the earlier company model, in which quality was regarded as a factor that could be controlled by inspection procedures *approval.*

9. In order to obtain continuous, significant improvement in a company's functioning, the *maximum quantity of company resources* must be activated. *Maximum involvement* is essential for improvement from within.

10. Mobilizing a large number of employees will not, by itself, ensure improvement. A company must *organize* the improvement activity, and must *train* employees for the *new skills that are required for improvement* (policy deployment, problem identification, problem solving).

The Japanese Union of Scientists and Engineers (JUSE) has provided another way of defining CWQC. They offer 11 points representing "ways of thinking" that should be introduced within a firm. This is a cultural approach that emphasizes the concept that CWQC is essentially a "people-building" mechanism.

1. *Put product quality first.* Everyone within a firm must be aware that quality is more important than any other objective of the firm, including costs and service.

2. *Cultivate market-in.* The market must be brought into the company. The quality characteristics of the company's product or service must be recognized and pursued by everyone within the company, to the extent that these characteristics are compatible with the goal of customer satisfaction.

Principles	Operational Consequences
First Principle One principal and fundamental motivation, namely customer satisfaction, must guide employees at all levels. Customer satisfaction is the company's highest priority.	Management must transmit this value to the entire work force in a highly convincing way.
Second Principle The company's fundamental process is improvement of quality and, as a result, improvement of the level of customer satisfaction. Every employee must be involved in this process, which shall occur in an ongoing and unlimited way.	Having found that the *quality improvement* process allows improved productivity, Japanese firms use quality as a way of boosting productivity.
Third Principle Quality control methods and techniques, which must be applied by the entire work force, are the fundamental way to improve quality.	Among all of the business resources offered by American culture, the Japanese have chosen statistics, because, in their opinion, it is the most important in a company's quest for excellence *("statistical thinking")*.
Fourth Principle Activities in terms of providing knowledge and training concerning quality control techniques must be precisely defined and continuous, and they must involve all of the firm's employees.	Training is a large-scale endeavor that must be precisely planned. The most advanced techniques must be used whenever necessary.
Fifth Principle A company's management, namely, its highest executives, must exercise leadership with respect to its mechanisms for achieving quality, and they must provide coordination in terms of the company considered as a whole.	Management must define policies and goals in terms of quality. It must plan activities and provide organizational coordination.

Figure 1-2. The Five CWQC Principles

Contrasting Principles in Western Companies	Slogans
Profits and establishment of pecuniary incentives are priority motivations.	"The customer is the king." "Quality first, not profits." "The downstream department or division is your customer."
Quality has a cost, and the optimum equilibrium must be pursued. There are limits to quality. Productivity and quality are conflicting objectives.	"Do the right thing the first time." "Productivity through quality." "Avoid placing blame upon others."
Knowledge of quality control methods and techniques should be the specialized domain of a small number of persons within the firm. Executives do not share awareness of the fundamental importance of these techniques for the firm's success.	"Analyze data and use facts when you speak." "Apply the seven tools." "Apply the PDCA *(Plan-Do-Check-Action)* process." "Emphasize a few important factors, and disregard the many unimportant factors."
Training in quality control techniques should be limited to quality specialists. A gap emerges between persons responsible for quality and those who are responsible for production.	"Total quality control begins with training, and it ends with training." *"Many* small brains used properly are better than *a few* large brains."
A firm's management is only marginally involved with quality. Quality mechanisms within various sectors of a company are not properly coordinated.	"Apply management by policies." "Decisions from the bottom up, instead of from the top down." "Quality audits must be a permanent activity."

3. *Treat downstream departments and divisions as customers.* Customer satisfaction must be pursued by developing a network of "suppliers" and "customers" within the company. Their relations should be defined by the effort of each department or division to satisfy its own customers (downstream departments and divisions).

4. *Focus on the vital few.* Everyone should concentrate on a few important factors and disregard the numerous factors that are of little importance (the "trivial many").

5. *Control by facts and data.* Everyone must learn to abandon the habit of spewing directives and rendering opinions willy-nilly. Facts and data should govern decisions and actions. Anything else is a waste of time.

6. *Apply in-process control.* Control must be applied during processes. Companies must control, manage, and upgrade operating processes, instead of controlling quality in the final product ("counting inanimate objects").

7. *Aim for standardization.* A high level of reproducibility must be established for the operating conditions that have been defined as most favorable. This requires standardization, namely consolidation, or systematic organization.

8. *Conduct dissemination control.* The reliability of procedures must be continuously improved. This means that statistical analyses of their effects and results must be conducted continuously, and these records must be communicated to all the appropriate people.

9. *Practice upstream function control.* Before starting production, it is always necessary to ensure that requirements for customer satisfaction are being fulfilled. This process may involve modification of policies, strategies, and plans, but it will enable a company to avoid launching production ventures that are doomed.

10. *Use statistical methods.* Everyone should use available statistical resources in making their contributions to improvement. In other words, they should develop the habit of statistical thinking.

11. *Institute Q.C. circle activities.* Quality circles are essential for introducing this model, and they should be applied within every sector of a firm.

Figure 1-2 presents another way of envisioning this strategy — one that contrasts Western operating principles with five basic CWQC principles, their operational consequences, and their associated support slogans.

Kaizen

As a direct consequence of the CWQC strategy and large-scale *participation* by employees, the activities of Japanese firms have a powerful *continuous improvement* dimension. In Japan, this participation concept is expressed by the term *kaizen.**

This participatory dimension is not entirely new; certain Western authors had already formulated it before it developed in Japan. Likert's participatory management is one example, but kaizen is more strongly oriented toward continuous improvement than toward management. This feature and the methods and techniques that have been developed for achieving continuous improvement represent innovations.

Training and mobilizing employees of Japanese firms for total quality has developed according to the phases indicated within Figure 1-3.

As the figure suggests, the CWQC model developed in relation to continuous cultural evolution. On the other hand, this type of development, which affected companies' structural characteristics at the same time, is not clearly indicated by chronological presentation of this kind, even though the development was directly associated with the events being cited.

Indeed, the structure of Japanese companies developed according to participatory management models. This phenomenon means that, in Japanese companies, there is actually significant delegation of authority to lower levels, and that decisions are made by spontaneously formed groups of persons who are directly involved. This fact has led Japanese executives to regard a group approach to problem solving as natural, and systematic organization according to project groups (which the Western model requires, as we shall explain presently) as superfluous. As a result of the automatic organization of executives in relation to problems in the kaizen model, improvement

---

* Masaaki Imai, *Kaizen*, Random House, New York, 1986.

1949 The low quality of Japanese products generates interest in quality control of a statistical type.

1950 The American expert W. B. Deming gives seminars on statistical quality control techniques.

1951 The first nationwide quality control conference takes place, and the Deming Prize (an award for quality) for companies is established.

1953 Companies begin to provide quality control training for middle management and workers (more than 30 years ago).

1954 J. M. Juran, an American expert on quality, arrives in Japan for a series of lectures.

1956 Radio broadcasts pertaining to quality control are introduced under the sponsorship of the JUSE. The earliest experiments in applying CWQC begin.

1960 Quality Month is proclaimed on a nationwide level. Television broadcasts are introduced. The JUSE publishes a book entitled *Quality and Middle Management*, and more than 500,000 copies have been sold thus far.

1961 CWQC has been fully delineated and is gradually being adopted by leading Japanese firms.

1962 The periodical *Gemba to Q.C.* ("quality control for middle management") is introduced, and it begins to promote the concept of quality circles. The forerunner of a national quality circles organization is established, and it accepts the first member quality circle in May.

1963 There are 10,000 quality circles in Japan that are registered with the JUSE. Two years later, there are 20,000; by 1970, there are 30,000; and by 1971, there are 40,000.

1964 Earliest Policy Deployment *(Komatsu)* applications.

1965 Announcement of introduction of a "management by policy" system at Bridgestone.

1968 The first Japanese quality circle visits the United States, and a series of conferences takes place.

1970 The JUSE launches a series of publications concerning establishment of quality circles.

1971 CWQC has gained full acceptance and has been extensively adopted while continuing to expand rapidly among all of the leading Japanese firms.

1980 There are 1 million active quality circles in Japan (nearly 10 million members).

1983 Development of the MBP System (Toyota, Nippon Steel, NEC).

1985 The quality strategy has been decisively adopted within the principal Japanese firms. By the end of the 1970s, JUSE has already begun to promote the new approach for small firms. Even trading companies and those which provide services, as well as the banking sector, have introduced the new approach. Japanese companies are using the same approach in companies they have established or acquired in the United States, Europe, Asia, and Australia.

1987 Use of second-generation policy deployment methods (Sumitomo, Sony, Mitsubishi Heavy Industries).

Figure 1-3. Development of CWQC in Japan

programs are directly included in operational management (*control by policies*). Nevertheless, for the bottom level, namely, workers and supervisory personnel, Japan has developed a specific mechanism: *quality circles*.

Quality Circles

Within the mode of organization developed by Japanese industry for promoting improvement, quality circles are a vital ingredient. Nevertheless, Westerners have probably overestimated their importance, because they have not fully understood that quality circles are merely the tip of an iceberg. Indeed, they represent the smallest visible portion of a far more extensive phenomenon. The most important aspects are not observable because they are interwoven with companies' control and management systems.

Although one should consult the vast body of literature that already exists in order to investigate specific aspects of quality circles, the following overview of their structural features may be useful at this point.

Definition and Objectives

A quality circle can be defined as a group of workers or employees who meet voluntarily and regularly to identify, analyze, and solve problems pertaining to their own work. The principal objectives pursued through quality circle activities are:

- Improvement of a company's processes
- Improvement of communication, especially between the lower levels and executives
- Improvement of occupational qualifications and upgrading of individuals' skills
- Improvement of employees' motivation

Conditions for Participation

Participation in quality circles is entirely voluntary. Topics are chosen in a free and autonomous manner. (Usually, members are asked to refrain only from discussing such topics as hiring, dismissals, salaries, and assignments.) Whenever problems with participation exist as a result of the functioning of the technological process, activities take place outside working hours. The standard commitment is usually two hours per month per employee.

In most instances, substantial direct monetary compensation for participation in quality circles is not offered. On the other hand, bonuses or other tangible forms of compensation may exist, but the scale is usually very limited. More often, the rewards are indirect. The most significant reward is the satisfaction that members of a quality circle receive from exercising an active and decisive role in solving problems and from observing that proposed solutions are implemented, with the expected positive results. Another significant indirect reward is the satisfaction quality circles gain from submitting their own plans directly to their superiors.

Organization and Structure

Quality circles consist of four to ten persons who share the same work area. The composition of the circle generally remains over time (except for voluntary departures). Coordination of the group is entrusted to a *leader*. The circle leader is usually the direct supervisor of the group members' work area, or is a worker elected by the group members. Sometimes participation in quality circles and coordination of their activities within a company is entrusted to *facilitators*. (This practice is common in Western QC programs.) Facilitators may be given responsibility for managing training programs for participants and for solving organizational and operational problems.

Training is the most important activity in initiating a quality circle program. Training essentially enables circle members to understand and use the *seven tools* and PDCA (described in Figure 1-4).

Data Concerning Activities of Quality Circles

The following data was obtained by the JUSE in 1981. For our purposes, it has been subdivided into six categories:

Areas of the firm in which quality circle activities have been introduced:

- Production 100%
- Maintenance 72%
- Materials management 69%

- Administration 64%
- Technical area 58%
- Marketing area 20%

When meetings are held

- During working hours 68.4%
- Outside working hours 31.4%
- Average number of meetings: two per month
- Average length of meetings: one hour

Topics discussed

- Cost reduction 47%
- Quality improvement 30%
- Additional topics: improvement of resources, organization, safety, atmosphere/morale, and environment

Selection of topics

- Free selection 70%
- In keeping with company structure 20%
- Other forms of selection 10%

Average number of projects completed by quality circles

- Three per year

Remuneration for activities

- Covered by normal compensation (work schedule) 30%
- Special compensation 39%
- Educational assistance 17%
- Social activities 8%
- Other forms of compensation 6%

Results

Quality circle activities can produce improvements in the following areas:

- Quality of finished products
- Defects in semifinished items
- Reliability of processes
- Maintenance requirements

- Safety and other working environment conditions
- Production costs/productivity
- Employees' problem-solving capabilities
- Absenteeism

Nevertheless, the principal results that have been reported involve the human element and interpersonal relations.

Effects on participants' personal characteristics

- Development of skills
- Increased self-esteem
- Improvement of certain personality traits
- Development of individual potential (for advancing within the company)

Effects on interpersonal/interhierarchical relations

- Increased respect for colleagues among supervisory personnel
- Increased understanding on the part of executives in their dealings with lower-level employees, and improved relations with them
- Greater understanding among lower-level employees of problems that their superiors may encounter in performing their duties, and vice versa
- Improved contact among individuals

Effects on the working environment

- Reduction of potential for conflict within participating departments/divisions
- Greater understanding of difficulties encountered by colleagues, by other groups, or by co-workers
- Greater involvement/participation in operational management
- Greater understanding of the role of product quality
- Improved communication

Problem-Solving Methodology

The methodology that the Japanese developed with the assistance of the American expert, Professor Deming, requires use of a specific method, PDCA (Plan-Do-Check-Action), with seven tools.

The PDCA method is a guide for effective completion of the phases of an improvement project, and the following seven tools can be applied within this context:

- Data collection sheets
- Histograms
- Pareto analyses
- Stratification
- Cause-and-effect diagrams
- Control charts
- Correlation diagrams

These tools correspond to specific requirements of the problem-solving process, as indicated in Figure 1-4.

Requirement	Tool
To obtain a precise image of the initial situation by means of data (the only scientific method for defining situations).	Data collection sheet
To verify the statistical validity of available data so as to ensure the correctness of each successive deduction.	Histogram
To identify the most important factors in regard to a given problem in order to be able to proceed by priority.	Pareto analysis
To allow seemingly flat and meaningless data to speak by finding a key that can provide significance.	Stratification
To initiate a search for possible causes of the problem being examined	Cause-and-effect diagram
To verify the existence of a link between two parameters (between a cause and an effect, for example).	Correlation diagram
To express the functioning of a machine, process, or system in statistical terms.	Control chart

Figure 1-4. The Seven Tools

2

Organizing Production

Priority Objectives

The snapshot of the Japanese organization model that has been developed by Western authors is particularly oriented toward identifying the priority objectives pursued within this model. They have concluded that, in contrast to Western firms, the highest priority objective is not *efficiency* in terms of direct resources (hours of production/hours of work), but a set of operational objectives oriented toward *total productivity*. These objectives, which can be expressed in terms of "zeros" to be pursued (unlimited objectives), include:

- Zero defects
- Zero inventories
- Zero setup time
- Zero downtime
- Zero paper

These goals are the so-called *five zeros* that shape Japanese methods of organizing production.

Actually, a "sixth zero" — *zero human labor* — has been identified, but it is more attributable to strategy than to an organization model. This objective is in part a result of today's high labor costs in Japan, which make automation more economical than human labor. It also derives partially from the need for high quality and reliability in processes, and this objective can be attained more effectively by using robots.

Having identified these priority objectives, Western authors tried to confirm their validity by comparing the results obtained by Japanese industry with those obtained by American industry. Whether for reasons of absolute importance or because managers within the automobile industry were the principal doubters who needed to be convinced, the automobile industry has been the sector most closely scrutinized in making the comparison.

Zero Defects

Most of the world is well aware that the Japanese organizational model has produced astonishing results in the electronics industry. Japanese firms are now achieving output with levels of defects measured in *p.p.m.*, *p.p.b.*, *p.p.t.*, (items per million, billion, or trillion), whereas our Western companies are still producing output with defects in the range of items per thousand, or at best, items per million.

What is not so widely known, however, is that as early as 1977 a significant difference in the defect rate had emerged in the automobile industry. The repair and maintenance data that Hertz supplied for its automobile fleet for that year is highly significant, as Figure 2-1 shows. Toyota's product was already six to eight times superior to the other makes in 1977. The defect reduction objective had been pursued successfully.

Brand	Number of Repairs for Warranty Period (per 100 automobiles)
Ford	326
Chevrolet	425
Pinto	306
Toyota	55

Figure 2-1. Hertz: Automobile Repairs and
Maintenance during 1977

Zero Inventories

Two hours of inventories between departments as an average figure at Toyota and 144 cycles as an annual turnover figure for manufacturing supplies at Suzuki are results that do not require comments. An objective has been pursued successfully.

Zero Setup Time

Setup time (the time required to tool up for production or to change from one production process to another) is directly linked to flexibility and responsiveness in production. It also exercises a strong influence on inventories, determines not only how much time will be required to fill an order (lead time), but whether a particular lot can be produced economically.

The 1980 data presented in Figure 2-2 enables us to compare average changeover times at Toyota with those in the United States, Sweden, and Germany. These data are for one of the most time-consuming setup operations in the automobile industry: changing stamping presses for automobile panels.

Figure 2-3 shows the reduction in setup times for all of Toyota's production activities, for the period 1977-78.

	Toyota	U.S. Firm	Swedish Firm	German Firm
Setup Time	10 min*	6 hr	4 hr	4 hr
Setups/Day	3	1	—	$\frac{1}{2}$
Size of Runs	1 day	10 days	1 month	—

* Currently less than 5 min

Figure 2-2. Production Changeover Time for Stamping Operations for Automobile Panels (1980)

We can draw certain conclusions from the data provided in these figures. Figure 2-3 shows the extent to which Toyota considered production flexibility an important objective, as indicated by the company's success in reducing setup times over a 12-year period (1976-1988). By 1988:

- Setup times of more than 10 minutes had been virtually eliminated
- At least 85 percent of all setups were being completed in less than 100 seconds

Setup Time	1976	1977	1980	1988 Estimated
> 60 min	30%	0	0	0
30-60 min	19%	0	0	0
20-30 min	26%	10%	3%	0
10-20 min	20%	12%	7%	1%
5-10 min	5%	20%	12%	5%
100 sec-5 min	0	17%	16%	9%
< 100 sec	0	41%	62%	85%

Figure 2-3. Reduction in Average Setup Times at Toyota 1976-88

This data also suggests that Toyota must have achieved a very high level of employee participation in this effort. Thousands of operations must have been studied intensively in order to achieve these reductions; they could not merely have been reviewed by a time and methods department. This objective had been pursued in an extremely successful way!

Zero Downtime

Japanese plants operate with proverbial efficiency and reliability, but available data is not always easily interpreted. One interesting study completed by the University of Kyoto in 1981 compared Japanese metalworking firms with equivalent firms in northern Europe. This survey revealed that "overall efficiency" was more than 50 percent greater in Japanese plants. (For further information on this subject, consult Chapter 16, "Total Productive Maintenance.") Another objective had been successfully pursued.

Zero Paper

The following data reported by Toyota speaks for itself:

• Scheduling and dispatching is done without computers.

- The need for an "initial production" office has been eliminated.
- The need for machining labels has been eliminated (labels were replaced by the flow of kanbans).
- Management is "by sight" instead of by issuing documents.

It is natural to wonder about the consequences of such an absence of paper and procedures. We shall see how this situation has arisen, but it cannot be denied that this particular objective has been successfully pursued.

Zero Human Labor

U.S. data pertaining to the level of robotization in industry and to the difficulties associated with selecting types of robots indicate that ratios vary from 5:45 to 1:2, depending upon the source. When the different manufacturing volumes are taken into account, however, the ratio is extremely favorable to the Japanese. The situation is possibly better in certain European nations (in the Italian automobile industry, for example), but, in most instances, ratios remain favorable to the Japanese. Another objective has been successfully pursued.

The Reference Model

Apart from stated objectives and accomplished results, Western observers have been impressed during their visits to the best Japanese factories with the exceptional orderliness and cleanliness of the working environment.

In Western plants, raw materials, semifinished products, and finished products are typically present at the same time in production units. This is not the case in Japanese factories, which have been characterized as having bare floors. Only small amounts of materials that are expected to be used within a period of several hours are to be found in these units.

Western experts who visited Japanese factories during the 1970s could see with their own eyes that materials and supplies in production areas were always there for imminent use, that is, *just-in-time.* The expression *just-in-time,* in reference to the Japanese organization system, has, in fact, been used more often by American authors than by the Japanese, who prefer other expressions, such as *stockless production.*

Despite the Japanese preference for other terms, *just-in-time* is the slogan that, for Westerners, captures one of the fundamental differences between the Japanese model and their own traditional models, which have been characterized by a tendency toward *waiting* a while for everything, from resupplying raw materials to processing. In fact, American authors have sometimes used the term "just-in-case" to characterize the American approach to materials management. In other words, materials inventories in Western factories are not justified by imminent use, but by precautionary considerations, such as contingency supplies or advance production "just-in-case" something happens.

If we apply analogous logic to the term *stockless production*, we can say that, in the West, it might often have been more accurate to speak of "productionless stock," namely, the existence of abundant inventories and limited production.

Leaving slogans and attempts at humor aside, let us examine the basic principles of Japanese just-in-time production. Above all, we should consider the operational objectives, which can be expressed in the following form:

- *Eradicate all waste*. Anything that does not add to the value of the product is waste, which can be reduced to a minimum.
- *Continuously improve the product quality and the reliability of processes*. This objective is derived directly from the total quality strategy.
- *Minimize allocations for production*. Financial wastefulness is regarded as the worst form of waste.
- *Minimize lead time*. Maximizing the firm's capability to respond to the market is directly related to minimizing the time required to fill orders.
- *Maintain flexibility in terms of the product mix*. Production flexibility is essential if a firm is to take advantage of every business opportunity and achieve significant diversification of products.

In Japan, these objectives have been pursued by using a so-called *minimum energy* organization model, which allows continuous improvement of production cost factors and of their elasticity. Indeed, this system should be regarded as an improvement system instead of a management system.

One effective way to illustrate the concept of minimum energy management, as other authors have done, is to portray the production system as the bottom of a lake and production management as sailing upon the waters of this lake. If we confine ourselves to the problem of inventories, for example, we can illustrate the situation with the two diagrams shown in Figure 2-4, which describe both high and low levels of work-in-process (WIP). The contingencies, which are indicated at the bottom of the lake, represent production problems that prevent the bottom from being perfectly flat (a condition representing "perfect" production).

According to the Western approach, which the Japanese have defined as a *maximum energy* approach, the measures introduced to overcome these production problems involve generating sufficient inventories (water) to completely submerge the consequences of these problems (contingencies).

The relationship between production problems (contingencies) and inventories (the necessary water level) in the Western model can be described in the following way:

- A scheduling system that grants priority to saturation of resources automatically produces goods that are not immediately needed. (The excess of inventory stems from the need to saturate productive resources.)
- The inability to anticipate or to plan correctly systematically requires production in advance.
- The risk of having to shut down certain machines or plants requires establishment of contingency inventories.
- The existence of a certain level of defects requires routine production of excess goods, so as to avoid risks, or the presence of semifinished lots awaiting approval, or systematic work-in-process for anticipated inspection procedures (inventories).
- Shortages of suitably trained personnel disrupt the equilibrium of the production process, resulting in the generation of intermediate stock, or a need to continuously relocate personnel throughout the process, resulting in the generation of additional quantities of semifinished goods (inventories).
- Long setup times require companies to produce large inexpensive lots and, as a result, to maintain high average supply levels (inventories).

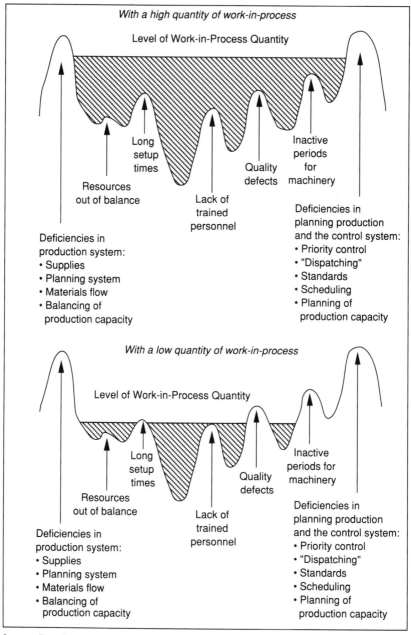

Source: Ryuji Fukuda, *Managerial Engineering*, Productivity Press.

Figure 2-4. WIP and Production Problems

- Imbalances in production resources produce a need to stockpile resources (inventories) so that they will not be depleted too quickly.
- A poorly planned production system involves unfavorable flows of supplies and imbalances in the productive capabilities of different departments, with a corresponding need for intermediate inventories.

So, what inventory levels are necessary in traditional Western systems? The answer is, amounts that are adequate to cover all possible contingencies. Even with levels considered adequate, if problems arise on a given day, an increase in inventories is promptly requested so as to prevent any further interruptions of production ("Efficiency above all!"). This is the "curative" approach (inventory as a cure for potential problems), which the Japanese have dubbed maximum energy management.

In minimum energy management, seeking remedies means identifying the causes of problems and removing them. Contingencies that cause problems must be uncovered — made visible — rather than "covered" with inventories. This is done by always keeping the "water level" at a minimum, or at a level that allows the most important contingency to be identified at a given moment.

This approach is used to achieve the objective of continuous improvement of processes. For improvement to occur, problems must be eliminated, and in order to be eliminated, problems must be visible, not buried. Only when the water level is low are the hazards on the bottom of a lake visible. In the minimum energy model of production, inventory levels must be kept low enough for problems to be visible.

Indeed, control of the "water level" can become the principal tool for operational management of production, with the goal of keeping the water even with the contingencies of the particular moment. This approach enables a firm to pursue the twofold objective of keeping downtime to a minimum and continually improving production, with problems being identified and solved as they arise. Internalization of this approach can be promoted by introducing an outlook affirming that at least one problem per day must arise if a significant level of continuous improvement is to be maintained. This means that at least one interruption of production must occur every day, as a result of depletion of the work-in-process inventory. A day in which

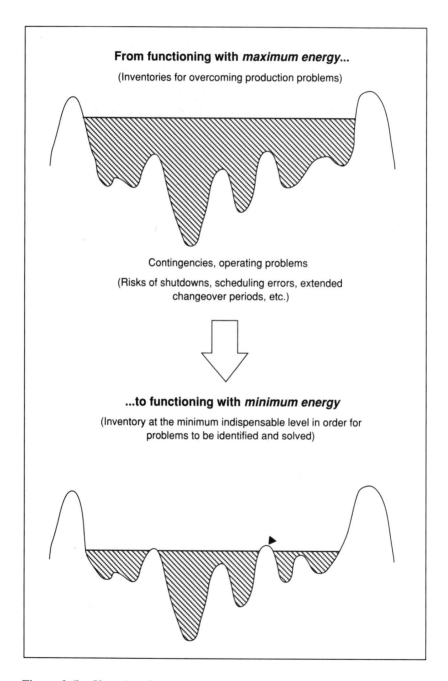

Figure 2-5. Changing One's Approach

no problems have been identified is a wasted day on the path of continuous improvement.

Thus, the water level must be controlled in real time, which means that direct sight control must be used instead of a computer. As we have already noted, leading manufacturers of computerized information systems, such as Hewlett-Packard and IBM, are using visual kanban systems in their own plants, without using computers for departmental scheduling and dispatching.

The main point of the Japanese version of the water level model is that it does not focus on reducing difficulties at the outset so that it will be possible to reduce inventory levels. Instead, it aims to reduce inventories continuously, and then to confront problems that arise. Figure 2-5 illustrates this distinction.

According to the minimum energy method, inventory that is removed is placed "in the bank" for several months, for safety's sake; if none is used during that period, it is withdrawn. This approach has currently been adopted by many Western firms, even though Western firms nearly always refrain from keeping removed inventory "in the bank" for a certain period of time. In the West, there is no time for hesitation; lost time must be recovered. It has now become a widely held opinion that waiting for problems to be mastered before being able to reduce supply levels would be a whimsical strategy: the culture of urgency, which is so widespread in Western industry, would never allow anyone to find the necessary time for approaching these important but nonurgent problems.

Organization Principles

The reference model for organizing production according to the Japanese just-in-time system can be summarized by the following seven principles:

1. *Production according to a flow*

    Criteria:

    - Organization should be determined by the process.
    - Products should never be "taken out" of the process.
    - Process speeds should be adjustable.

This principle means that optimizing the production flow — not efficiency — should be the main objective of organization. This means that production must be organized according to departments that operate in parallel with one another, instead of being arranged sequentially or according to product lines. This model also proposes adoption of a pipeline concept, whereby anything that enters at one end should exit at the other end, without stopping inside the pipeline. In other words, products should never be taken out of the process. Lastly, production systems must be highly elastic in terms of volume. Their speed and output must be adjustable, instead of being limited to rigid on-off logic.

2. *Piece-by-piece production*

Criteria:

- Defects should not be brought forward to the next phase.
- Any worker should be able to halt the process.

This principle is particularly consistent with the objective of maximum production quality, inasmuch as the intent is to prevent defects in the process from continuing. When items are produced one at a time and when they are intended for immediate use, defects or flaws can be easily detected and the risk of producing many defective items is limited. In addition, workers are much more strongly motivated to identify causes of defects as soon as they occur instead of several days later, when it would be necessary to determine whether specific defects were being produced in extensive production runs.

Workers are responsible for controlling the quality of processes, and they have the right or duty to halt the entire upstream process whenever a defect is observed. They must use this opportunity to diagnose the causes of defects; shutdowns will be offset over time. This system of halting production when defects are identified is called *jidoka*.

3. *Elimination of "aqualung" inventories*

Criteria:

- Inventories are a drug with respect to production.
- One hour of inactivity is better than an hour of production that must be sent to a warehouse.

Two significant management revolutions are evident in this principle. The first pertains to the minimum energy concept, which provides a pragmatic basis for regarding inventories as a drug that must be taken away as soon as possible. Inventories are drugs in that they prevent workers from identifying the real problems and because workers become accustomed to continually increasing doses. (Inventories never seem to be large enough!)

The second revolution involves the problem of emphasizing operational management factors. The reward systems and the industrial accounting techniques developed in conjunction with the Taylorist* approach in the West are intended to promote attainment of optimal production efficiency — the standard by which the performance of departments and managers is usually measured.

In the West, the cost of outlays for inventories is normally regarded as a cost to be placed under the heading of general expenses, or, even worse, within the domain of financial management. This situation produces a paradox: Although we urge production supervisors not to accumulate inventories, we often continue to evaluate them in terms of efficiency (hours of production in relation to hours of work). Under these circumstances, production supervisors may resort to creating false production reports instead of halting production, and they are very likely to complete work in advance of actual needs, so as to obtain maximum efficiency. This situation inevitably generates work-in-process (WIP).

Our Western management methods display similar deficiencies with respect to lead time and production flexibility. Although these are two extremely important strategic factors, they are not emphasized from a management standpoint. Consequently, a department that succeeds in producing with a lead time of one day, for example, is not considered superior in accounting terms to a department that produces with a lead time of two days (a 100 percent difference). Does this situation mean that lead time is not worth very much? Try telling that to the marketing managers of our companies!

---

* Fredrick Winslow Taylor (1856-1915), an American industrial engineer, called the father of scientific management, developed the time and motion study to analyze factory operations toward increasing efficiency. (Theory X approach to management.)

Similarly, if rewards are only provided for efficiency, no incentive exists for improving production flexibility; resistance to reducing production lots will be strong. Only within the framework of general accounting principles can we see clearly that "one hour of production that must be sent to a warehouse costs more than an hour of inactivity"; traditional industrial accounting does not capture this fact.

Western firms that are adopting just-in-time organizational changes have found it necessary to use global (activity-based) accounting to overcome this problem. With global accounting, production is managed according to "profit centers" and "cost centers," and each department is evaluated on the basis of its total results (overall productivity), instead of its efficiency. Only payments for by order production — the portion of production that is requested by the market — are treated as revenues; the value of unrequested output is not counted. Production by order is credited only on the specified delivery date. Costs that must be debited to a particular profit center are those that have actually been incurred (materials, labor, etc.), plus financial charges associated with the use of WIP and with the production of advance inventories of finished goods.

Production in advance is penalized because costs of the materials used must be debited as soon as they are used, whereas no counterpart revenues emerge until the specified time of delivery. This penalty exerts pressure to reduce lead time as it allows proportionate WIP reductions, with corresponding reductions in financial charges and materials-handling charges (space and transportation).

4. Economical production run: one item

Criteria:

- Setup times should diminish toward zero.
- Setup is the priority objective in identifying waste.

The ultimate objective in the Japanese just-in-time system is to become capable of producing a single item economically. This goal obviously becomes possible only when setup time reaches zero. The results described in the preceding chapter indicate that the Japanese have had remarkable success in achieving this goal. However, setup time has never been a high-priority objective within the Taylorist Western model, which emphasizes optimizing the consequences of problems instead of eliminating their causes. We have been satisfied with minimizing costs of the remedy, where the remedy consists of producing as many items as needed to amortize time lost during a change in production. (This has been the Western definition of an economical run.) Instead of eliminating the costs of lost production, we have added another type of cost — the cost of products being generated (finance, management, obsolescence).

Today, when flexibility in production is essential, the Western system finds itself in a state of crisis. The advantages of reducing setup time are linked not only to the size of lots and, thus, to reduction of inventories, but to greater flexibility, less lead time, and lower risks of rejection. The sophisticated methodology that has developed in response to the challenge of reducing setup time will be summarized in Part II.

5. *Micro mix = macro mix*

Criteria:

- The product mix in each small unit of production should match the total mix demanded by the market.
- Leveling of production is necessary.

If the market consumes a certain mix of products at a given daily rate, production on the basis of a monthly mix (for example, lots equivalent to requirements for one month) will require maintenance of equivalent supplies on average, to 50 percent of the monthly requirements for each category. At the same time, an estimated risk equivalent to one month must be taken into account (although once the monthly product has been produced, the same category will not be produced again until the next month).

Ideally, it should be possible to produce sequentially at the unit level a mix that would precisely represent the total product mix. This would ensure that production maintained almost perfect consistency with the flow actually required by the market, without generating stockpiles of finished goods, and would thus allow management of these two distinct mixes (the production mix and the sales mix). A firm's supplies of finished goods are nothing more an indicator of the extent to which its production activities are unsuited to accommodating the firm's field of business.

This principle (micro mix = macro mix) is well illustrated by the example of Toyota, where, on any given line, automobiles have been produced since the 1960s according to the following sequence: sedan, hardtop, sedan, wagon, sedan, hardtop, sedan, and so on. One can see that not even two production runs of the same car are undertaken sequentially! Thus, supplies for this mix are reduced to zero.

This type of production control is based upon the concept of leveling production. The meaning and structure of the leveling process is discussed more fully in Chapter 10.

6. *Units instead of work locations*

Criteria:

- A unit's output matters more than the workers' efficiency.
- Systems that provide individual incentives must be avoided.

The productivity of a unit or department consists of the value — billable output — that it succeeds in creating within a given period of time. According to this perspective, as already articulated by the third principle, advance production or excess production cannot be regarded as value; it represents costs. Thus, it is clear that the crucial factor in productivity is not the efficiency of the individual worker (or an individual machine), nor the average efficiency of the entire group of workers (or all of the plant's machines), but the minimum level of efficiency that can be identified during the process. In other words, the crucial factor is whatever bottleneck exists at a given moment.

A department's efficiency, when it is understood as a contribution to creation of a process that generates billable value, is therefore represented by its ability to identify and remedy production bottlenecks. In terms of a hydraulic analogy, the value produced by a plant consists of the flow rate that it can achieve, not the pools that can be produced along the way. The flow rate for a process is determined, of course, by bottlenecks which may arise at specific points.

In order to obtain high productivity, it is therefore necessary to control the efficiency of the entire process, instead of the efficiency of individual workers or machines. This concept actually means "managing production according to bottlenecks."

Any incentive system established to promote efficiency must be consistent with this principle. For example, bonuses according to production or piece work must be awarded to departments, not to individuals. Such incentives heighten each worker's sensitivity to bottlenecks within his or her department.

Whereas the Japanese JIT structure does not allow for a system of providing individual incentives, Taylorist systems are based upon controlling the efficiency of individual workers. Such systems have provided output incentives indiscriminately throughout the process — even upstream from the bottlenecks that inevitably arose. The result was that, in a production chain, a worker who, along with his downstream co-worker, found it temporarily impossible to dispose of the volume of items that he was producing, was nevertheless given incentives to produce as much as possible, and he was rewarded on the basis of his output, even though he was generating more costs than value at that particular moment.

7. Inexpensive run for resupplying: one item

Criteria:

- There will be no warehousing of raw materials.
- A comprehensive relationship with the supplier is essential.
- Fixed purchasing costs shall be eliminated.

A just-in-time structure requires direct resupplying from suppliers on a real-time basis — in keeping with actual needs at a given moment. There is no reliance upon a preestablished components warehouse. Resupplying every one to two hours (and, in some instances, every ten to 20 minutes) in small lots, with direct delivery to production departments, is already a reality in many Japanese firms. It is a reality even in some Western firms, including Italian firms.

Obviously, the entire process must occur without allowing materials to pass through a raw materials warehouse and an acceptance department. This is possible because quality is guaranteed by the supplier. The manufacturer's reliance on that guarantee is based not upon written attestations, but on a relationship with the supplier that is characterized by demonstrated loyalty and reliability, rooted in the interests of both parties. References to a few "wedded" suppliers and to a comprehensive relationship with these suppliers (co-makership) are not exaggerations. The system allows bureaucratic elements to be reduced to the indispensable minimum (accounting and fiscal requirements), and the practice of seeking at least three offers for each purchasing transaction to be eliminated. Purchasing by the bid method is replaced by purchasing based on such functions as knowledge of the market and approval of suppliers. Simplifying the purchasing procedure also eliminates or reduces fixed costs associated with purchasing excessively large lots of supplies — even supplies of simple consumable items that can be easily obtained.

Although comprehensive relationships with suppliers are essential in the JIT system, one should not assume that an organizational transformation of the JIT type will inevitably emerge from a firm's relations with its suppliers. On the other hand, some Italian firms proceeded precisely in this way, seeking JIT service from their suppliers even though the suppliers did not initially know how to furnish this kind of service. To some extent, this maneuver is a form of seeking solutions. It is comparable to saying, "The solution for my raw materials inventory problem is to shift it onto the supplier's shoulders." This approach only displaces the problem. Making the best of the consequences of problems does not solve them; their causes must be identified and eliminated.

In developing its JIT system, Toyota has treated suppliers as one of the last elements to be approached: "Only when we understood how things should be done, when we had the necessary organizational know-how, did we make requests to our suppliers."

The Toyota Production System

For several years, the just-in-time system par excellence has been the system developed by Toyota. Toyota was the first company in the world to develop a comprehensive JIT system, and it is therefore the only firm that can claim more than 10 years of experience with systems that many Western firms have not yet adopted. Toyota also invented some very original control techniques to make this system possible, and many observers regard the firm as still unparalleled in applying these techniques.

The purpose of this subsection is not to provide an exhaustive description of Toyota's system, but to portray it qualitatively, with the following objectives:

- To provide examples of certain principles presented within the preceding chapter
- To highlight certain aspects of Toyota's approach
- To examine certain specific techniques developed by Toyota

The first aspect to be emphasized is that the main objective pursued by the Toyota production system, according to the firm's vice president, Taiichi Ohno, is *to produce small quantities of many different models of automobiles.*

In other words, the system arose in order to allow Toyota to achieve efficiently the high level of diversification required by today's markets. It is important to bring this fact to light, because some Western authors have claimed that the JIT-kanban system was suitable only for mass production of extremely standardized products.

The second aspect to be emphasized is that Toyota's JIT system is not merely a series of techniques that were developed to solve organization problems. It is a comprehensive management system that is directly associated with strategic principles.

In summary, we can say that the six principal operational objectives pursued by this system are:

- To eradicate any form of waste (which is defined as anything that does not add to the value of a product)
- To reduce lead time
- To eliminate down time
- To minimize WIP
- To balance the production flow to the maximum extent
- To identify existing problems automatically and systematically

Eradicating Any Form of Waste

Toyota has identified various forms of waste: overproduction, rejected items and repeat work, waiting time, transportation time and charges, inventories, and wasted motion. Among these forms of waste, the first two — overproduction and low quality — are considered the most serious. Consequently, the following two elements are paramount in Toyota's waste-elimination program:

- It is impossible for defects to be carried forward to the next phase, and every effort must be exerted to ensure that a given defect will no longer occur (these efforts include stopping production for proper diagnosis).
- It is impermissible to produce an item in advance of the time it will be used, or to produce quantities that exceed immediate needs.

Toyota has initiated countless activities and measures designed to eradicate waste. Some will be discussed more fully in Part II:

Waste on account of overproduction

- Analysis of operations and methods
- Production leveling
- Production in small lots (item by item)

Waste resulting from having to wait for machines

- Production leveling
- Analysis of preparatory steps

Waste associated with transportation time

- Analysis/improvement of the layout
- Analysis/reduction of transportation activities
- Improved efficiency of transportation methods

Waste related to time required for processes

- Value engineering
- Value analysis
- Reliability of the process

Waste on account of inventories

- Analysis of delivery time and lead time for production.
- Reduction of production lead time
- Production leveling
- Production in small lots (item by item)
- Analysis of preparatory measures

Waste on account of motion

- Analysis of methods, equipment, and motion
- Analysis of principal operations
- Mechanization
- Standardization

Waste due to defects

- Prevention and improvement activities
- Analysis of operator-controllable errors (OCEs)
- Foolproofing measures
- Self-inspection, sequential inspection

Reducing Lead Time

Toyota regards lead time and throughput as crucial strategic factors. It is not physically possible to attain substantial diversification of products if inventories for each category of items must be kept in the warehouse. Such a policy would lead to financial disaster for the firm. A firm must be capable of producing goods in sufficiently brief periods of time to allow starting of production or, at least, of final assembly procedures only in response to confirmed orders. While this approach may involve certain forms of inefficiency, they are offset by the nearly total elimination of storage costs (financial and operational costs), by elimination of the risks of obsolescence of finished products or semifinished items, and by the increased business efficiency that this situation generates.

Today, Toyota's plants produce according to the following principle: Orders are to be filled within five business days, with a total lead time of eight business days. This capability does not depend on the presence of vast supplies of semifinished items. Instead, the entire production chain (suppliers included) is exceptionally short and flexible. The firm's commercial units make the five-day lead time possible by proportioning orders every day — they control delivery dates to ensure that the required daily output will not exceed capabilities to fill every order within five days. Thus, lead time is brief and invariable. Delivery dates are solely controlled by the sales division, and the entire process of managing orders has been significantly simplified.

Eliminating Downtime

Every stoppage affecting the semifinished product during the process is regarded as waste and as a source of costs, notably costs for managing the supplies associated with any given stoppage. Whenever the process has begun, the product should never be taken out (the *pipeline* concept).

Minimizing WIP

Western industry has shared this goal for some time, so detailed explanation of the goal itself is unnecessary. However, the West appears to have pursued the goal less successfully than Japan.

Maximum Balancing of the Operating Flow

Toyota does not try to keep every unit and every machine operating continuously at peak efficiency, so the firm does not have to create the associated problems with "aqualung" or contingency inventories. Instead, the firm's main objective has been to achieve a production flow in which each unit's output is perfectly balanced with the capabilities of the next downstream unit and in which the total output is perfectly balanced with orders. Maximum resources are focused on the real problem: bottlenecks. Employees ask at Toyota: "What is the purpose of achieving high production with a machine if it cannot be handled downstream? It is better to slow down the machine and to avoid having to handle extra output at a later point."

This approach may create a victim, namely, the efficiency (hours of production/hours of work) of certain machines. Nevertheless, the most important consideration is total productivity, which is strongly influenced by bottlenecks. It is possible to improve the ratio between revenues and costs only by reducing bottlenecks.

Automatic and Systematic Identification of Existing Problems

Toyota wanted a system whose primary objective would be to identify problems instead of merely solving them when they are discovered. For problems to be solved, however, they must be visible and quantified, instead of being defined by hypotheses and estimates. "It is better to lose two hours of production today in order to solve a problem, than to shut down for five minutes every day during future months or years," goes the slogan at Toyota.

Subsystems

The Toyota Production System consists of many subsystems. Considered most important are the following three:

- *Kanban.* Kanban can be defined as "an automatic system for scheduling, starting, and controlling production." It shall be described in more detail presently.
- *Jidoka.* Jidoka refers to the act of stopping the entire production when a defect is discovered, so that the defect will not affect the downstream process. The basic concept is that when problems occur, it is better to shut down a line or a machine

than to continue production. "Jidoka temporarily reduces production efficiency, if production efficiency is understood as the number of items being produced, but there is an extremely rapid recovery on account of the improvement capabilities associated with the respective interruption." Production may be halted either automatically (by sensors installed on the machine); or manually (by any operator who considers halting necessary).

- *Andon.* The andon subsystem embodies the principle that "problems must be seen in order to be solved; hence, it is necessary to attempt to render every activity along the line visible." The most elementary form of andon consists of a board displayed within a unit in a location where it is visible to everyone. This board can provide a schematic portrayal of the production process, and it can allow those who are working within a given department to remain aware (by means of signal lights) of the status of the entire line. Andon can be described under the broader heading of *visual control systems* (VCS), or "sight management," which will be more fully described in Part II.

Kanban, jidoka, and andon have been extensively adopted by Western firms. The schedule provided in Figure 2-6 conveys an idea of the sequence of steps completed by Toyota in developing its system. This sequence emerged logically, instead of in a random fashion, and it was only marginally susceptible to modification. It is appropriate to observe that, as indicated heretofore, suppliers are regarded as a point of arrival instead of a point of departure.

The mode of reasoning which constitutes the basis for this system shall be discussed in the second section, along with the meaning of the respective steps.

Something which becomes evident from this brief description of the content and modes of application of the new production system is the high level of synergy existing among the approaches and mechanisms which are unique to JIT and to TQC. Indeed, the implementation processes developed simultaneously and in a combined form. (Figure 2-7 indicates the parallels which exist with respect to the most significant features.)

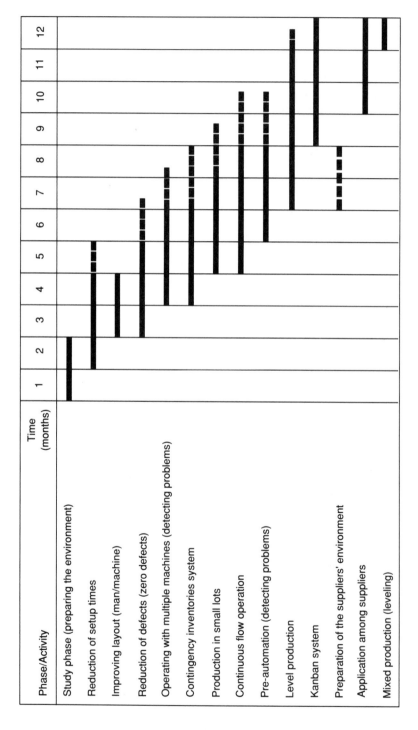

Figure 2-6. Schedule for Introducing the Toyota Production System

Kanban

The kanban system has already been discussed extensively in existing JIT literature. The following description is intended only as a summary.

The kanban system has already gained exceptional popularity, even in Western nations, and in some instances, its popularity has fostered the belief that it is the secret underlying high productivity in certain Japanese plants. While the importance of this system must be acknowledged — on account of its innovative and revolutionary approach if for no other reason — some of its popularity is perhaps undeserved.

The kanban system is only one component of the just-in-time production system. Indeed, kanban is of limited importance in relation to JIT as a whole, and it is only useful as a production management system in situations where a certain repetitiveness of production is assured.

The necessary level of repetitiveness is actually extremely low: some Western firms use kanban in the production of machine tools that involve small numbers of components. Accordingly, it is more accurate to say that kanban constitutes an extremely effective JIT production management system for precoded products (namely, products characterized by differing basics and a predefined product structure). Nevertheless, kanban is merely an operating technique, whereas just-in-time is an entire management and organization system.

These observations are not intended to diminish the importance of kanban in any sense, because kanban must be described carefully. The following definition of kanban may be useful:

> The kanban system consists of an extremely simplified production control system that is *capable of being adapted for modifications in production* and *capable of maintaining a self-regulating function* for production within a given department.

Thus, it is a system that allows automatic real-time monitoring of anything occurring during production, with adjustment of total output according to the bottlenecks existing at a given point. These goals are met without generating production orders and even without using computers.

The concept of *pull* constitutes the logical basis for kanban, in the sense that production controlled by kanban is pulled forward, instead of being moved by traditional *push* methods.

"Push" scheduling procedures consist of anticipating flow between departments and the various points of contact that are necessary. Afterward, the necessary documents are issued, and attempts to "push" production ahead occur — in this system expediters are designated even for physical pushing — until the desired output leaves the plant. This process occurs with a heavy burden of feed control functions intended to regulate the actual status of the flow in addition to various work orders.

In *pull-kanban* management, much of the scheduling, feed control, and expediting functions become superfluous.

"Pull" procedures are based on downstream control instead of upstream control. This situation is not as unusual as it may seem. In fact, it could be affirmed that a kanban system is nothing more than an industrial version of the system used in the meat departments of supermarkets. Toyota's system was actually inspired by supermarkets. Who schedules the work of butchers in a supermarket? Who tells them which items or which quantities to prepare? The scheduling department? No, the butchers' output is controlled by the selections that customers make in the meat display areas.

Even the more advanced computerized simulation systems cannot effectively regulate product mix in small quantities, because small numbers cannot be processed statistically. Although the required output for a given period (one week, for example, in the situation under consideration) can be estimated by a scheduling system based upon projected statistical data, output during brief periods (days or hours) must be regulated on a sight basis, in response to downstream control (customers). In other words, production is "pulled" forward.

Introducing the kanban system in a plant consists of developing an operating chain that begins with the actual client (the dealer) and travels upstream to suppliers of raw materials. Toyota uses the following principles, which are now widely recognized in Western industry as well:

- Monthly advance scheduling with computerized *Master Production Schedules* in order to ensure monthly leveling

- Operational scheduling with sight control (kanban) or synchronized control

This system, for example, enables the plant that produces the Celica model to accomplish operational management of 120 finished product categories for each production line, with 100,000 subassembly codes, and with shipping guaranteed for five business days following receipt of orders.

The Kanban System

Kanban means "ticket." With its various changes of location throughout the process, the kanban controls production flows by controlling the necessary procedures through a "pull" principle. In other words, the necessary downstream subassemblies or procedures are requested according to the needs of the moment. Requests flow upstream throughout the process, and the needs encountered at each step are communicated to the next upstream unit by attaching kanbans to the containers that are removed. The kanbans therefore constitute documentation for completion of the preceding steps (see Figure 2-7).

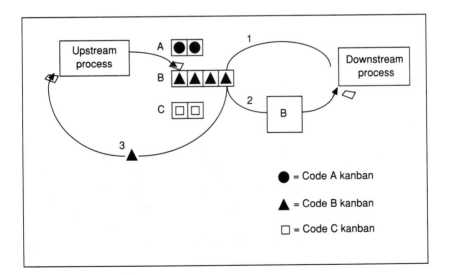

Figure 2-7. How Kanban Functions

When all production units are interconnected through kanbans, pull is created, and each phase of production is drawn downstream. Even the suppliers are affected by the pull, as they must deliver supplies according to existing needs (see Figure 2-8).

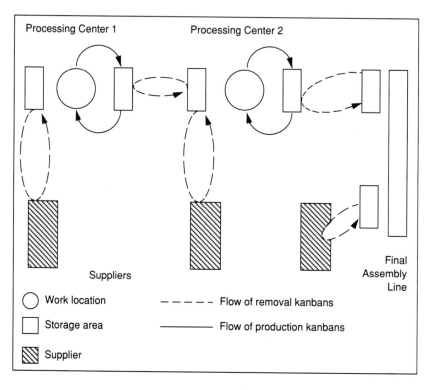

Figure 2-8. Production Controlled by Kanbans

Thus, a process controlled by kanbans is self-regulating, because each phase of production is activated by needs. The flow of kanbans is initiated by the last unit in the process, namely, the final assembly department, which obtains the necessary components in response to production orders transmitted by the order control department. Thus, output flows are balanced and harmonized, with economical assembly lots equivalent to one item, whereas lots corresponding to prior phases may be greater than one.

Toyota uses a two-kanban system, where the two basic types of kanbans are:

- Removal kanbans
- Production order kanbans

This system is illustrated in Figure 2-9.

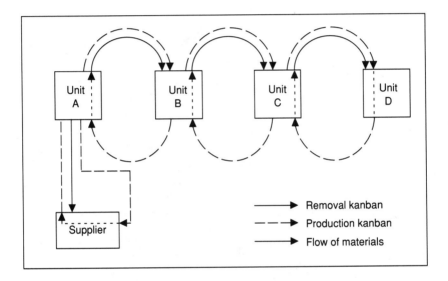

Figure 2-9. Flow of Materials and Kanbans (2 slips)

Figure 2-10 provides an example of both types. Removal kanbans contain the following information:

- Code for contents of container
- Kanban number and the total number of containers (kanbans) for the respective code
- Container capacity
- Supply center (production unit or external supplier)
- Storage location from which container is obtained

Item: Gear 712,913,400			From Unit *105* Machining *(2)*	To Unit *108* Assembly *(1)*
Container:			Storage Location *A-3*	Storage Location *C-3*
Type *B-2 red*	Number *4 (of 8)*	Items per container *20*		

Unit:	*105, Machining (2)*	
Item:	*Gear 712,913, 400*	*20* items
Materials to be Removed:	*Forging, 712,913,300*	
Removal Location:	*Unit 102 Forging*	Storage Location: *A-3*
Taken to Unit:	*108 Assembly (1)*	Storage Location: *C-3*

Figure 2-10. Removal Kanbans and Production Order Kanbans

Production order kanbans contain the following information:

- Component code
- Container capacity
- Kanban number and total number of kanbans
- Supply center
- Storage location upon release from supply center
- "Customer" center
- Incoming storage location for customer center

The roles of the two types of kanbans are indicated in Figure 2-11.

Operational functioning of the kanban system is subject to the following rules:

1. Downstream processes must remove products from upstream processes in the numbers equivalent to the numbers of kanbans that have been removed.

2. Upstream processes must produce products according to the quantities, quality, and sequence indicated on the kanban that is to be removed.
3. Defective items should never be transferred to the next process.
4. The numbers of kanbans must be reduced to a minimum (continuous reduction of stock).

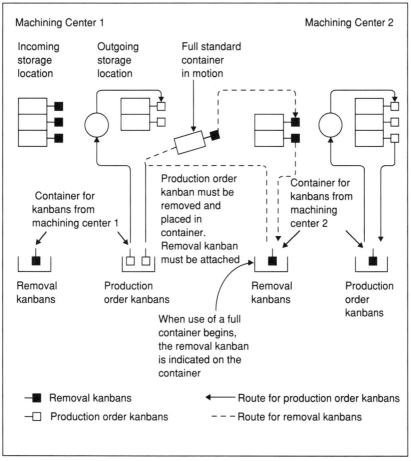

Source: Robert Hall, APICS, *Zero Inventories.*

Figure 2-11. Flow Patterns for Containers and Kanbans

Rule one carries some subrules:

- Any removals in the absence of a kanban are forbidden.
- Any removal of numbers of items exceeding the number appearing on the respective kanban is forbidden.
- Kanbans should always be attached to the product (or to the container).

The second rule likewise entails subrules:

- Production in excess of the number of kanbans is forbidden.
- In the event that different types of items may be required in the preceding process, production of these items must be consistent with the sequence for which each type of kanban has initially been provided.
- When a kanban is not present, transporting and processing of items must stop.

In order to allow management of specific situations, there are also other types of kanbans, which shall not be discussed within this context:*

- Emergency kanbans
- Special kanbans
- Warning kanbans
- Materials kanbans
- Combined kanbans

---

* For specific discussion of these types, consult the texts cited in footnote 1.

3

New Strategies

Where is Japan going now? Many Westerners expected Japan to undergo a settlement of accounts: "When their labor costs exceed those of Western nations and when the standard of living improves, productivity will decline and they too will enter an economic downturn." The appointed time for such a decline appears to be shifting further into the future, however, giving rise to certain doubts about the validity of that prediction.

Not only has the prediction failed to materialize, but a new industrial revolution, which has been designated *super-industrialism*, has been occurring in Japan for the past three years. This revolution has tended to discredit many beliefs about industrial development and about replacement of industry by services. In response to revaluation of the yen *hendaka*, Japan has adopted measures that are giving new life to industry, including mature sectors such as materials (steel, nonferrous metals, chemical products, and paper). Even the sectors that have been most profoundly affected, such as electrical equipment, electronic products, appliances for domestic use, semiconductors, and multipurpose motors, have been able to perform brilliantly.

The strategy that has been adopted is one of pursuing *product innovation* and *obtaining optimal yield from investments*. Product innovation has generated high levels of consumption. In 1987, 3.77 million refrigerators were sold in Japan; in 1988, 4.3 million were sold. During the same period, the number of washing machines sold increased from 3.68 million to 4.36 million.

In 1987, Japan invested 19.5 percent of its gross domestic product in plants and equipment, whereas the peak level during the most favorable years of economic growth — the 1960s — had been 18.8 percent. These large-scale investments support a prediction that Japan will remain the most productive industrial force in the world for at least a few more years.

What strategy is now being adopted with respect to manufacturing in Japan? Waseda University in Tokyo has initiated research (Manufacturing — 21: Research Project),* whose goal is to develop a new production system for Japanese industry. The research has defined a scenario and a strategic approach for the future. Figure 3-1 contrasts the scenario within which the new strategy is expected to operate — a mature global market characterized by slow economic growth — with the rapidly expanding market of the recent past.

The following strategic possibilities have been envisioned as means of achieving leadership in this scenario:

- Develop and produce new products that are competitive by virtue of their newness rather than price. (The manufacturers shift to major positions as developers of new products/technologies.)
- Gain a position as a low-cost producer with world-class competitiveness.
- Gain a competitive advantage through flexibility in manufacturing.
- Develop a "new multinational system."

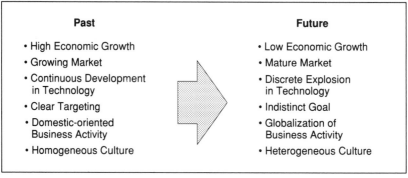

Past	Future
• High Economic Growth	• Low Economic Growth
• Growing Market	• Mature Market
• Continuous Development in Technology	• Discrete Explosion in Technology
• Clear Targeting	• Indistinct Goal
• Domestic-oriented Business Activity	• Globalization of Business Activity
• Homogeneous Culture	• Heterogeneous Culture

Source: Jinikiro Nakane, Waseda University

Figure 3-1. Key Elements of Change in the Environment and in Manufacturing Competitiveness

---

* Jinikiro Nakane, "World-Class Manufacturing," Napa Valley Convention (Coopers & Lybrand), November 1988.

Within the general outlines of this scenario, decisions are expected to depend largely on the sectors and products in which companies will be pursuing activities. When specific sectors are considered, mid-term and long-term strategies can already appear easily defined.

- *Auto Industry*

  - Rapid development and introduction of new products
  - Realization of efficient "make-to-order" production
  - Development of a new product design concept for low-volume production
  - Development of a new manufacturing technology for low-volume production

- *Electronics Industry*

  - Rapid introduction of new products and new technologies, with short life cycles
  - Development of just-in-time and flexible production systems
  - Major target of "minimization of total lead times" by removing all waste

- *Machinery Industry*

  - Development of a "higher level" of value-added products
  - Development of an automated and integrated manufacturing system with flexibility (CIM)
  - Development of a worldwide production network to realize flexible, low-cost manufacturing for a global market

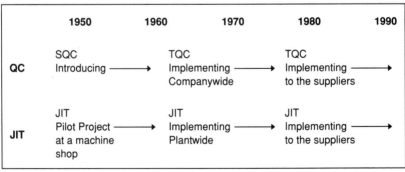

Source: Robert Hall

Figure 3-2. Toyota Motor Company: From QC to JIT

As Figure 3-2 indicates, the strategic factors that Japanese industry appears to be giving priority are, in general terms:

- Rapid development and introduction of new products
- Flexibility (to permit efficient and economical make-to-order production and/or low-volume production)
- Globalization (total business and total manufacturing management)

In Part II, the strategies being adopted by Japanese industry are compared with those used in Western firms. In addition, possible differences in approach and interpretation are explored.

Part II

The New Reference Model for Organizing and Managing Production

4

The Origin of Just-in-Time in Western Industry

The "discovery" of just-in-time by Western industry is not closely associated with the Japanese stimulus. Indeed, the term *just-in-time* was introduced in the United States at the end of the 1960s, and it was defined as follows:

> Producing finished products just in time to deliver them; producing semifinished items and resupplying oneself with purchased materials just in time to use them.

The definition indicates that the concept was already relatively clear at that time. It also reveals the motivation behind adoption of the new model: financial problems arising from the existence of large inventories.

Between 1965 and 1968, managers of American firms began to believe (correctly) that the financial burden derived from their production management and scheduling systems was excessive. Efficiency in production, or maximum saturation of resources, constituted a priority objective for these systems. Idleness among workers or machines was regarded as an extremely serious lapse, which it was absolutely necessary to avoid.

This outlook, which was of Taylorist origin, had arisen during the 1950s, when direct labor costs actually constituted the highest operating costs for companies and were therefore regarded as a high-priority area for improvement. Delivery periods and product quality were relatively unimportant factors during those years, when the market was still unsaturated and quasi-monopolistic patterns existed in many sectors. Buyers were prepared, for example, to pay a deposit for an automobile that arrived six months later (even the most standard type), with the color and optional features to be selected by the manufacturer. The manufacturer, meanwhile, could afford to reduce costs solely by seeking the most appropriate economies of scale (a few models, a few colors, with production efficiency as the priority objective).

The 1960s and 1970s brought new influences to bear on business profits — factors such as inventories, delivery periods, diversification, and product quality. Within this new context, the traditional, Taylorist model, which had been designed to grant priority to efficiency, lost its relevance, sending business into a crisis.

As stated earlier, the primary impetus for the just-in-time approach in the United States was the financial burden associated with the presence of large inventories. This situation produced a revolution in production scheduling. The priority objective for the new scheduling system became avoidance of producing anything in advance or in excess, relative to actual needs at a given moment, even at the expense of resource saturation. The new attitude was, "Only what is needed should be produced. An hour of inactivity is better than an hour of output that goes to the warehouse."

In the United States, one of the products of this revolution was the "MRP crusade," which changed scheduling methods for every company.

The MRP system (which means *materials requirement planning* in the initial version, MRP 1, and *manufacturing resources planning* in the second version, MRP 2) calls for the scheduling of materials requirements and activities on the basis of data concerning actual needs. Thus, one proceeds in reverse by scheduling whatever is necessary for producing these goods "at the latest possible time." The resulting work load for various work locations is nothing more than a consequence of these needs, and it is subsequently defined in optimal terms.

Because this system does not take into account the production capacities of various departments, it is defined as an infinite-capacity scheduling system, in contrast to the finite-capacity approach of scheduling systems in which resource saturation is a priority.

In Europe, the problem of inventories was decisively approached later, in the late 1970s and early 1980s. Possible explanations for the delay are culturally based as well as speculative. In cultural terms, the problem stemmed from widespread uncritical acceptance of industrial accounting systems based upon cost centers. In European industry, these systems, apart from being used for management control and forecasting, have often constituted a reference point for operational decisions. Thus, decisions concerning what to produce or how much to produce are made on the basis of budgets instead of actual needs. In many instances, the outcome is establishment of warehouses for unsold goods or large quantities of WIP, which may have been generated so as to avoid adverse effects upon efficiency.

Another factor behind the delay may have been the rapid inflation of the 1960s and 1970s, which affected costs in certain nations (such as Italy). In this situation, investments in warehousing could be financially advantageous. Unfortunately, these speculative warehouses were often created within factories or even in production departments (WIP), thereby narcotizing production with large inventories that would be difficult to dispose of at subsequent points.

In the United States, the MRP crusade produced such a significant impact that, by 1973, 47 percent of the manufacturing companies in the United States had adopted the new scheduling system (Figure 4-1).

Technique	Percentage of Companies
ABC	62
Economical Lots	56
MRP	47
Point of Reordering	32
Mathematical Models	30
Finite Capacity	30

Figure 4-1. Production Management Techniques
in the United States in 1973

The conviction that MRP was the answer to the just-in-time challenge survived until approximately 1976. At that time, the confrontation with Japanese industry began to inspire doubts about the effectiveness of MRP. Manufacturers wondered why, if MRP was equivalent to JIT, Japanese firms operating *without* MRP obtained results that were as much as ten times better than their own.

Notwithstanding these reflections, the MRP system, on account of the amount of time needed for implementation, reached its highest level of use in 1981, at which time it was being employed by 73 percent of all American firms. The earlier doubts about the validity of MRP had prompted closer study of the Japanese mode of organization that was producing the "snapshot" cited within the first portion of this book. The following conclusions gradually emerged (1978-1980):

- The Japanese production model is considerably simpler.
- It is not sufficient to adopt various scheduling systems for achieving actual JIT production: the Japanese have demonstrated that, in order to attain this goal, new approaches must be introduced throughout a company.

Since 1976, Westerners have attempted to develop and to consolidate a new organization model for production, having drawn certain lessons from the Japanese experience. The chronology of this transformation is indicated in Figure 4-2.

1968-75	• Revolution in production scheduling systems with movement toward JIT (MRP)
1975-79	• Contemplation of the Japanese organization model: discovery that JIT approaches should be introduced throughout a company • Initial applications of TQC strategy
1979-81	• Development of JIT company model: initial versions of the system
1981-present	• "Revolution" in production organization

Figure 4-2. Just-in-Time in the United States

As stated in the introduction, the revolution in organizing production is already yielding significant results. Their impact could be greater if JIT were understood to the fullest extent. Indeed, the Western approach to JIT is still influenced by an overly technical outlook in which the cultural and organizational dimension is not fully taken into account. The diagnosis presented by Robert Hall, as indicated within Figure 4-3, underscores the differences between the Japanese and American approaches.

In this section, the comprehensive just-in-time model recommended for Western industry will be examined in terms of its strategic, organizational, and technical aspects.

Concept	Japan	U.S.
Total Quality Control	Strengthen people's capabilities	Techniques
Total Productive Maintenance	Improve equipment capability	Avoid unplanned downtime
Standardization	Methods often standardized by workers	Methods usually set by IE
Visibility	All people can read shop floor data	Supervisors keep data

Source: Robert Hall

Figure 4-3. Comparison of JIT/TQC Concepts as Understood by Americans and Japanese

5

Changes Occuring in Organizing Strategies

The origin and development of the just-in-time system obviously did not occur accidentally. This phenomenon is a reflection of clearly defined strategic needs that this chapter is intended to interpret.

The organizational changes occurring in industry throughout the world may be explained by means of an interpretative model consisting of four reference configurations that are correlated with specific strategies for organizing production.

These four configurations correspond to four important points in the history of manufacturing, inasmuch as it is possible to regard them as coinciding with the predominant organization models of the past four decades. They are:

- The Western Taylorist-functional company of the 1950s and 1960s
- The marketing-oriented company of the 1960s and 1970s
- The Japanese company of the 1970s
- The world-class company of the 1980s and 1990s

The Interpretative Model

The reference model being proposed for interpreting the current phase of strategic development in industry on a global scale consists of the matrix appearing within Figure 5-1.

The dimensions of this matrix consist of two alternatives for relationships with the market, and two alternatives in internal organization strategy. A general explanation of each component follows.

		Internal Organization	
		Bureaucratic Dynamics (Product Oriented)	**Group Dynamics (Process Oriented)**
Relationship with the Market	**Operations Oriented**	**A** Bureaucracy/ Product-Out	**C** Involvement/ Process Improvement
	Market Oriented (Market-In)	**B** Marketing/ Product-In	**D** Venture/ Market-In

Figure 5-1. Organization Strategy for Companies: The Four Alternatives

Operations-Oriented

An *operations-oriented* strategy is directed toward incremental changes in the company's environment by means of:

- Improvements or innovations in company processes (technology)
- Improvements or innovations in products

This strategy is developed within a company as the cumulative result of continuous response to the market. It treats the firm's existing capabilities (the technology and know-how for its products) as both the strong point and the point of departure for its business activities.

Market-Oriented

A *market-oriented* strategy is developed through continuous analysis of business opportunities offered by the market. It involves response to the environment on the basis of planning or organization that identifies the internal activities to be pursued and the measures to be initiated.

The firm's ability to seize and make use of market opportunities is regarded as the strong point and as the point of departure.

Product-Oriented (Bureaucratic Dynamics)

In the strategy termed *bureaucratic dynamics*, organizing emphasis is placed upon the *product*. Internal organization is wholly instrumental, and it is fundamentally based upon differentiation of duties according to functions, as well as formal delineation of authority and responsibilities; the activities to be pursued are standardized as formally approved procedures, with control through specific systems. This mode of organization:

- Assures systematic and impersonal action
- Promotes efficient and logical activities

Process-Oriented (Group Dynamics)

The organizing emphasis in a *group dynamics* strategy is placed upon the *processes* a company may introduce in order to pursue its business activities. As a result, the organizational units (groups of people) intended to manage these processes are emphasized. Company members are encouraged to share values and information, but the organizational structure is not precisely defined. The necessary form of management is of a comprehensive or entrepreneurial type. Internal roles are often group-oriented. This type of organization:

- Allows autonomous responses to situations by all organizational levels
- Uses information originating from every organizational unit
- Generates a high level of mental energy among its members

As shown in Figure 5-1, convergences among the four possible approaches provide a basis for four reference models that offer specific strategic choices in terms of internal organization and relationships with the market.

The four models are:

- Bureaucracy/product-out (the Western company, 1950s)

- Marketing/product-in (the Western company, 1960s and 1970s)
- Involvement/process improvement (the Japanese company, 1970s)
- Venture/market-in (the world-class company, 1980s and 1990s)

These four models are theoretical. They are derived from comprehensive and correct application of operational principles associated with strategic choices adopted according to the two axes of the matrix. It is unlikely that a company's operational realities would coincide precisely with the principles embodied by one of these models. While strategic choices are usually extremely clear, practical application often represents a compromise among these choices, the existing company outlook, and contemporaneous situations. Moreover, perceptions based upon models are static, whereas reality changes constantly.

Nevertheless, the reference model acquires exceptional operational importance. The strategic and operational decisions adopted by a firm's management are actually inspired by these models or, more frequently, by the principles that correspond to them. In turn, these principles evolve into the management culture (the entire set of beliefs and values) that underlies company decisions.

Each of the four models shall be described in terms of the principal distinguishing features, namely:

- Relationship with the market
- Organization and management approach
- Conditions favoring success
- Manufacturing strategy

The Bureaucracy/Product-Out Company

The *bureaucracy/product-out* company (Figure 5-1, area A) results from application of *operations-oriented* strategic assumptions and organization principles of a mechanistic type.

This type of firm was predominant in industry (especially in Western nations) during the 1950s and 1960s.

During this period, industry had entered the so-called technological phase, using Taylorist organization principles. The characteristic features of this model are described below.

Relationship with the Market

The guiding principles of the bureaucratic/product-out company comprise several beliefs or attitudes:

We do business with the product or technology. Technological or product know-how is regarded as the priority factor in doing business: "The important thing is to have technology." Business is pursued by spotting needs that the firm's product or technology can satisfy. Thus, the company's product, along with its ability to develop technological know-how, is its point of departure.

Accordingly, in order to do business, it is sufficient to possess the product or the technology. All other areas of business sales, procurement, production, distribution, and deliveries are secondary.

The market wants our product. The bureaucratic/ product-out company functions and usually excels in an unsaturated market (such as existed the 1950s). The clients come to the company for the product, because supply lags considerably behind demand.

In such a situation the marketing structure is restricted to simple order management functions and customer relations. In addition, firms can pursue their own internal cost-cutting measures, allowing the market to suffer in terms of deliveries, quality, and prices, because there is no serious risk of losing sales volume.

We know what customers need. Operational leadership for relations with the market is entrusted to technical specialists who are not challenged, as they decide the market's needs and the value of product functions. Market feedback is taken into account only if it is explicitly sought by technical personnel. In other words, it is considered only in exceptional situations. The attitude is, "The product is good and will stay as it is until *we* decide to change it." Also defined by technical personnel are the necessary levels of product quality.

Products are expressions of technological capabilities. To summarize, the marketing approach of the bureaucracy/product-out company consists of preparing suitable products and launching them into the market. Products are designed "technically." Success depends upon the degree to which the market is capable of accepting the product (if a product is not accepted, either consumers are ignorant of it or they have failed to understand it, according to the technical specialists).

Organization and management approach

The product precedes organization. In the same way that business is determined by products, so the operational structure is defined by the product line, in a bureaucracy/product-out company.

Thus, whenever a product is created, one begins with the prototype and anticipated volumes. Next on the drawing board come the necessary technological processes for industrial production (in order to define methods and, ultimately, time), as well as the necessary structure (organization diagram and staff).

As soon as the optimal organization diagram has been developed, efforts are undertaken to fill the anticipated positions with persons whose occupational and psychological or attitudinal profiles are most appropriate.

When the product becomes available, business is conducted according to a predesigned structure which ensures performance of all necessary, and thus specified, functions.

The fundamental belief is that "It is *organization* that allows business activities to be pursued."

The organizational design is static, being modified only in the event of changes in the product or (occasionally) in scale of production.

The organization takes precedence over people. The assumption is that, after the product and the type of organization have been defined, resources shall merely constitute a means of achieving the objectives indicated by predetermined requirements. Likewise, individuals at all levels are seen purely as elements who perform the tasks that have been determined and perfected beforehand by the mode of organization. In other words, employees constitute precoded operational resources whose functions can be compared to those of machines.

Thus, the organization model is a Taylorist one (in the restrictive sense of the term), requiring allocation of organizing responsibilities (job design) to specific entities, such as a "time and methods" department, an "organization and procedures" department, or similar subdivisions.

Technical specialists and planners are regarded as the vital element. In keeping with the emphases on technology and organization, the most valued positions in the firm are those associated with product technology and organizational functions. Thus, not only does the firm attempt to recruit the best technical specialists and planners that the market may offer, but the persons working in these areas are the firm's most highly paid employees. Moreover, the largest investment budgets tend to be granted to their departments.

The most important operational and cultural aspect, however, is that *de facto* operational power is given to these departments. Technological specialists are the *dei ex machina* for the firm's business activities, while planners are the designers and interpreters of indices that are used to evaluate the performance of operational units, managers, and workers (through "allocated time" and "jobs").

The organization system is of the mechanical type. As expected, the organizational design is of the Taylorist type, and it is therefore a mechanistic design. Beginning with predetermined products and volumes, the organization department, or, indeed, an "organizing" mind, defines all of the required steps for completing basic business processes (for example, procurement, production, distribution, and sales).

As can be seen if one examines the resulting organization diagram (in a Taylorist firm, the organization diagram is usually developed according to functions) these procedures are the source of all functional responsibilities.

A comparable form of classification applied rigorously to units at the second and subsequent levels leads to definition of individual positions, namely, the duties that are specified for each person, according to the opening or position he or she may fill. Such an organization produces descriptions of responsibilities, or job descriptions, that entail a mechanistic listing of employees' functions.

The emphasis is upon control systems. The need for generally applicable controls is likewise rooted in the Taylorist approach, which specifically allows for planning, organization (methods), and control functions, in conjunction with line functions.

For each production worker, for example, there must be someone to plan his work, someone to develop the method, and someone to regulate his output.

Control functions are essential to this management approach, but the most representative of these functions is quality control, which is to be understood as inspection (determining the acceptability of work performed by others).

Note that, in cases where organization diagrams resemble the matrix type as opposed to the functional type, and where the managerial approach continues to be Taylorist, the matrix functions tend to acquire an inspectional role. For example, according to the Taylorist approach, the materials management function (a matrix function) becomes the inspection unit. Its role is thus to ensure that every other unit possessing a relationship to creation of inventories shall respect the corresponding standard budget.

Occupational qualifications equal specialization. The occupational qualifications required by a mechanistic system are incontestably oriented toward specialization. The company system tends to cultivate and give priority to specialized skills when designing predefined positions. This approach promotes use of employees as "spare parts," by training them for specific positions.

This outlook, which was widely applied during the 1950s and 1960s, particularly in the manufacturing sector, led to the viewpoint that *occupational qualifications equal specialization* and to the ensuing rise of many specialized but few entrepreneurial managers.

The entrepreneurial role was paradoxically subsumed by organization, which anticipated anything capable of occurring and specified how to respond to events (business controlled by procedures).

Another outcome of this approach was the development of careers solely within the framework of positions. This phenomenon led to high personnel turnover because the difficulty of growing within the same firm ("pyramids" of positions). The reality that emerged was characterized by frequent migration of managers and executives from one company to another, although within the same positions. The consequence was an increase in specialization and in functional approaches.

Another paradox that arose was the equation of hermetic language with specialization and, hence, with professional qualifications. The situation was such that the harder it was to understand a person using specialized terminology, the more professional and highly regarded that person was seen to be.

Sales personnel are blamed when business suffers. The emphasis on technical functions in a bureaucracy/product-out company has repercussions on the sales force. In this situation, there is an effort to accomplish as much as possible without relying upon basic business skills. When the market becomes more saturated and thus gives rise to increased competition, the firm is obliged to introduce significant market-oriented positions (initially sales, and then business and marketing positions). Nevertheless, attempts are made to isolate these positions as much as possible and to prevent them from gaining access to the control room.

Business personnel are regarded as a necessity for responding to changing conditions, but it is difficult for them to advance to strategic roles. Indeed, if the latter objective should be met, cultural acceptance will, nevertheless, be slow.

If business suffers, there is a tendency to attribute blame to sales personnel. The attitude is, "The technical people created perfect products, but the sales people failed to make best use of them," and, "The sales people are unprofessional, unimportant, poorly organized, and incapable of planning effectively."

Management is based on cost centers. The managerial product of a Taylorist outlook, which is wholly based upon the priority of ensuring that operational functioning coincides with standards extrapolated from expectations, is the budgeting and budget management approach, which is understood as the ability to achieve maximum curtailment of allocations in order to avoid placing the entire system in a state of crisis.

This viewpoint led to management according to cost centers, and, when carried to its logical extremes in an unsaturated market during the 1950s and 1960s, it gave rise to management according to efficiency standards. The following logical process ensued:

- Business (revenues) is obtained through the product and organization. The firm's employees must guarantee the required volume, and they must concentrate upon the denominator, namely, costs.
- Costs are to be planned at all levels, and they are to be assigned according to responsibilities.
- Because the firm's operations allow only for management of costs, it is necessary to establish budgets according to homo-

geneous organizational centers (known during this period as cost centers). These centers are responsible for achieving maximum curtailment of costs ("to place the smallest possible burden upon the company").

- Sales volume, prices, and, as a result, revenues are predetermined through analysis of the supply-demand ratio, as are possibilities for investing in technology and in operating resources.
- In a stable milieu, it is easy to proceed with an *a priori* definition of cost standards for raw materials, labor, and operating output.
- Within this perspective, operations are directed toward producing the required volumes at minimum cost.
- Because the costs to be managed within this context are essentially direct labor costs or plant and machinery costs, it is sufficient to manage and control output and efficiency (which is also a way of guaranteeing desired volumes) in order to control these costs.
- In terms of production, management according to cost centers becomes management of efficiency.
- If direct labor costs or direct plant costs constitute significant components of operating costs, it is possible to use them as a basis for controlling all types of costs through so-called hourly rates consisting of direct costs and overhead, which are "dumped" onto direct production hours.

Although the impact of direct costs upon hourly rates was relatively high during the 1950s and 1960s, it is relatively limited today (the real cost for "assigned" hours is now less than 5 or 10 percent of total manufacturing costs). Nevertheless, control of manpower efficiency is still employed by many companies today as a means of controlling manufacturing costs. It is also occasionally used as a factor in the adoption of operational decisions, and it is even used for "make-or-buy" analysis (every firm must still give consideration to hourly rates as well as to marginal costs).

Conditions Favoring Success

The bureaucracy/product-out company thrives in conditions favoring operational priorities.

As indicated above, such a company pursues high efficiency with respect to direct resources through attempts to predetermine its optimal operating parameters.

It is most successful, therefore, in an *unsaturated market,* when it can define volumes and prices autonomously, and when it can pursue internal improvement without taking significant risks within the market (in regard to delivery times, quality, and diversification).

Stability of the milieu constitutes another indispensable aspect, because improvements on the drawing boards must be based upon standards, which should be reliable. The success of these endeavors depends upon the predictability of, for example, labor costs, raw materials, social and economic conditions, and foreign exchange rates. The 1950s and 1960s satisfied these requirements to a significant extent, thus favoring the success of this type of firm.

The designation of this particular company model as *bureaucracy/ product-out* gives expression to two fundamental beliefs that govern the model:

- *Product out* as an approach to the market
- *Bureaucracy* as a management tool (vertical organization)

Manufacturing Strategy

The manufacturing strategies of this type of company take a relatively simple form, serving limited operational priorities that are nevertheless defined in great detail.

These priorities can be identified as:

- Maximizing production volume (the only limit being the financial resources for investments in technology)
- Maximizing production efficiency (with an emphasis on operating costs in general and labor costs in particular)
- Investing in innovation (technological R&D, product R&D) and organization as a means of maintaining business

The Marketing/Product-In Company

The *marketing/product-in* (Figure 5-1, area B) organizational model represents the company that is inspired by market-oriented strategies and is managed according to mechanistic perspectives.

This type of company became successful during the 1960s and 1970s, the most noteworthy applications being found in certain leading American firms. The model emerged when markets were close to saturation and were characterized by high purchasing power and, in some instances, by excursions into pure consumerism.

As such, the marketing/product-in company represented a natural outgrowth of the bureaucracy/product-out model, evolving only when the external context moved toward saturation of markets.

In many instances, this type of evolution led to internationalization of companies (to provide outlets for excess production capacity).

Relationship with the Market

The greatest difference between the marketing/product-in model and its predecessor lies in its relationship to the market. Indeed, this type of company represents a completely reoriented perspective, which arose as a result of a revolution that can be characterized as cultural.

Whereas the bureaucracy/product-out company had found its point of departure in its own product and technological know-how, the marketing/product-in firm looks beyond the product to market need. Its strategy can be summarized in the following points.

The firm must do business by identifying and developing market opportunities. The most important business factor is the firm's ability to detect opportunities within the market (in some instances, this aim can be achieved only through sales). Having a product is not enough. Above all, it is necessary to identify and define the market's needs. With such an outlook, a firm might legitimately suspend consideration of its technological capabilities. Indeed, no limits are to be placed upon its capabilities. If necessary and appropriate, a firm might also launch new activities, or it might restrict activities to the marketing of existing products, or entrust production to other firms. After all, if business is pursued primarily by identifying or creating sales opportunities, then production is somewhat marginal — and indeed, merely instrumental.

The company must promote and develop market needs. Whenever opportunities — namely, clients or segments of the market — are discovered, the company must utilize them to the maximum extent. It can do so through an intelligent and profitable policy of technical assistance for durable goods, or through a policy of sharply accelerated obsolescence for semidurable and durable goods.

Aggressiveness and determination on the part of a firm's sales force are decisive factors.

When seeking new opportunities, a company must sharpen its marketing techniques so as to generate new needs in a market where supply exceeds demand. Hence, according to the particular sector, the marketing division must develop advertising techniques, product obsolescence policies, or even commercial adventurousness when necessary.

The dominant goal is to tap the market to the fullest extent. The basic approach is to maximize annual income with short- and mid-term strategies, while long-term strategy (which is never even defined in some instances) is inevitably de-emphasized.

Market needs define product development. Another point of difference between the marketing/product-in model and its predecessor lies in its approach to product development. Here again, the point of departure is perceived market needs.

The process of development allows for expression of needs in terms of functional and even aesthetic requirements, followed by identification of technical and, ultimately, manufacturing requirements.

Such a reversal in logic was not painless for technical specialists, whose technological arrogance, cultivated during prior years, had led them to believe that they could dictate market needs.

Products must fulfill market needs. In conclusion, the strategic perspective of the marketing/product-in company, insofar as its relationship to the market is concerned, is that business is conducted by identifying market needs and by then producing products that meet those needs (product in).

Organization and Management Approach

The product precedes organization. Although the definition of products takes place in a different form in the marketing/product-in model from that of its predecessor, the development of company structure nevertheless follows the same pattern.

Indeed, it is appropriate to observe that, within the reference matrix, this type of firm is situated within the same column as the previously described type, and it therefore relies upon the same structural principles.

For this aspect, the observations that were previously offered with respect to bureaucracy/product-out companies are therefore pertinent, with the clarification that, in this instance, the same principles are being applied to a significant business component that is practically absent from the former model.

The organization takes precedence over people. The emphasis on organization over people, discussed in regard to the previous model, applies to the marketing/product-in model as well. In the latter case, however, the ramifications of this approach on sales personnel became even more critical.

Although it is true that plausible and rational arguments for Taylorist principles exist in the domain of production, it is not possible to apply the same principals to sales, where the system must turn outward, and where internal procedures and standards cannot by themselves respond to the extremely diversified configurations of customers and markets.

Thus, procedures and standards are experienced in a decisively critical manner by sales personnel (restrictions upon sales possibilities), and crises involving rejection are not uncommon.

Marketing and commercial activities are regarded as the vital element. In the marketing/product-in model, marketing capabilities are regarded as the principal form of operational know-how that is needed for pursuing business.

Extensive efforts are therefore undertaken to increase the capabilities of managers and employees in this area, with the result that schools may even be created on an ad hoc basis. For a time, the motto Managerial Know-How Equals Marketing Know-How was even incorporated within companies' perspectives. The field of marketing becomes increasingly specialized and sophisticated (sprouting branches in marketing concepts, marketing intelligence, strategic marketing, operational marketing, etc.).

In keeping with their new prominence, marketing executives are generously rewarded and highly valued.

In general, company perspectives are significantly enriched during reorientation to this "gust of fresh air" from the market.

The organization system is of the mechanical type. The predominant organization system continues in the Taylorist tradition, undergoing significant transformation in systems or procedures.

Nevertheless, expansion of the business area creates a need for effective control, and the firm is therefore obliged to organize this sector of its activities to the fullest extent. Responsibility for the job is entrusted to the organization department (the counterpart to the time and methods department for production), whose growing importance often transforms it into the "organization division," which shares control of commercial activities with the administrative division (in some instances, the organization division and the administrative division constitute a combined hierarchical stronghold).

It should be observed that more widespread use of EDP systems during this era, along with their technical possibilities (T.P., for example), caused the organization division to acquire even greater importance.

Budget management is based on cost centers. During the 1960s and 1970s, significant reasons emerged for emphasizing the budget management methods that had been introduced in Taylorist-functional companies. These reasons varied from greater organizational complexity to difficulty in controlling costs (which had now become more difficult to identify) to the significant management possibilities offered by information systems (which were more advanced at this point), and to the rise of managerial perspectives that were more attentive to management.

Cost centers continued to play a structural role. The concept of reducing costs, which produced a significant impact on those who were responsible for cost centers, created certain motivational and managerial problems.

In many instances, the aesthetics of the system prevailed over management needs, giving rise to overly complex or detailed "spider webs" (even "cost entries" emerged).

The emphasis is upon control systems. The need for rigorous control is a natural consequence of the management system described in the preceding subsection. In the marketing/product-in model this need is expressed by development of an ad hoc system that is an outgrowth of the Taylor-functional model: organizational structure (development of management control), information systems (hardware and software), specific procedures, audits, and so on.

The controller acquires exceptional power inasmuch as his or her input constitutes the most important parameter in evaluations of executives' performance.

Indeed, the entire power structure has changed dramatically in the marketing/product-in configuration. Production personnel (including the time-and-methods specialists who are now assigned to various departments) must surrender the scepter of importance to commercial personnel — but the organization managers (who sometimes overlap with personnel managers) and controllers, who actually become assistant general managers, are the ones who possess the real power.

The emphasis is upon sales structure. The importance of the sales system accounted for significant investment in this area, not only in terms of resources, but in terms of systems and facilities.

Furthermore, the structure of companies was often revisited on an ad hoc basis.

Regard for a firm's relationship with the market as the point of departure for conducting business led to reconsideration of management responsibilities.

Firms that had originally been organized in terms of principal functions (production, planning, scheduling, purchasing, marketing, etc.), began to adopt models that more closely reflected business processes. In this way, divisions and product lines emerged, as channels to which "slices" of primary functions could be allotted, or as means of pursuing specific types of business.

The internal structure of a division could continue to be of the functional type, or it could be modified according to the same principles.

This organizational restructuring definitely offered the advantage of shifting companies toward more entrepreneurial and management-oriented concepts. Nevertheless, in some instances, the marketing emphasis led planners to excesses in the application of authority. For example, attempts were made to subdivide certain production departments according to business divisions, even though these departments were indivisible on account of problems in terms of minimum technological thresholds or excessive diseconomies in terms of production (the latter problems can now be avoided with production of the flexible/elastic type, which is oriented toward just-in-time systems).

Production personnel are blamed when business suffers. The strategic perspective of a marketing/product-in company leads to a de-emphasizing of production functions, as explained above. The phenomenon has various nuances in market sectors and entrepreneurial concepts.

On consumer goods, the impact has been extremely pronounced, less so on semidurable goods, and to a lesser extent still on industrial goods (including those emanating from engineering firms that manage "turnkey" plants and subcontract for production activities).

One general consequence has affected everyone to some extent: For a decade, investments in production systems have been decisively curtailed — relegated solely to innovations regarded as indispensable for introducing new products. Obviously, this situation provides an advantage for the sales area and for products.

Now that production was no longer fashionable, production managers were penalized economically in relation to other positions. Certain multinational firms, accustomed to promoting future managers from within, actually abandoned this policy for several years with respect to production.

Within the context of company operationality, production was often seen (perhaps deservedly so) as an obstacle to potential business, on account of its rigidity and slowness in responding.

In sum, the tables had been turned in the marketing/product-in company. The attitude now was, "The sales people have identified perfect sales opportunities, but the technical people failed to make use of them." (It will be recalled that, in the bureaucracy/product-out companies, the opposite attitude prevailed.)

Interdisciplinary professional qualifications are needed. The organizational complexity of marketing/product-in companies inevitably exposed the limitations of the Taylorist-functional structure. Notwithstanding the prolific endeavors of the organization department, company procedures were incapable of handling the entire range of company problems.

The conclusion was that "people need to talk more," especially in order to cope with the exceptions and problems that were becoming so numerous.

Thus emerged the era of meetings and committees designed to cover specific problems and areas: a production committee, a planning committee, a quality committee, a committee for modifications, and so on. This was in direct response to the inherent defect of the functional model, in which the operational process had been subdivided into multiple specialized responsibilities (functions).

However, because the new approach was designed to *remedy* problems, not remove their causes, it was neither highly effective nor economical.

One outcome of this phase of development was that it kept managers extremely busy with meetings that, keep in mind, were attended by as many as 20 people and consisted essentially of discussion (as opposed to decision-making or planning).

The positive side of this phenomenon, however, was that it made evident the need for greater diversification of functions on the part of managers, if for no other reason than to make them capable of communicating effectively with their co-workers.

Situations requiring interdisciplinary activities became more frequent, and interdisciplinary planning groups also emerged (although they were not trained with suitable methodologies).

The diversification phenomenon also became observable at lower organizational levels, where terms such as *polyvalency, job rotation, job enlargement, job enrichment,* and *socio-technical systems* (*work units*) came into being.

Actually, this was merely a chronological coincidence, in the sense that the motivating factors for these changes at the workers' level were principally other factors, as is already known.

For managers, the ability to communicate effectively in many disciplines took on a remunerative value. Those who were talented in this regard were the ones to get ahead, because they were the most successful in conducting meetings and promoting decision making. Thus, within the context of this organizational design, they were the most useful to the company.

Management by objective is the rule. Another deficiency of the Taylorist-functional organization model was that it did not ensure effective overall supervision of business, inasmuch as this function was entirely entrusted to the general manager.

Management by objective (MBO) was developed to correct this deficiency — to orient management more effectively toward results.

The strengths of the Taylorist-functional system in this area were significant, however, and MBO was not readily accepted in every instance. Indeed, the static type of budget management that had arisen during the prior decade often limited the intrinsic effectiveness of MBO, since this form of budget management was also used as an instrument of companies' compensation systems.

Many firms attempted to ensure that budgets coincided with objectives, notwithstanding all of the risks involved. An extremely common solution was maintenance of two budgets, namely, an "official" budget that coincided with the firm's stated objectives, and a more prudent "confidential" budget, intended for high-level decision making.

This ambiguous situation, which obviously causes the system to lose credibility, generated bureaucratic inclinations whereby managers measured their performances with their own budgets, for better or worse, without considering the consequences of such an approach on general business objectives.

The critical period, then, became the month of October when a manager's ability to "sell himself" during establishment of his budget would strongly influence his performance evaluation.

Everything else a manager did was of little importance, since beyond that point, operating margins capable of allowing dramatic changes in anticipated profits were extremely limited.

For this reason, there would be several managers at the end of each year devising explanations for their failure to adhere to the budget while obtaining specific operating results. Indeed, two typical forms of behavior emerged during the final portion of the year:

- Managers who failed to attain their objectives dedicated their time to preparing justifications instead of to efforts to attain these objectives at a later point (72 percent or 74 percent is always failure in relation to the 100 percent objective).
- In anticipation of stepping far over budget, managers attempted to limit the results to avoid setting an overly ambitious goal for the following year.

Nevertheless, MBO ushered in a significant conceptual range and constituted a forerunner of the more entrepreneurial management models being introduced today (management by policy or MBP).

Conditions Favoring Success

The scenario favoring success for a marketing/product-in company is a "first-generation market," namely, a situation in which business can be done on the basis of a firm's ability to identify market needs and to market its product effectively. Thus, the situation involves a *saturated (though still immature) market* characterized by ntense competition.

In contrast to the *efficiency* era that characterized the earlier context (high volume, low costs), this was the *product* era (diversified products that met customers' needs).

Such are the primary ingredients of success for the marketing/product-in company.

The inherent structural limits of this type of company, however, establish a need for a limiting factor, namely, *predictability of the economy and the market*. Indeed, the mechanistic principles derived from a Taylorist-functional approach — in which management is based upon precodified standards and procedures — could not be applied successfully in a context characterized by abrupt changes and turbulence, since these phenomena hinder standardization.

This model is nevertheless better adapted than its predecessor to markets that are approaching saturation, and are marked by intense competition; it is also better adapted to *internationalized markets*.

The marketing/product-in firms experienced their heyday in the late 1960s and early 1970s. The designation *venture/ market-in* alludes to the operational capabilities of this kind of firm, namely, intensive marketing activities and the identification of products that are to be designed and produced *product-in*.

Manufacturing Strategy

Whereas the strategic emphasis of bureaucracy/product-out companies consisted of production efficiency, the principal operational lever in a marketing/product-in company is explicit operational communication of the need to increase *sales volume* and *profits* to every level.

One could engage in sophistry and point out that in some firms sales volume became the number-one priority (especially in the United States), whereas for other firms (generally in Europe and particularly in Italy), profits were the highest priority.

Indeed, whereas the prevalent objective in the United States was a constant increase in output and sales volume, certain historical and socioeconomic phenomena oriented some European managers, and notably Italian managers, toward maximizing profits while limiting risks (and, for that reason, toward limiting volume if necessary).

In this situation, the overseeing of continuous changes in the scale of a firm's activities so as to increase or at least avoid reducing profits was regarded as a successful strategy. Accordingly, there developed a school of managers and consultants who specialized in "profitable adjustment of scale."

Despite the obvious hazardousness of such an approach in macroeconomic terms, or for the economies of individual nations, it has not entirely lost its grip.

The emphasis upon income (sales volume and/or profits) was an innovation that gave meaning to the concept of the *value* of various functions. In the bureaucracy/product-out companies, where only denominators (costs) were being controlled, the extrapolation of *value* has not been so easy.

Another strategic characteristic of marketing/product-in companies is the importance attributed to *market research*, which actually becomes the point of departure for industrial strategies (within a short- or mid-term context, obviously). From an operational point of view, an effective industrial strategy was extensive *diversification of products*, and nearly every firm began to rely upon this strategy.

Insofar as organization may be concerned, the strategy adopted in most instances was one that allowed for segmentation of companies into *business units*, especially for marketing purposes (divisions, product lines, etc.).

In fact, a tendency toward *marketing alone* often arose.

As can be observed, an actual manufacturing strategy does not exist within this type of firm, except insofar as such strategy may contribute to short-term satisfaction of market needs. Indeed, in general terms, the 1960s and 1970s saw few changes in manufacturing strategy, a consequence of the limited emphasis placed on production.

The Involvement/Process-Improvement Company

The involvement/process-improvement company organization model (Figure 5-1, area C) is inspired by an operations perspective, as was true of the bureaucracy/product-out model. However, the management and cultural principles of the two models differ decisively.

Indeed, this type of firm falls within the *group dynamics* column.

As indicated earlier, this particular model was most effectively interpreted by the Japanese during the 1970s. Hence, the ensuing description is actually a description of Japanese manufacturing firms during that period.

Relationship with the Market

The operations orientation of Japanese firms during the 1970s is distinguished by significant peculiarities, discussed below.

Business is done by continually improving processes in terms of technology and capabilities. The statement above encapsulates the entire belief system of Japanese firms, namely, a system that emphasizes:

- Continuous improvement as an operational priority (kaizen)
- Operating processes and production processes in particular as the objective of improvement efforts (*process oriented*)

The emphasis of processes over products requires greater concentration upon causes than upon effects. In other words, improvement of output is guaranteed through control and improvement of processes. Hence, the orientation requires continuous management and improvement of process capabilities.

According to the model, this particular approach provides the possibility for continuous improvement in the quality of products and services (outputs), as well as effective pursuit of the following objectives.

Customer satisfaction is essential. In fact, customer satisfaction is regarded as the only relevant objective for ensuring stable and continuously increasing business (the Japanese CWQC strategy is explained in Chapter 1).

Quality is the priority factor. The strategic assumption that quality is the priority factor for business affects every aspect of the company system — management methods, perspectives, control methods, organization, and technical factors.

Indeed, the company is permeated with the principles of TQC, in such a way that the inherent priority for every operational activity is quality.

Market feedback promotes process improvement. An ability to manage and to increase business depends upon this approach. If business consists of the ability to provide quality, and if quality means appropriateness for purposes (the customer's purposes), then appropriateness must be verified and upgraded on a continuous basis.

Hence, it becomes necessary to gauge customer satisfaction with each product and to modify the products accordingly. Applied to departmental performance and to productivity, this approach became the source of just-in-time systems.

Organization and Management Approach

The process precedes organization management by process. Whereas *products* constituted the point of departure for companies of the Western type (in categories A and B of Figure 5-1), and whereas functions provided the basis for assigning operational responsibilities, now *processes* became the critical dimension of the organization system.

In terms of macro-organization, the vital processes according to the Japanese are those which are correlated with *quality, delivery,* and *costs,* whereas these are the principal activities that confront units at a micro level.

Accordingly, whereas the parameters for operational management in Western firms were essentially budget indicators defined according to functions and cost centers, the indices adopted by Japanese firms for management and evaluation of performance were performance indicators associated with operational processes.

Supplier to customer chains form an organic system. Because the processes that determine company performance and produce the greatest impact upon business results are interfunctional factors associated with quality, delivery, and costs, controlling and improving these processes requires prudent activation of all elements involved.

The "optimizing" approach employed by the Japanese consisted of linking every element to a downstream unit, with the goal of providing satisfaction (within a total quality perspective, satisfaction = quality = appropriateness for purposes = suitability for the needs of customers, or downstream units). The quality of work is thus evaluated by the downstream unit, and not by the organization (in the generic or centralized sense).

This supplier to customer concept at the operational level is employed at a macro-organizational level as well.

Japanese companies are actually structured as *organic systems* (not *mechanical systems* of the type associated with companies in categories A and B), where various components are in contact with one another as if they were suppliers and customers within the market, according to an operational network whose channels are activated on the basis of company needs and specific circumstances.

There is exceptional subdivision of responsibilities, constituting overall responsibility on the part of multiple operational units, which are more comparable to profit centers than to cost centers (industrial accounting was still less sophisticated than in the West).

Organization is based on improvement. The principal organizational dimension of the involvement/process-improvement firm is certainly the aspect of continuous improvement (kaizen). In this respect it differs sharply from companies in categories A and B.

Indeed, whereas the latter types of firms adhere to static standards emanating from the central organization, standards are continually developed and improved by the units that operationally control the same standards within companies belonging to category C.

The structure for promoting such improvement developed during the 1970s. It allowed for individual suggestions, group improvement activities (quality circles), interdisciplinary study groups, and, in particular, daily improvement measures on the production line ("day-to-day management," or "daily routine work").

Although consolidation in the form of an organization model had not yet taken place, methods that were shaped and defined by top management (management by policy) would nevertheless develop during the 1980s.

Frequent rotation breeds total professionalism. A management system that is oriented toward improvement generated from within — in other words, from the company operators — presupposes a capability on the part of those operators to determine the upstream and downstream implications of any changes being introduced. Moreover, not only improvement but operational decision making of any kind presupposes a capability to perform comprehensive evaluation instead of one based on functions.

Accordingly, Japanese executives and managers, along with workers, are given maximum possible rotation in all company positions. This practice enables them to obtain the broadest level of occupational skills while discouraging attitudes and forms of behavior that are determined by specific functions. While specialized occupational skills were being cultivated in the West and careers were being pursued vertically within the framework of various functions, Japanese firms had already introduced highly effective mechanisms for promoting comprehensive approaches.

Operational authority is delegated to lower levels. The cultural milieu of managers and executives provides numerous possibilities for delegating decision making and operational authority to lower levels. According to the Japanese, although continuous improvement is the most important operational dimension for companies, individuals at higher levels must also fully dedicate their efforts to improvement. This ensures that sufficient time will be devoted to these efforts while also establishing a need to delegate authority for routine supervision. In contrast to Western firms, the Japanese have shifted authority for routine management downward while substantially altering the nature of operational interaction at the managerial level.

Whereas the flow of information needed for operational decisions is essentially top-down in Western firms, it is predominantly bottom-up in Japanese firms. Decisions are adopted by operating personnel and reported or recommended for approval to managers.

The top-down dimension nevertheless allows for an abundant flow of policies, or criteria for adoption of decisions.

Authoritativeness is encouraged. Collective social values in Japan are based upon esteem and respect. Thus, it is essential that managers be esteemed and respected by their co-workers; indeed, they represent their co-workers.

Within this context, authoritativeness is emphasized, and it thereby generates authority and acknowledgment of hierarchical levels.

This is far different from the Western meritocratic system, which features hierarchical promotions that are based on the evaluations of superiors and/or possession of absolute specialized skills.

Conditions Favoring Success

A firm that is oriented toward customer satisfaction through continuous improvement of product quality is certain to succeed within the context of a mature market, namely, a market where buyers are able to appreciate product quality.

This situation presupposes a product with which the customer is familiar. Indeed, it is appropriate to recall that during the 1970s, the Japanese developed their industrial sector by placing specific emphasis upon products that had already been invented and placed on the market by Westerners.

Approaching the client as a "second wave," the Japanese were able to apply a comparison strategy by supplying products of higher quality — in other words, products that were more appropriate for their purposes. Indeed, the Japanese could not gain competitive advantages in marketing or innovation, and they therefore limited themselves to taking advantage of situations created by others (Western companies).

Nevertheless, their improvement-oriented approach (not only to quality, but to manufacturing processes) allowed them to achieve significant expansion of markets for individual products, with the formula *greater volume* → *lower costs* → *greater volume*. Thus, significant advantages in terms of domestic employment levels were obtained.

The decision was therefore to supply familiar products that offered high potential volumes.

Application of the improvement lever for every area of a company (not solely for quality) nevertheless allowed conquest of products and high volume markets that had traditionally been controlled by Western firms. This situation occurred in the automobile industry, for example, where the Japanese combined flexibility with prompt filling of orders (industrial and commercial leadtime).

To summarize, the conditions under which Japanese firms of the 1970s succeeded involved markets where quality and service were in demand. The method they employed for attaining these objectives essentially consisted of maximum employee *involvement* in continuous *process improvement* (*involvement/process-improvement*).

Manufacturing Strategy

Whereas the basic strategy for firms within category B had been essentially marketing-oriented, Japanese companies within category C sought to apply an essentially industrial strategy.

The predominant perspective, at a philosophical level as well as an operational level, was companywide quality control (CWQC), which emphasized:

- Customer satisfaction
- Quality
- Continuous improvement
- Maximum employment/maximum volumes
- Consolidation of sales volume

From an industrial viewpoint, this outlook is distinguished from that of its predecessors by certain priorities. These priorities can be identified as follows:

- Continuous control and improvement of process capabilities, with strong emphasis upon process control as a result (extensive process-control know-how, even at lower levels)
- Development of effective quality assurance systems based upon maximum participation (rather than upon certification documentation)
- Significant verticalization of production processes, with reliance upon organizing techniques that promote simplification (just-in-time, non-stock production, visual control)
- Plants focusing upon product families, with high flexibility in terms of product mixes
- A search for "waste" in every operational activity (the "five zeros")
- Maximum use of equipment (total productive maintenance)
- Prompt industrial development of products, with an emphasis upon quality (quality deployment techniques and organization)

- High decentralization of production and close integration with suppliers

The Venture/Market-In Company

The *venture/market-in* model (Figure 5-1, area D) represents the characteristics of successful companies during the 1980s and 1990s.

These characteristics emerged as a result of an analysis of those companies which currently offer the most favorable mid-term and long-term trends. The reference firms are international firms, in the sense that they operate throughout the world. Today it is no longer valid to speak of models in terms of geographic areas. In fact, there exist greater differences between the successful and unsuccessful firms within the same nation than between the typical Western firm, for example, and the Japanese firm.

The interesting trait of "D" companies is that they embody both the Western and Japanese approaches, constituting a combination of the best features of each. Yet it is precisely the interaction of these elements that distinguishes this model from the others. Its position in the reference matrix shown in Figure 5-1 expresses its unification of the market-oriented approach of Western firms with Japanese management principles.

The predominance of this model today is suggested by the efforts of Japanese firms to overcome their weakest point — namely, marketing capabilities — and the efforts of Western firms to introduce participatory principles into their management organization systems.

Relationship with the Market

One could say that the venture/market-in model's relationship with the market combines strategies of Japanese origin (mid- and long-term orientation) with approaches of Western origin (market analysis, innovation, and product diversification).

The principal features of this type of firm are outlined below.

Customer satisfaction is essential. A strategy that seeks to satisfy customers instead of merely extracting short-term profits from them is designed to ensure reliable sales volume and favorable results for the mid- and long-term.

Business is done through chains, supplier-customer chains, and "value" chains. The Japanese and Westerners have independently arrived at this concept, although their ways of doing so were entirely different.

Whereas production was the usual point of departure for the Japanese, the market was the point of departure for Westerners.

In this way, the Japanese arrived at the conclusion that, in order to raise processes and quality to optimal levels, it is necessary to think in terms of *groupwide quality control* and maximum improvement of the entire chain of suppliers and clients for a given business. In the United States, meanwhile, the most widely accepted approach (Michael E. Porter's "value chains") asserts that the strength of a business depends on the strength of each link in the chain constituting the respective business.

The impact of these perspectives is substantial, because the implication is that a "perfect" company in a chain of limited value (in absolute terms, or in terms of the partners' strength) is doomed to failure, whereas a merely adequate firm in the proper chain shall be successful.

Actually, it is probable that both results shall be obtained quickly: being in the proper chain, and acquiring appropriate partners who are highly effective and efficient.

Quality, flexibility, and lead time are the key features. At present the most significant operational factors for success within the market are quality, lead time, and flexibility of the entire logistical chain (from development to production to delivery). This condition will prevail throughout the century.

Information flows from the market to processes. The vital relationship between the market and processes, which has been borrowed from the Japanese model, will ultimately become more prominent and will occur as a result of real-time information and feedback obtained from development of networks, expansion of a market-in outlook, and the development of principles for market-directed production.

Continuous improvement and innovation are equal partners. Attempts are being made to combine the Western propensity for innovation with the Japanese strategy of continuous improvement.

Indeed, it is no longer sufficient to innovate and then to accept mediocre manufacturing development (Westerners), nor is it sufficient to pursue manufacturing development and continuous improvement without innovation (the Japanese).

Sony's situation is relevant in this sense. Sony is perhaps the only Japanese firm to have relied in the past almost entirely on innovation. In this regard, its approach was typically Western. Nevertheless, in 1986 Sony, a rarity in Japan for never having promoted an intensive participation-based improvement program, introduced one of the most effective kaizen programs in the world.

Made-to-order (personalized) products will gain prominence. A new phenomenon is emerging. The market has become so abundantly supplied that mass production will enter a crisis. Not even extensive diversification shall suffice. For durable and semidurable goods (from automobiles to clothing), customers will seek (and in some instances, already are seeking) custom-produced goods.

Thus, the current reality of the custom-tailored apparel produced by Melbo in Japan (custom-tailored clothing within five days, with the customer's name sewn on the inside) shall exist tomorrow for custom-made shoes and made-to-order automobiles. Consumers can then bid farewell to mass-produced goods.

Organization and Management Approach

The business chain precedes organization. The approach is definitely of the Japanese type: business processes above all. This includes not only company processes but processes constituting the entire business.

In this way, the company is viewed as an open system that is linked to upstream and downstream partners, with the general procedures for business prevailing over any other management criteria: "Business-related flows must be given priority."

Companies are open systems. Within this perspective, partner firms must be directly linked with respect to the most important operating procedures. A fuller explanation of the cultural aspect of this principle follows.

Conceptually, the objective is to overcome a relationship between two companies that submerges the functions of both firms in bureaucracy, which is time-consuming and inefficient. Instead, the objective is to force close linkages between the analogous functions of both firms (see Figure 5-2).

Let's say that Company B needs a subassembly that can be produced by Company A. The two companies enter into a relationship. How would such a relationship be managed within the functional-Taylorist bureaucracy/product-out company?

Under the assumption that production to order (to adopt one category as a point of reference) is required, the process would occur in the following manner:

1. Company B's production division determines that an excessive work load prevents it from making a certain subassembly, and it is decided that this item should be externally produced.
2. The scheduling department determines the needs and defines the necessary supply dates.
3. A request is transmitted to the time and methods department, which must define the component's characteristics and provide appropriate information for evaluation.
4. The technical planning department defines the tolerances and technical specifications that are to be indicated to suppliers.
5. The quality department supervises acceptance of items being supplied.
6. The documentation is sent to the purchasing department, which then seeks offers (at least three) from potential suppliers.
7. The purchasing department or another channel evaluates the offers.
8. A supplier (Company A) is selected.
9. An entirely analogous procedure begins for the supplier, starting with the sales department. (In the interest of brevity, the steps will not be described.)
10. The supplier produces and delivers the necessary item.
11. Acceptance testing by Company B uncovers various problems with the component.
12. A ping pong process begins between various departments within the two firms; an extended period of time may be required.

13. A decision is adopted to systematize the component. This is done either by the supplier or under the supplier's supervision.

The product resulting from such a process is usually barely adequate in terms of certain characteristics and decisively superior in terms of others. At times, it is different from the product envisioned by the original department.

Certain observations about this process can be made:

- Although the objective was certainly otherwise, the process did *not* provide the best component as promptly as possible and at the lowest possible total cost.
- Even when every department involved in the process (with the total number of departments being at least 13) is acting in good faith and is demonstrating an adequate level of competence (which is far from guaranteed), such a lengthy communication process creates significant risks of unacceptability.
- The process does not easily accommodate modifications in scheduling or content.

This type of relationship between two firms can be defined as an *end-to-end* or *series* relationship, where the various functions are arranged "head-to-head," disallowing for any direct dialogue between like departments (Figure 5-2).

Open companies develop "side-by-side" relationships (Figure 5-2) according to the principles outlined below:

- Companies A and B are already operationally integrated, with Company A being one of the suppliers to whom Company B is "wedded."
- When it is necessary to resolve a problem in prices, Company A's purchasing department and Company B's sales department speak to one another.
- Similar dialogues occur as necessary between the two firms' technical departments, time and methods departments, the scheduling departments, and production departments.
- Open communication channels are maintained through contact and open procedures.

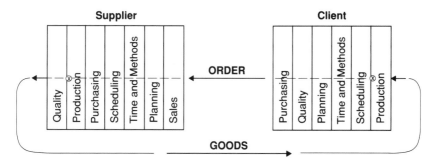

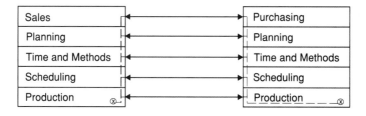

Figure 5-2. End-to-End or Side-by-Side Supplier Relationships

Companies develop as organic systems, with profit centers and global accounting. The organizing system is based upon the concept of *organic systems,* consisting of units that maintain supplier-customer relationships with one another. This system likewise allows maximum decentralization of responsibility. These factors lead to a replacement of cost centers by *profit centers,* in which the details of analytical accounting are de-emphasized.

Today, overhead is increasingly attributed to activities, and the practice of expressing it in cost percentage levels is being abandoned.

At the same time, other accounting principles intended to emphasize actual business factors, namely, flexibility and lead time, are emerging. Some companies are imputing overhead to products in proportion to throughput time or relative inventory rotation, instead of according to the value of the respective products (thus, distribution of expenses is determined according to the length of time a product remains with the firm).

Entrepreneurial skills and rotations are emphasized. Whereas model A emphasizes specialized occupational skills, model B interfunctional skills, and model C general skills, model D seeks and encourages entrepreneurial skills. Thus, qualities necessary to an entrepreneur, such as general management capabilities and ability to manage risks, are encouraged.

In some companies of this type, managers can share directly in business earnings (portions of stock, or "entrepreneurship"). In addition, job rotation becomes indispensable for allowing managers to acquire general occupational know-how.

Management by policy. Management by objective has been found to be excessively oriented toward obtaining short-term results, insufficiently process-oriented, and heedless of the means by which results are obtained. These factors mean that MBO is considered risky within a long-term context. Management by objective is now being superseded by so-called management by policy, which was developed by Japanese companies.

Chapter 7 offers a comprehensive definition of this system, but its basic characteristics can be indicated here:

- Translation of the entrepreneurial logic of "managing by priority, applying long-term policies to the short-term" into an operative management system
- Direct link to business plan
- Focus on a few vital priorities with important goals
- An integrated interfunctional process oriented toward these goals
- Involvement of numerous people
- Continuous and active management of the process intended to attain goals
- Strict application of PDCA cycle
- Emphasis on cause-effect relations

Operating units manage the improvement of operating systems and procedures. Along with profit centers, decentralization, management of processes and continuous improvement of processes comes continuous improvement of operating procedures.

This need should not be examined by central organizational units, which are remote from operations, but by actual operating units, which must propose the modifications and improvements they wish to introduce to the firm's management and to central units responsible for organization. The contributions of central units consist of ensuring uniformity and offering consulting services, but only if operating units consider these services worthy of being "paid for."

Conditions Favoring Success

The most favorable milieu for a firm of this kind consists of features that are predicted for the future:

- Mature/affluent markets
- Globalization of all business activity
- Intense competitiveness
- Economic turbulence
- A demand for customized products
- A need for rapid adaptations/changes
- A marketplace in which "time to market" is a competitive advantage

In such a context, the other three models would encounter serious difficulties in remaining competitive. Even the Japanese model of the 1970s (involvement/process-improvement) is undergoing significant modifications (see Introduction).

Only model D can offer the necessary breadth of approach to respond to a situation requiring a real-time market orientation (*market-in*), and significant delegated entrepreneurial capabilities (*venture*).

Manufacturing Strategy

Marketing strategy and operations strategy tend to merge, forming a comprehensive approach (from *market-in*, with operations as a business tool, through *time to market*). Beyond these levels is a master strategy of mid- and long-term profits (in contrast to the short-term profits of the 1960s and 1970s), with the aim of preserving and developing a company's position.

An overall vision of the company (value chains and groupwide quality control) is associated with verticalization of processes. The result is that firms will seek either actual internal verticalization (reunifying areas of production that have been previously decentralized), or (more frequently) integrated logistical configurations (comakership and information networks). The entire process shall occur within the context of *global manufacturing*.

Nevertheless, the current operational watchwords in leading firms are *flexibility* and *lead time*. These aims will be pursued in every possible manner through technological changes. During this effort just-in-time, CIM (computer-integrated manufacturing), and TBI (total business integration) will play leading roles, becoming the actual organizational point of arrival during the final portion of this century.

The marketplace will be oriented toward buyers who want increasingly individualized products within the shortest time possible. Accordingly, methods of reconciling automation with flexibility and personalizing of products with efficiency will be prevalent topics of discussion during future years.

6

Emerging Strategies

The manufacturing strategies adopted by venture/market-in companies are nothing other than prototypes of the strategies that will emerge by the year 2000.

Successful firms will be those which have best managed, combined, and refined the strategies emerging today.

These new strategies form three currents of activity that are independent, yet interactive. They are:

- Time-based strategy
- Global manufacturing
- Total business integration

It should be kept in mind that these strategic priorities are extremely similar to those which were defined for Japanese industry by Waseda University in Tokyo, as indicated within the first section of this book. The difference lies in the degree of emphasis placed on flexibility. Whereas time-based strategy allows for significant flexibility in terms of production systems, it is not given the same priority in Western countries as it is in Japan.

For example, CIM configurations, which have been introduced in the West, are only slightly (and not always) more flexible than prior systems, whereas Japanese production systems have become "significantly" more flexible. Indeed, it may be that limited awareness of the extensive level of improvement that is required to achieve flexibility is the Achilles' heel of Western industry.

This limited understanding may partially stem from the prevailing notion that automation is a means of transcending JIT rather than fully achieving it. The risk we Westerners face consists of creating CIM production systems that lack sufficient flexibility and are extremely complex from any planning or management standpoint. Indeed, the factors that render CIM applications truly effective are simplification of production flows and organization, as well as flexibility of product mixes and volume. In some instances, failure to consider these principles leads to development of CIM production methods and production lines of the "on-off" type, in other words, production at a constant output level, instead of self-adjustable production whose output varies according to the volumes actually needed. This type of error even negates the logic of responding to the market.

One cause of this lack of overall awareness is certainly the overly technical orientation that Westerners have adopted in relation to JIT and CIM. Thus, the most important dimension of these approaches, which is the cultural-organizational dimension, has been eclipsed. This phenomenon is more fully examined in the Chapter 8.

This chapter is concerned with the other strategic approaches that form the basic structure for total manufacturing management. A brief summary of each concept follows.

Time-Based Strategy

Time is becoming the principal factor in business. The way in which firms manage time in production, new product development, sales, and distribution represents the principal tool today for obtaining competitive advantages.

If it is assumed that the best firms in the world manage such factors as productivity and innovation in more or less comparable ways, then quality and time become the factors that distinguish the absolute leaders, and time by itself becomes the factor capable of distinguishing firms that are leaders *and* that maintain high profit levels.

Indeed, the ability to bring products onto the market before competitors do allows a firm, for example, to obtain high profits through high prices.

On the other hand, a delay of only six months in comparison with competitors appears to cause a reduction in profits by at least one-third during the first five years of a product's life span.

The ability to deliver products promptly contributes indisputably to sales increases and therefore to sales volume, because firms that have that capability will be preferred over their competitors. Furthermore, when ability to serve the market is equal, the firm with lower throughput times will require less WIP and less storage space. Thus, its costs will be lower, and its operating margin higher.

This observation is even more applicable in a company that is capable of producing individualized products to order in brief periods of time (high flexibility).

It should also be recognized that there is an objective value placed on time, in the sense that many clients are prepared to pay more in order to obtain products quickly.

A diagnostic approach based upon the time factor would allow easy explanation of why many of today's leading firms are successful.

The success of many Japanese firms, for example, can be explained in terms of their extraordinary ability to manage the time factor. Firms that can definitely be placed within this category are Sony, Matsushita, Sharp, Toyota, Hitachi, NEC, Toshiba, and Honda. Some of the statistics on these firms are indeed exceptional. A few examples follow:

- Matsushita: throughput time for producing washing machines is two hours (originally 360 hours)
- Honda: period for developing new automobiles is 36 months (originally five years)
- Toyota: production time is two days (lead time for filling orders in Japan)

Moreover, Japan outproduces the West by significant ratios for certain products (Figure 6-1).

Products	Ratios for Development Time	
	Japan	West
Televisions	1	3
Dies for plastic materials	1	3
Automobiles	1	2

Figure 6-1. Comparative Development Times

These differences are accompanied by planning costs that (unfortunately for us) offer similar ratios.

Probably one of the best Western interpretations of that "timeliness" factor is provided by the Italian firm Benetton, which is a world leader in knitted and ready-to-wear items.

In sectors where there is a higher technological content, Hewlett-Packard offers one of the best examples, because it has also interpreted just-in-time principles properly in the domain of organizing production.

As the firm's "number one," John Young, has indicated, Hewlett-Packard's corporate structure is currently oriented toward reducing time for every company process (by at least 50 percent) by introducing the concept of *break-even time* (time that must elapse between the moment when an idea arises and the moment when the product becomes capable of generating net income for the firm).

The following statistics, which have been recently obtained by leading firms, demonstrate the importance now being attributed to the time factor, even in Western nations:

- General Electric: time for filling orders for electrical switches is from three weeks to three days
- AT&T: time for developing a new telephone set is from two years to one year
- Motorola (Florida): ability to produce and to ship pagers is within two hours of receiving an order (originally three weeks)
- Hewlett-Packard: development time for a new printer is from 4.5 years to 22 months. Production time for electronic testing devices is from 35 days to five days
- Olivetti: development time for certain data processing products is from 12 months to six months

The "fundamental" periods of time available for improving a firm's competitive advantage involve various processes, and their relative importance varies according to sectors of the market. These periods can be identified as follows:

- Development and engineering time for new products (R&D, design, and engineering)
- Start-up time for new production ventures
- Production time (scheduling, throughput time, setup time/flexibility)
- Distribution time (shipping, transportation)

The two principal operating components for any process therefore consist of *throughput time* ("physical" time) and response time, or changeover time, which corresponds to *flexibility*.

These two aspects are widely considered as the two operational priorities for just-in-time systems, and thus as significant contributors to a competitive advantage.

Global Manufacturing*

Manufacturing organization strategies evolve according to the development of business strategies.

Today, it is no longer possible for business to avoid thinking on a worldwide level. Indeed, companies are either operating directly in international markets or are feeling the effects of international competition indirectly.

Also emerging to an increasing degree is a global economy. This development has been characterized by the following stages:

- Domestic business (before the 1950s)
- International business (1950s — 1960s)
- Multinational business (1960s — 1970s)
- Global business (1980s — 1990s)

For manufacturing firms, these stages possess the following meanings:

- Domestic business

  - Local production
  - Local market

- International business

  - Local production
  - International markets

- Multinational business

  - Production in different nations
  - Local markets (local for local)

- Global business

  - International production
  - International market

---

* The content of this subsection is based on a study completed by Patrick McHugh and William Wheeler III of Coopers & Lybrand.

The corresponding industrial strategies can be identified as follows:

Domestic Business. The "traditional" type of manufacturing organization is employed, with sporadic application of JIT and CIM. Product quality and stability of design do not constitute fundamental strategic factors. Investments are undertaken for rapid financial returns. Company structure is of the Taylorist-functional type, and it is static. Manufacturing activities are pursued on the basis of technology that is already "available."

International Business. Operating in international markets while producing in only one nation leads to complications in terms of marketing and logistics. Improvement of logistics becomes the operational priority in firms of this type, while products must undergo significant diversification according to various markets.

This problem is accompanied by the problem of compliance with different quality and safety standards for products intended for various markets.

The industrial strategy that was adopted during the 1950s and 1960s depended upon economy of scale, achieved through centralized management of companies' business activities and production facilities.

Multinational Business. The concept of local production for local markets resulted in the presence of different approaches and focuses for each nation, with local development of products and processes.

Multinational management nevertheless encompasses a need to establish many staff and general coordination units and interface units (on a local level).

Transferring of technology from one nation to another is impeded by differing national standards and technological perspectives. This situation sometimes leads to development of unsuitable technology.

Global Business. Global business, which arises from increasing uniformity of markets, economic situations, and standards, also offers opportunities for global manufacturing. However, this principle is applicable only to products of the international type (namely, products with worldwide usability), for which a certain coordinated technological effort is desirable.

Usually, the context involves production that is based upon original processes and bears a significant technological core. The ideal situation is one in which a core embodying advanced technology and originality is present, along with a parallel need for aesthetic or truly marginal individualization of the product for the local market. In this instance, the core can be developed at any given center, and it can then be introduced at every production center.

Usually, there is a high degree of reliance upon the CAE-SC combination (Computer Aided Engineering and Strategic Cells), or upon CIM.

Development of production strategy through the four steps described above may also be a function of the level of maturity or development for a product/market relationship.

In this regard, it may be pertinent to examine the strategy employed by Sony, as depicted within Figure 6-2.

Product Life Cycle	Local Production	Local Production International Market	Multinational Production	Global Production
Mature	◯			◯ ◯ ◯ ◯
Growth Phase		◯		
Introduction	◯			
Development	◯			

The size of the circle is proportional to the production capacity that is allocated

Source: Coopers & Lybrand

Figure 6-2. SONY: Example of Production Strategy for a Product

Development of Production Systems

Organization of production systems is influenced by development of industrial strategies, on the one hand, and by the opportunities afforded by development of technology, on the other hand.

Obviously, the strategic problem is one of coherence in strategy, organization system, and technological system.

Indeed, it is pointless to speak in absolute terms of whether or not introduction of CIM is appropriate, for example. Instead, it is necessary to adopt the most effective and coherent system possible for the business that is to be managed.

One critical situation that arises relatively often in highly automated Western companies (high tech production systems) is, for example, the absence of a suitable organizing management system to provide support (low tech management).

In this instance, it is easy to observe forms of wastefulness that are significant enough to offset a major portion of any technological progress that has been achieved. At times changing over to a CIM configuration may indeed be unadvisable, because it would be wasteful and too risky.

Development of production systems in terms of logic and time can be depicted as shown in Figure 6- 3.

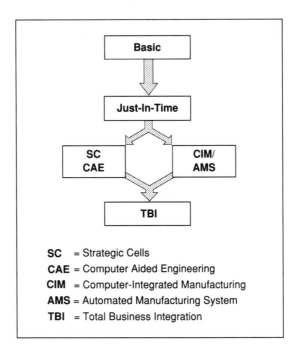

Figure 6-3. Evolution of Manufacturing Systems

A strategic decision concerning selection of the most appropriate production system for one's own company must take into account certain specific determining factors:

- Level of complexity
- Potential productivity
- Difficulty in terms of managing:
  — people
  — plant
  — logistics
  — cash control
  — information system

- Return on management effort

Basic Manufacture

As a general rule, many basic manufacturers employ relatively sophisticated ways of working. The major inhibitor to global manufacturing is the lack of a unifying or integrated approach throughout the value chain. They may have MRP2, CAD/CAM, and CNC equipment. But, they have piecework incentives that necessitate automatic storage and retrieval systems in their stockrooms. Piecework, MRP2, and job costing tend to force asynchronous, batch processing. Shop floor data systems and storerooms are then required. There is often a heavy reliance upon inspecting quality into the product rather than building it in. The net effect of the above is the exaggeration of overall lead times which, in turn, is not conducive to the flexibility and rapid response required of a truly global environment.

Lacking a unified approach, improvement tends to be task-driven. At this level, justification is based upon efficiency rather than overall effectiveness. Given this environment, functional boundaries tend to be more clearly delineated. The benefit of EMI teams is lost.

Most multinational companies are either at the basic or JIT phase of the manufacturing migration.

Just-In-Time (JIT)

JIT is a philosophy that strives to eliminate waste and therefore significantly reduce lead times (improved responsiveness). In its purest sense, JIT is a people-oriented approach to simplification. Since people in multinational plants have different value sets and ideas, different solutions are offered. By imposing a worldwide standard upon each multinational plant, the sense of individual contribution and creativity may be stifled. The concepts of continuous improvement and quality at the source can be inhibited. JIT can be an appropriate philosophy for any given plant, but it is only uniform for products made in that plant.

JIT does, however, force significant improvements that support the migration to TBI:

- Parts rationalization
- Quality improvement via process control
- Work simplification
- Breakdown of functional barriers
- Process flow definition and redesign
- Increased flexibility via setup reduction
- Supplier networks and cooperativeness
- Compatible cost and performance measures
- Lead time reduction

Without the discipline of JIT and the simplification process, it is difficult to realize the transition to the global manufacturing technologies of MS or Strategic Cells.

Strategic Cells

The concept of *strategic cells* (SC) is new to most of the manufacturing community. Basically, it combines the flexibility of JIT and the precision of automated manufacturing. Core or strategic technologies are automated and optionality is built in via the application of JIT principles.

Strategic technologies are those significant value-adding operations that differentiate the product from the competition and/or core processes. For example, the manufacture of fractional horsepower motors is a core process in the manufacture of hand-held power tools. It matters not whether the motor will be incorporated into a drill or a grass clipper. In an SC environment both the drill and the clippers would be assembled on the same line by applying the concept of homogenous production. The soap formula developed by P&G is clearly a competitive differentiator. In both cases the manufacture of the motors or the mixing of the formula would be automated. Inherent to this approach is the clear understanding of, and, therefore, control of, the process variables.

To the uninitiated a strategic cell looks similar to a properly functioning JIT cell. Parts and subassemblies are pulled to the homogeneous assembly line (Figure 6-4). Wherever possible, one piece lot size fabrication is directly linked to the assembly process. The physical position of the final assembly scheduler is critical to flexibility. Theoretically, the *Final Assembly Schedule* (FAS) represents the sequence in which the incoming orders arrive. For some processes the random sequence may not be appropriate because of fabrication cycle time variation, but the concept of making every option every day is still applicable. The scheduler is usually located near the end of the assembly process. In this manner options can be assigned to core technology or process(es). In some cases the final configuration is determined at the beginning of the line. Hewlett-Packard assigns options to the ink jet printer at the end of the line, whereas optionality is determined at the first step when the appropriate contact circuit board is selected for the manufacture of computer keyboards. In both cases the core process for manufacture is the same. In the former process the base printer is assembled in a standard manner; the latter employs the same technology of inserting, laser etching, and testing keys. If there are a few options to the core technology, the final assembly scheduler must also have a means of controlling the automated manufacture of the strategic process so that the appropriate sequence of assembly is preserved. As opposed to AMS, the sequence signal is under the control of a person who is part of the operation.

The development and implementation of strategic cells require significant planning efforts. While not as rigorous as AMS implementation planning, SC still requires foresight beyond the "discovery and adjust" approach espoused by JIT methodologies. There are three critical success factors to SC development:

1. EMI teams must manage the design and implementation.
2. Optimized quality capability for the core processes is key. Automation enhances quality yields. The process variables, their interaction, and subsequent management must be clearly understood and managed in order to assure synchronous production.

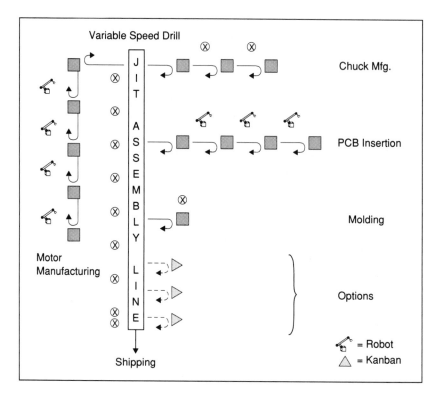

Figure 6-4. Example of a Strategic Cell

3. The fewer the base designs, the greater is the flexibility for simple automation. The identification of strategic technologies and their subsequent rationalization are difficult and often require courage in the marketplace. Consequently, design rationalization should be transparent to the customer. This is usually accomplished by making the products feature-rich or by upgrading the customer at no additional cost. An example of the latter is a transformer manufacturer who offers a limited range of KVA options. If a customer wants a 125-KVA transformer, the supplier will offer a 150 base with a stepdown option. The customer usually chooses the 150 model at the 125 cost. By rationalizing the base offerings, the cost to produce the upgraded model is lower than the competition's cost of the 125 model.

The technologies to implement and manage strategic cells are the same as JIT, plus some degree of local area networks (LAN) for the automated portions of the SC. The characteristics of adaptive manufacturing are similar to AMS enablers. These include NC machines (CNC or DNC), plus advanced robotics. But, these technologies are in support of manual JIT lines for ultimate flexibility of final product configuration. Finally, the engineering data base must be managed by Computer-Aided Engineering (CAE) systems. CAE is a prerequisite for rapid new product introduction or modification. The CAE systems include design (CAD), functional and physical analysis, standards, and group technology archive data bases. As globalization is achieved, CAE becomes the only system for assuring uniformity of process as well as serving to collapse the time-to-market cycle.

Automated Manufacturing Systems (AMS-CIM)

Much has been written about AMS. Definitions differ enormously, but all agree on the basis of integrating the shop floor execution, product and part planning, and engineering data bases. For purposes of this article, we are describing AMS as the "lights out factory," where the management of the factory is essentially under the control of a central processing unit with minimal support by operators on the first shift. It is better to avoid using Computer Integrated Manufacturing (CIM) as a descriptor because there does not appear to be a universally accepted definition of the boundaries of CIM.

AMS requires significantly greater dependence upon computers and their operating systems/software packages than does SC. While flexibility can be programmed into the operations, it is usually difficult to assure the complete range of worldwide product optionality on the timely basis that globalized manufacturing requires. Core technology or process rationalization improves the flexibility, but high optionality often forces other means (people) to achieve the necessary flexibility.

The technologies required of AMS are similar to SC; there is just more and greater dependence upon them. In addition to LANs there are requirements for Wide Area Neworks (WANs), and the base technology of making pumps, motors, agitators, drums, backguards, metal stamping, etc. is the same regardless of final configuration. Certain process industries have high optionality and local preferences. The dessert pudding industry (process industry) has thousands of formulations for local tastes and an even greater number of packaging combinations. The same even holds for pet foods. Production runs are short and frequent. SC is the choice of approach for both industry types.

Conversely, products with low optionality or national preferences can realize with relative ease the full benefits of AMS. Aluminum smelting or rolling (process) or CRT interface box manufacture (repetitive) have few options with which to contend. Both successfully operate in a global environment and apply AMS technology.

Total Business Integration (TBI)

Regardless of which approach is most appropriate, SC or AMS, globalization is not complete until the worldwide business is totally integrated. While TBI relies heavily upon global information networks, the basic objective is to provide a common way of working so that flexibility and assets are optimally managed on a worldwide basis. In order to achieve TBI, certain ways of working must be adopted:

- Realtime and complete visibility of the entire product value chain
- Recognition of performance indicators that emphasize the Return on Total Assets (ROTA)
- Global gainsharing
- SC or AMS
- Strong business focus with no functional biases
- EMI teams
- Recognition of centralized and decentralized activities

Fully integrated hardware/software systems provide the information flows that enable the technology to be globalized. Remote diagnostics are an enhancement, as are information MAPS. The critical enabler is the Asset Manager (AM). Basically, the AM's function is to accept worldwide orders, to review the condition of each manufacturing site, and to establish an optimized Final Assembly Schedule (FAS) for each plant.

The enormity of such a daily task is too great for an individual or a centralized department. Therefore, the AM is an expert scheduling system. The following parameters must be reviewed frequently:

- Monetary parity
- Capacity availability
- Logistics
- Planned shutdowns
- Political events
- Raw material stocks
- Suppliers
  — proximity
  — capacity
  — quality

- Shipments from previous FAS
- Backorders
- Tooling availability
- Finished goods stocks
- Local promotions
- "Local content" and/or tariff requirements

Strategic Cells or AMS should provide the means to make every product every day (or at least all of the A items every day). The AM provides the mechanism to accept and schedule every order every day for manufacture on the same or next day. By reducing the lead time to a minimum the point of manufacture becomes relatively inconsequential. The AM is "free" to schedule each plant in the worldwide network to its optimum. For instance, assume the demand from a geographic sector upon the nearest plant is 1,200 capacity units of production. But, the plant has a demonstrated output of 1,000 units. In a multinational environment local stocks or overtime would have temporarily buffered the demand surge. Neither panacea is an effective use of assets. Applying the rule-based logic in the expert system the AM would assign the demand surge excess to alternate site(s) and trans-ship the difference. Thus, SC or AMS and the AM become technological enablers to TBI.

Air freight costs have been declining over the past seven years. For many industries, logistics costs are not as critical as they used to be. The cost of excess resources (inventory, redundant support personnel, capacity, and space) are usually considerably higher than transportation costs.

Supporting the AM and the manufacturing sites would be key information data bases. At a minimum, the data bases would include:

- Manufacturing and design specifications
- Quality requirements, procedures, and results
- Accounting requirements
- Sales administration
- Procurement requirements
- Personnel

Some of the data points required by the AM would be updated real time from the data bases. Others, such as shipments or local promotions, would be updated locally.

Expectations

Figure 6-5 indicates the relative expectations from each manufacturing approach. As with any commitment to new approaches there are tradeoffs until one achieves the full benefits from the new philosophy. From the figure it can be noted that neither SC nor AMS as a stand-alone in each plant are as effective as JIT, but when synergized with TBI they become far more effective to the corporation or division than JIT.

	BASIC	JIT	SC/ CAE	AMS/ CIM	TBI
Quality	L	M	M	H	M - H
Service	L	H	H	H	H
Safety	L	L - M	M	M - H	H
Flexibility	L	H	H	M	H
Response Time	L	H	H	M	H
ROA/Plant	L	H	H - M	M	M - L
ROA/Overall	L	M	H	M - H	H

Source: Coopers & Lybrand

Figure 6-5. Comparative Expectations: Low, Medium, or High

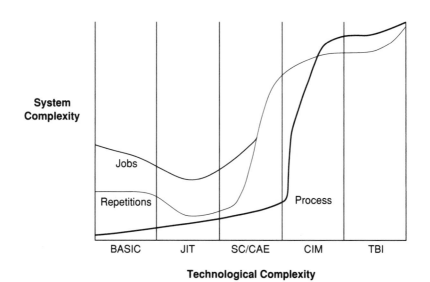

Source: Coopers & Lybrand

Figure 6-6. Industry Evolution

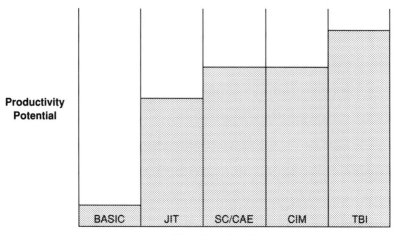

Source: Coopers & Lybrand

Figure 6-7. Comparative Productivity

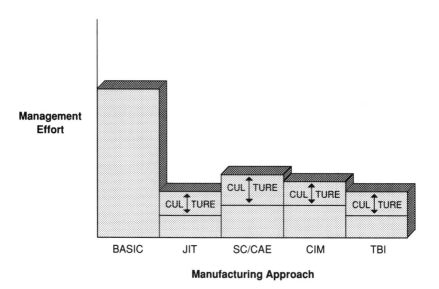

Source: Coopers & Lybrand

Figure 6-8. Degree of Management Effort Required — People

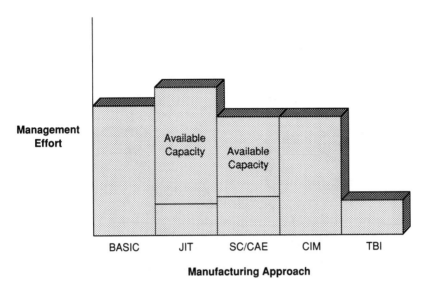

Source: Coopers & Lybrand

Figure 6-9. Degree of Management Effort Required – Plant

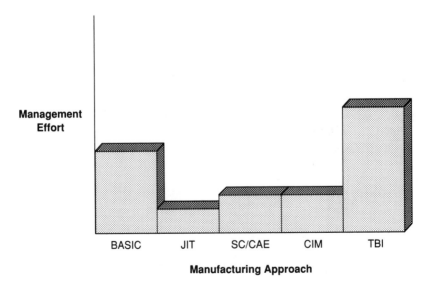

Source: Coopers & Lybrand

Figure 6-10. Degree of Management Effort Required — Material Logistics

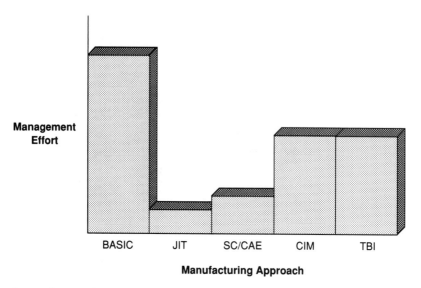

Source: Coopers & Lybrand

Figure 6-11. Degree of Management Effort Required — Cash Control

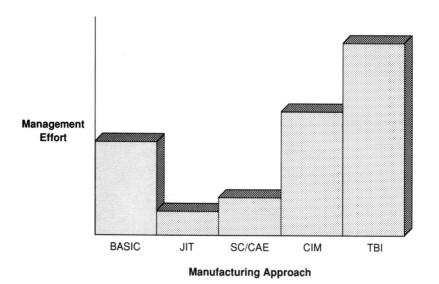

Source: Coopers & Lybrand

Figure 6-12. Degree of Management Effort Required — Data Breadth/Usage

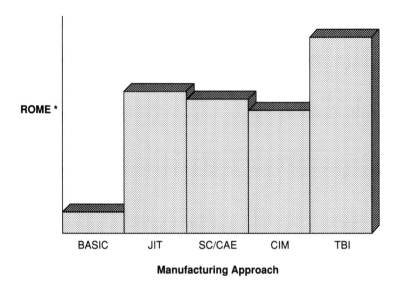

ROME *

Manufacturing Approach

BASIC   JIT   SC/CAE   CIM   TBI

* Return On Management Effort

Source: Coopers & Lybrand

Figure 6-13. Aggregate Return on Management Effort

7

Western Industry and Companywide Quality Control

As indicated in Chapter 6, companywide quality control constitutes the fundamental strategy for the changes occurring in manufacturing. The principle of granting priority to customer satisfaction,
quality, and participation actually constitutes the entrepreneurial and
conceptual basis for development of operating strategies.

As is known, the total quality orientation was predominantly developed in Japanese industry under the approach described in the first
section of this book. What kind of model is being developed in the
West, however, and what is the level of application?

Policy Aims

The political aim of pursuing the path of total quality in the West
is demonstrated by the campaigns and initiatives that emerged in
many Western nations. The most significant endeavors were those initiated by the United States, Great Britain, and France.

The United States

The about-face probably occurred in 1984. During that year, the
largest American firms, with assistance from the American Society for
Quality Control (ASQC), attempted to increase congressional aware-
ness in order to promote a national quality campaign. In July 1984
Congress enacted a law authorizing the president of the United
States to proclaim the month of October in that year as National
Quality Month.

President Reagan's ensuing proclamation included a vitally important sentence: "Quality in industry and in services contributes to

121

increasing productivity, reducing costs, and satisfying consumers." Such a concept is precisely the opposite of the one that had constituted the basis of the predominant corporate outlook for many decades. Within the old perspective, quality was negatively associated with costs; indeed, it was believed that improvement of quality tended to *increase* costs and to *reduce* productivity.

Subsequent to President Reagan's proclamation, the first quality campaign took place during October of 1985. The campaign was designated The Rebirth of Quality In America. Since that time Fortune magazine has published the promotional document for the annual quality campaign in its September issue each year. The campaign's slogan for the following year was The Quality Imperative.

In January 1988 President Reagan announced the establishment of a yearly national award, the Malcolm Baldridge Award, for companies that excel in the area of quality. Some fifty auditors were trained to select winning firms, and a private foundation was established with contributions from leading American corporations. Each year, a maximum of six companies is to receive awards, with the president taking part in the awards ceremony.

The slogan selected for the 1988 campaign was Beyond Customer Satisfaction through Improvement of Quality.

Great Britain

Great Britain was the first nation in the Western world to sponsor a national quality campaign. Prime Minister Thatcher launched this campaign in May 1983 with a message to the nation.

The source of the campaign was a white paper entitled *Standards, Quality, and National Competitiveness,* which was issued in July 1982.

The white paper identified four areas of activity:

- A nationwide campaign to stimulate quality-consciousness, along with promotion of independent certification programs
- Close cooperation with the British Standards Institution for defining an effective series of standards for maintaining competitive capability
- A commitment by the government to use the series of standards in enacting statutes and regulations
- A major effort by government agencies to confirm adherence to standards by their own suppliers

During the first two years, the quality campaign concentrated upon publicity efforts and an extensive series of conferences and seminars on a nationwide scale. More recently it has focused on encouraging the new approach to quality within various sectors and upon promoting new relationships between clients and suppliers.

Within the context of this campaign, the ministry of trade has promoted development of a supporting structure for quality efforts undertaken by British firms.

Through the Institute of Quality Assurance, the National Quality Information Centre was established for assisting British firms in improving quality at every level of their activities.

The government has also promoted creation of the Association of Quality Management Consultants, in order to aid training of specialized consultants in quality. Finally, the Business and Technical Advisory Service on Quality pays two-thirds of the expenses incurred for use of consultants by companies (with fewer than 500 employees) seeking to introduce a total quality approach.

France

Promotion of quality at a national level is definitely more advanced in France than in any other European nation.

Quality circles, which were introduced in France after 1979, have been a significant factor in promoting quality. At the present time, there are 40,000 active quality circles in France, more than in any other European nation.

Development of quality circles began with the leading firms in basic sectors (iron and steel, chemical, textiles, machinery), and it subsequently spread to small and intermediate firms as well as to firms within the tertiary sector (banks, insurance companies, trading companies, hotels).

Lastly, quality circles have been established in public administration and in public services (Telecommunications Authority, hospitals, prefectures, postal service, municipal agencies).

Quality circles are merely one component of a broader quality strategy that France is pursuing. In firms where quality circles have been established, 92 percent have adopted a total quality orientation.

From June 1 to June 15 during 1987, a national campaign to increase quality awareness took place (via newspapers, television, and advertisements). The slogan for this campaign was Quality — each individual tries for it, and everyone benefits.

Today, quality awareness has been achieved in every sector in France.

A poll (IFOP-Pechiney) conducted in 1985 and verified in 1987 offered the following results: Of those interviewed, 74 percent stated that they were aware of quality, and 28 percent indicated that they belonged to quality circles.

European Foundation for Quality Management (E.F.Q.M.)

In 1988, the European Foundation for Quality Management was established. Its objective was "to create conditions to enhance the position of European industry in the world market by strengthening the role of management in quality strategies."

The governing committee of this foundation consists of the presidents of the fourteen founding companies:

ROBERT BOSCH, GmbH. Federal Republic of Germany	Mr. M. Bierich
BRITISH TELECOMMUNICATIONS, p.l.c. United Kingdom	Mr. I.D.T. Vallance
BULL, S.A. France	Mr. F. Lorentz
CIBA-GEIGY, AG. Switzerland	Mr. H. Lippuner
AVIONS MARCEL DASSAULT-BREGUET AVIATION France	Mr. Serge Dassault
A.B. ELECTROLUX Sweden	Mr. A. Scharp
FIAT AUTO, S.p.A. Italy	Mr. U. Agnelli
KONINKLIJKE LUCHTVAART MAATSCHAPPIJ, N.V. The Netherlands	Mr. J.F.A. de Soet
NESTLE, S.A. Switzerland	Mr. H. Maucher
ING. C. OLIVETTI & C., S.p.A. Italy	Mr. C. De Benedetti

N.V. PHILIPS GLOEILAMPENFABRIKEN   Mr. C.I. van der Klugt
The Netherlands

REGIE NATIONALE DES USINES RENAULT   Mr. Raymond H. Levy
France

GEBR. SULZER, AG.   Mr. F. Fahrni
Switzerland

VOLKSWAGEN, AG.   Mr. Carl H. Hahn
Federal Republic of Germany

The Western Companies

During recent years, practically all of the leading Western companies have announced quality policies that are coherent with a total quality approach. Indicative of the changes under way are the following statements issued by some of these companies.

> If Quality is not the number one operating priority at General Motors, there may be a time when there is no General Motors. (F.J. McDonald, President, General Motors)
>
> Thirty percent of production costs are attributable to the fact that things are not done right the first time. (IBM)
>
> Quality is no longer an issue which solely pertains to production. Today, it is a problem which pertains to a company's entire economic system. (Carlo De Benedetti, Managing Director, Olivetti)
>
> We have to arrive at the same quality level as the Japanese: This is an obligation. This is foremost in my thoughts and in my concerns, and it is also the best way to defend ourselves against the Japanese. My commitment to quality and reliability shall be a total commitment. I wish to use a strong verb: I shall mobilize the entire company, from the first to the last of our employees, suppliers, and dealers. (Cesare Romiti, Managing Director, Fiat)
>
> The quality of products and services is of the utmost importance for the continuity of our company. By adopting a quality policy aimed at complete control of every activity, maximum quality, productivity, flexibility, and a reduction in cost prices will be achieved. Every employee must be imbued with an attitude directed toward a continuous striving for improvements. (Dr. W. Dekker, 1983, President, Philips)
>
> Our approach to CWQI must be businesslike, all-pervasive, and market-oriented. (C.J. van der Klugt, 1987, President, Philips)
>
> Overall operative quality is a central concept in Ericsson's strategy. Quality is necessary for our success in the market. It is also the key to efficiency in our internal work. (Bjorn Svedberg, President, Ericsson)

The Seven Reference Levels

In Europe, a reference model based upon seven levels of development is emerging.

This reference model, which was initially developed by Philips, is gradually being improved in each of its various components. The structure adopted by Alberto Galgano & Associati in preparing company programs (for self-diagnosis and for planning program implementation) follows. Seven reference levels are employed:

1. Technical approach
2. Quality improvement
3. Process control
4. Process improvement
5. Operational breakthrough
6. Strategic breakthrough
7. Excellence through quality

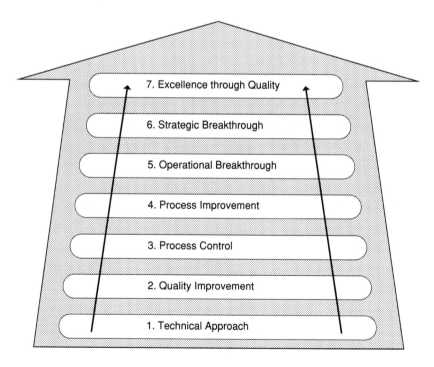

Figure 7-1. The CWQC Seven Steps

These levels correspond to the conceptual/cultural steps constituting the total quality scale shown in Figure 7-1. Activities relating to each phase are described below.

Level 1: Technical Approach

During this phase, quality is regarded as a technical problem, rather than a management problem. Hence, management attention is largely confined to product quality.

Activities pertaining to quality consist of seeking remedies whenever difficulties arise, so that problems can be delegated to specialists.

In this phase management does not seek reasons for unacceptability, nor does it contemplate development of preventive measures.

Level 2: Quality Improvement

During this phase, the company becomes aware of the importance of quality and of the strategic need for continuous improvement of quality. Campaigns to increase awareness and improvement campaigns are set in motion. Programs are based upon the activities of groups trained in problem solving, and managed according to the firm's hierarchical structure.

Level 3: Process Control

The company recognizes that, in order to obtain improvements in output, it shall be necessary to improve the processes whereby output is generated. This goal presupposes an ability to identify basic processes and their capabilities (process capabilities). Accordingly, analyses of processes are initiated, and process control techniques are employed. The line then takes charge of improvement programs, which are oriented toward control and upgrading of processes.

Level 4: Process Improvement

After having learned to upgrade (phase 2) and to control (phase 3) processes, it shall now be possible for improvement to be managed in the most highly developed form, with concentration on the firm's fundamental processes.

Improvements are planned and implemented through policy deployment activities and through management by the line.

Level 5: Operational Breakthrough

Far-reaching and dramatic operational improvements that give the firm a competitive advantage are obtained through concentration on the processes that are most closely linked to the firm's business factors. Improvement activities are guided by a deployment method directly derived from the business plan.

Level 6: Strategic Breakthrough

The competitive advantages derived from phase 5 directly influence a company's strategy. The company can now begin to take advantage of the strengths that have been developed and to pursue changes coherently. It will thus be possible to obtain further competitive advantages which can be employed in a new relationship with the market.

Level 7: Excellence Through Quality

Now that the company is capable of obtaining significant operational improvements and maintaining direct linkage to the market (market-in), it can continuously respond to the priorities of the given moment and thus maintain its competitive advantage.

A more accurate representation of this development can be seen in an operational configuration consisting of eight elements:

1. Cultural approach
2. Quality activities
3. Quality procedures
4. R&D and engineering
5. Results
6. Relations with customers
7. Relations with suppliers
8. Management system

A grid showing how these two models correspond can be seen in Figure 7-2.

Characteristics / Development Phase	Cultural and Organizational Characteristics	Quality Activities	Fundamental Procedures	Product Development and Industrial Production
1. Technical Approach	• Emphasis on product quality • Quality is perceived as a technical problem	• Tests (AQL) • Reimbursements • Certification	• Inspection and certification procedures • Quality assurance manuals	• Quality is not a planning priority • Quality technical performance
2. Quality Improvement	• Awareness that quality is important and that it must be continually improved	• Training • Improvement program	• Procedures for managing improvement programs	• Quality is important • Technical-technological approach
3. Process Control	• Quality of products and services is perceived and managed as the result of process quality	• Organization for controlling and improving process capabilities	• Analysis and management of process capabilities	• Quality = suitability for use • Emphasis upon structure for industrial development • Adoption of reliability-oriented techniques
4. Process Improvement	• Improvements planned and managed by the line	• Concentration upon improving priority processes	• Improvement programs managed according to improvement areas (priority deployment)	• Quality is planned according to customers' needs • Quality deployment • DOE
5. Operational Breakthrough	• Final development of the CWQC program according to company's operational priorities	• Extensive improvement programs guided by the business plan • Deployment activities	• Deployment procedures for business plan and "catch-all" objectives	• Quality as a point of departure and as a strategy • Reduction of costs and start-up time for new products
6. Strategic Breakthrough	• Search for excellence through market-in	• Concentrated improvement of processes that are most closely linked to the market • Management by policies extended to all middle management levels	• Procedures and systems for linking market and internal processes	• "Positive" planning • Full deployment of products and processes
7. Excellence through Quality	• Excellence is attained within the market every day	• Process of maintaining continuous excellence	• Procedures for real-time monitoring of the market	• Continuous automatic improvement • Product development is the essence of CWQC

Figure 7-2A. The CWQC Maturity Grid

Characteristics / Development Phase	Results	Relationships with Clients and Markets	Relationships with Suppliers	Role of Management
1. Technical Approach	• High costs for non-quality • Implantation of AQL	• It is agreed that minimum quality is acceptable	• Prices are "conquered" • Suppliers are not trusted	• Quality is not viewed as a problem
2. Quality Improvement	• Minor reductions in cost for lack of quality • Some improvements in products	• Customer satisfaction as a "must" • Internal supplier/customer chains	• It is believed that trusting the supplier may be beneficial	• Promotion, commitment, and budget for CWQC
3. Process Control	• Reduction of rejects • Honing of processes (reduction of problems)	• Customer satisfaction through control of internal processes • Quality assurance through control of process capabilities	• Self-certification is promoted • Vendor ratings according to total costs	• Announcement of quality policies • Management by processes
4. Process Improvement	• General reduction of costs for quality, especially inspection costs	• Processes are improved for customer satisfaction	• Firm develops linkage to best suppliers • Emphasis on improvement capability	• Management according to supplier-client chains through daily routine work
5. Operational Breakthrough	• Improvement of the firm's competitive position by improving key processes	• Concentration upon fundamental processes for customer satisfaction with guidance from management	• Comakership with principal suppliers • Significant improvements in quality of supplies	• Management by policies
6. Strategic Breakthrough	• Leadership through quality of the firm's processes	• Market-in approach • Autonomous capability of responding to changes	• Partnership agreements on business for excellence	• Management by market priorities
7. Excellence through Quality	• Continuous leadership through continuous customer satisfaction	• The firm provides real-time service for customers • Emphasis on positive quality	• Long-term agreements for continuous excellence	• Management guided by the market

Figure 7-2B. The CWQC Maturity Grid

Organizing and Managing Improvement

Organization and management of improvement within the context of a CWQC program corresponds to the firm's general approach and mode of organization.

The type of evolution necessary can be extrapolated from Figure 7-2, from the "Fundamental Procedures" and "Role of Management" columns.

A more detailed examination of the seven levels follows.

Level 1: Technical Approach

During this phase constituting the initial situation, a mode of organization and activities oriented toward improvement and designed according to a CWQC perspective does not truly exist. Improvement is pursued, whenever it does occur, through functions assigned to specific departments, such as a "time and methods" department.

However, in most instances, there is almost complete reliance upon innovation. Indeed, the approach consists of "desktop" research and planning, with customary reliance upon dramatic changes that, as much as possible, are based upon technical solutions (new systems, new procedures, new tools, automation).

There are no improvement activities at a group level.

Level 2: Quality Improvement

Improvement programs constitute the most significant dimension of this phase. Implementation occurs through an initial phase of promotion of awareness, a second phase in which training in problem solving (seven tools and PDCA) is provided, and, finally, an operational phase characterized by development of projects within improvement groups.

Themes chosen for these projects are elementary (Figure 7-3), in the sense that compartmentalization according to subprojects is not needed and completion of projects is possible with three or four months of work (two to six hours per person per week, with weekly meetings of one to two hours).

The program is supported by a promotional management structure (quality council, quality officers, facilitators), and it normally continues in conjunction with line control.

During this phase, the emphasis is on development of problem-solving abilities. The objective can be expressed as "learning how to develop improvement projects within groups."

Level 3: Process Control

While the firm's lateral structure for improvement is being consolidated with development of a second round of projects, a process control campaign, which is to be managed by the line, is initiated. The objectives are to increase acceptance of the process, to identify the firm's principal processes, and to promote line participation by indicating objectives in terms of removal of problems and/or improvement of process capabilities.

During this phase, the emphasis is on acquiring know-how for process control.

The firm's management provides support for these activities through process capabilities that are entrusted to the line.

Level 4: Process Improvement

During this phase, the operational approaches and know-how introduced during the two preceding levels interact so as to allow a significant advance — namely, completion of improvement programs with vital objectives, along with transferring of program management to the line and elimination of the need for a lateral structure. Indeed, the first actual results begin to emerge.

Implementation occurs through several measures. First, training in problem solving and deployment techniques is completed. Next, improvement projects are derived from "improvement areas," which are deployed according to operating projects by interdisciplinary project teams or by section leaders (Figure 7-3).

Improvement area (IA) is understood to mean an operating *process*, an area of *activity*, or an area with *problems* (in regard to quality, for example).

The objective is learning how improvement can be defined according to priorities and how it can be managed by the line.

If the total quality vocabulary is adopted, the objective is to introduce the so-called daily routine work (DRW) dimension, which is also known in the United States as quality in daily work (QIDW) (at Florida Power & Light, for example).

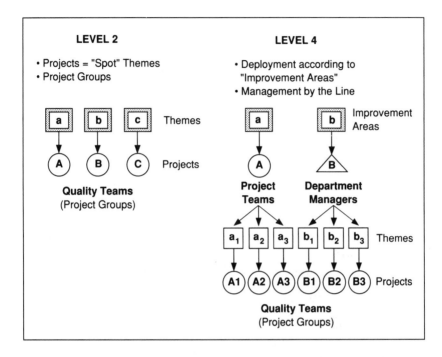

Figure 7-3. Managing Improvement

During this phase, management promotes the goal of satisfying "internal customers" throughout basic processes. This goal is accomplished through a rewards system for managers that takes into account the "evaluations" given by clients of the units that they administer. Bonuses or salary increases are granted on the basis of this criterion, and, ultimately, they are also granted as a result of audits that are intended to verify the policies being adopted at lower levels for obtaining results (coherence with the firm's quality policy).

Level 5: Operational Breakthrough

During this phase, improvement programs and the respective improvement areas are directly linked to the business plan. This means that all improvement activities are concentrated on the firm's priorities for the respective year, through effective preliminary policy deployment activity.

Indeed, the firm activates the management-by-policy (MBP) dimension, with important objectives being entrusted to its own structure each year. These objectives are developed at every level, and they are entrusted to the line, which pursues them through the structure developed for achieving improvement. In this way, it is possible to obtain significant results even during brief periods of time.

It should be noted that MBP is the essence of CWQC and that its characteristics can be identified according to the subsequent description (which illustrates how it constitutes a significant advance from MBO).

Management by Policy is a management method that:

- Allows development of a management system, structure, and culture intended to ensure implementation of the CWQC strategy within a firm
- Translates the entrepreneurial objective of management by priorities, "with short-term adherence to the firm's long-term policies," into an operating management system

Its characteristics are:

- Direct linkage to the business plan
- Concentration upon a few fundamental priorities (one to three, to be selected by top management), with important goals
- A highly interconnected multidisciplinary process that is oriented toward obtaining the previously cited results
- Involvement of a large number of persons
- Continuous and active control of the process that has been defined for pursuing objectives
- Rigorous application of the PDCA method
- Emphasis upon cause-and-effect relationships

Levels 6 and 7: *Strategic Breakthrough and Excellence through Quality*

At these two levels, the structure for improvement remains substantially unchanged from the level 5 structure. Evolution occurs, rather, in the firm's outlook (increasingly market-in) on the one hand, and its management system and management control methods (coherent with MBP and more comprehensive new approaches) on the other hand.

Operating Structure

As indicated previously, management of an improvement program on a systematic basis requires a specifically developed mode of organization. Nevertheless, as soon as this structure begins to operate, responsibility and authority for companywide quality improvement should be entrusted largely to the line. Improvement of a company's operating processes should be an objective for managers in the various sectors where these processes occur. The sole function of specific units and positions, namely, those which are to be suitably created, should be to ensure that the cultural and organizational development of CWQI will proceed according to appropriate times and forms. These specific units and roles are usually identifiable in relation to the following categories:

- Policy council (for defining policies)
- Steering committee (for program support)
- Quality officer (the "operational" protagonist for the program)
- Facilitator (for the quality circles program)

Operational capability pertains primarily to completion of projects by working groups, but there are also coordination needs and possibilities in terms of individual roles. The following organizational categories are employed most frequently:

- Coordinating group (project team)
- Improvement area (IA) manager
- Project group (quality team)
- Quality circle
- Self-improvement

There are also other organizational possibilities:

- Permanent study group
- Project leader
- Open project group (CEDAC group)
- Small group for improvement of abilities (SGIA)

These organizational categories can be described as follows.

Coordinating Group (Project Team)

This group is composed of the top executives within a given unit, who have been asked to assume responsibility for a specific improvement area. The group is responsible for improving a specific improvement area according to predetermined objectives and within a specified period of time.

Its functions are to:

- Provide an accurate "snapshot" of the initial situation within the respective IA
- Identify the most appropriate performance indicators for measuring improvements
- Formulate specific time-defined improvement objectives and obtain acceptance by the firm's management
- Complete a diagnostic analysis of problems while determining how many and which projects must be developed in order to attain approved objectives*
- Establish, activate, and coordinate the necessary quality teams for pursuing approved objectives
- Ensure coherent development of individual projects in terms of the objectives and the program formulated by the project team, and participate in the quality team by a member of the project team
- Manage and coordinate improvement activities planned by quality teams
- Inform the firm's management of progress and results

The Improvement Area Manager (IA Manager)

When an improvement area consists of only one sector or service, management can be entrusted to a sole individual whose responsibilities match those of a project team. This organizational form is adopted even more frequently when programs are already defined, because it corresponds to that configuration in which CWQI is directly controlled by the line (level 5, or the *operating* phase). Interdisciplinary improvement areas are always managed by project teams, however.

---

* The project team must be trained in use of the *seven new tools* and *window analysis* in order to pursue its project development activities effectively.

Project Group (Quality Team)

This group is formed ad hoc on the basis of specific themes to be considered.

- Its composition is approved by unit-level management, or it is defined by a project team or department head (IA manager).
- Its life span coincides with the length of the project.
- It mainly comprises middle managers and employees who are "significant according to specific skills." Members are drawn from various positions, departments, or units.
- Depending on the situation, this group reports to the departmental management (assisted by the coordinator), a project team, or an IA manager.
- All executives and employees at a certain level are potential participants in the program.

The objectives of the company in forming project groups are to:

- Improve company processes
- Mobilize the company structure
- Develop interdisciplinary attitudes and practices, along with a more comprehensive outlook
- Improve the company atmosphere

Usually, the projects to be initiated are interdisciplinary. In other words, they pertain to problems facing multiple departments or units (which are all represented within the group). They are also considered priority projects by management.

Projects are selected by one of four groups: (1) department head, (2) the steering committee, (3) the executive committee, or (4) a project team, according to its improvement area.

All projects must be completed within a maximum period of six months.*

Quality Circles

Quality circles are permanent groups, existing independently of individual projects. They are established on a voluntary basis, comprising employees or workers within the same department or unit. The firm's management only provides indirect support.

---

* The tools used for completing projects are PDCA and the *seven tools* with possible reliance upon some of the *seven new tools* or CEDAC.

The objectives of the quality circle are to

- Improve the atmosphere in the unit
- Improve relationships between workers at all levels
- Improve attitudes and behavior
- Improve communications within the unit as well as the company
- Develop greater awareness of quality among workers
- Improve operating processes

The projects initiated pertain to problems within the respective department or unit. Particular emphasis is given to improvement of customer satisfaction, with downstream departments or units being viewed as customers. Projects are chosen autonomously, within the context of company rules. There is no schedule (unless the quality circle establishes one). There should, however, be at least one proposal every six months.

Other Organizational Categories

Other organizational categories may also be used for managing improvement programs. These categories correspond to various operational needs or to possible use of more advanced *problem-solving* tools. A descriptive summary follows.

Permanent study group

The study group is a permanent working group that assumes responsibility for an improvement area requiring multiple systematic small steps that must be completed over time. In many instances, the product of a study group is a manual that lists accomplishments and possibilities associated with the improvement area being studied. Examples of improvement areas for study groups are sight management, housekeeping, eradication of waste, and so on.

Project leader

The project leader handles projects that are relatively simple, closely monitored, or highly technical. They are likewise expected to make use of contributions from their project groups.

Open project group (CEDAC Group)

The open project group seeks cooperation on its projects from other persons. This is done either from the outset or as a result of changes in the work of a normal quality team or quality circle. Sight management of projects with the CEDAC (cause-and-effect diagram with addition of cards) takes place. The CEDAC system is managed by a leader who is appointed by the firm's management or by the group. A project initiated on this basis has often been developed through *window analysis* (see Chapter 15).

Small group for improvement of activities (SGIA)

The small group for improvement of activities (SGIA) is a semipermanent project group whose membership may change over time. The group functions like a quality circle. Its membership often consists of workers and/or supervisory employees, although the group agrees to work on priorities that are approved or shared by the firm's management. Pursuit of this type of project often requires additional training in advanced problem-solving tools (such as the CEDAC system) and in specific forms of know-how (for example, techniques for total industrial engineering, stockless production, total productive maintenance, and process control). Depending on the skills needed for the projects, the group may become interhierarchical (in other words, composed of persons from a wide range of levels, including managers and workers.)

The Management System

The reference model for improvement and control of this structure can be considered according to a "two-dimensions" and "two-flows" perspective. The two dimensions are:

- Managed improvement
- Voluntary improvement

The two flows are:

- Top-down flow
- Bottom-up flow

A description of this model and its operational and management implications follows.

Managed Improvement

Managed improvement refers to improvement activities that are managed directly by the line. This dimension originates with top management and extends to all of the firm's intermediate executives and "important" employees, sometimes including supervisory employees and workers. This operational dimension is activated through completion of three phases, namely:

1. The training-cultural phase
2. The organizing phase
3. The operating phase

The first two phases must be completed before attaining the third phase, and they nearly always require assistance from an outside consultant. Hence, only the third, or operating, phase will be considered here.

The organization structure required for the third phase is based upon management according to improvement areas *directly from the line*. As was stated earlier, improvement areas (IAs) refer to company *processes* that possess a certain level of importance, areas of *activity*, or areas with *problems* — any of which can be identified and quantified in a specific form. Examples of improvement areas for *processes* include:

- Logistical flow (or a portion thereof)
- Lead time
- Stock
- Order processing procedures
- Purchasing procedures
- Collection procedures
- Sales procedures
- Shipping procedures

Examples of improvement areas for *activities* include:

- Production fall-off (defects)
- Billing errors
- Errors in computations
- Delays in activities

- Necessary work load for a given activity
- Structuring of work

Examples of improvement areas for *problems* include:

- Process quality
- Output quality
- Product reliability
- Process reliability
- Delays
- Systematic errors

Identification of priority improvement areas, or areas that are to be emphasized, takes place on a periodic basis (annually, for example). Some improvement areas may be designated for multiple consecutive periods. Priority improvement areas originate in two ways:

- They may be derived from the business plan (policy deployment).
- They may be identified by persons with specific line responsibilities (DRW or QIDW).

Figure 7-4 provides a reference diagram for defining and managing IAs.

Priority IAs selected by the management committee (policy deployment) are assigned to interdisciplinary project teams or to line managers (IA managers), according to their content (interdisciplinary IAs, or sector IAs). Project teams only manage individual IAs, whereas a line manager may manage multiple IAs (the ones which are assigned and any others he or she may identify). Project teams and IA managers both approach IAs through subsequent deployment and establishment of quality teams. Any input offered by quality circles in relation to IAs is self-managed.

Improvement can be measured and monitored by using *performance indicators*. Performance indicators (PIs) are units of measurement pertaining specifically to improvements. Because it is not always possible to select a single PI that is valid for an entire improvement area, more than one indicator is often used. Moreover, it is not always possible to measure every aspect of improvement; in such cases the respective IA must remain "open." In the absence of other indicators, it is still possible to express improvement in terms of the number or level of

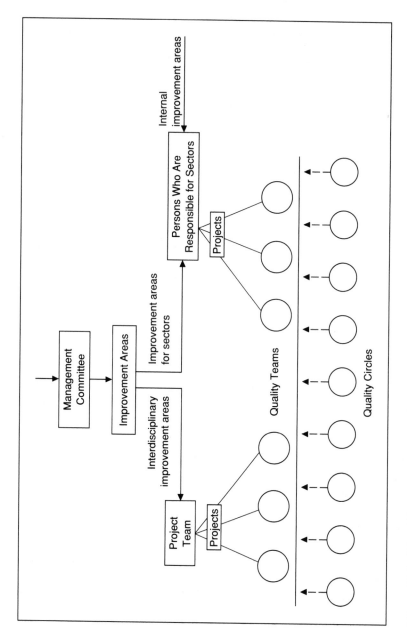

Figure 7-4. Identification and Management of Improvement Areas

complaints from "customers" (downstream units) for the respective activity. Examples of performance indicators include:

- Number of defects/errors
- Number or level of need for repetitions of processes or work
- Efficiency indicators (for example, documents or items per unit of time, or per person)
- Number of delays
- Duration of a given procedure or activity (time)
- Promptness of responses (time)
- Usability/cost ratio (value)
- Level of need to rely upon overtime work
- Level of changes in work load (factor derived from internal organization)
- Level of criticalness/vulnerability (of the system, for example)
- Level of standardization
- Number of unfinished documents

Under advanced conditions, managed improvement can be carried out in conjunction with development of extensive company projects. Thus, the managed dimension can be divided into two subdimensions:

- Improvement that is systematically managed on the basis of deployment and improvement areas
- Improvement that is carried out in conjunction with large-scale company projects, including innovative projects (a just-in-time project, for example)

A configuration of these dimensions, along with the corresponding organizational aspects, can be seen in Figure 7-5. Note that it is possible for an individual to be participating in several dimensions simultaneously.

Voluntary Improvement

The voluntary improvement dimension is the level achieved on an individual basis by quality circles and by a possible suggestions system. It is governed by a specific set of rules (for quality circles). Western firms have basically adopted the Japanese organizational model of quality circles (see Chapter 1).

	Autonomous/ Voluntary Improvement	Managed Improvement	
		Systematic	According to Company Projects
Operating Units	Quality Circles Individual suggestions	Coordination Project teams Line managers Mode of operation: Quality teams CEDAC projects Project leaders	Coordination Project teams Project leaders Mode of operation: Project groups: — Closed — Open Study groups SGIA
Com- position of Group	Same area Volunteers "Ranks"	Interdisciplinary Appointees "Executives"	Interdisciplinary/ Interhierarchical Appointees "All levels"
Completed Projects	Independent selection	Generated by improvement areas Assigned or approved projects	Generated by company projects Assigned projects
Project Objec- tives	Maintenance or improvement (minor to moderate)	Maintenance or improvement (moderate to major)	Improvement or innovation (moderate to major)

Figure 7-5. Improvement Dimensions

Two Types of Operating Flow

Operational management of improvement involves two types of flow: *top-down* and *bottom-up*. Their meaning and content can be understood in relation to the two previously cited operating dimensions, namely, voluntary improvement and managed improvement.

Voluntary improvement

This dimension — that of quality circles and individual improvement — is based entirely upon bottom-up flow. In this program, relations between the ranks and management consist largely of the submission of improvement proposals to management by the quality circles. Top-down flow is limited to support activities for efforts to launch and manage programs.

Managed improvement

Higher executives and middle managers usually participate according to this dimension, which is the dimension of policy deployment, project teams, and quality teams. The top-down process pertains to organization (selection of groups) and content (selection of improvement areas and project themes).

Part III

Total Manufacturing
Management

8

The TMM Model

The emerging manufacturing strategies described in Chapter 5 require significant changes in managerial, organizational, cultural, and production systems. At the same time, a coherent and balanced development of all components is essential.

Because of its premises and content, the total manufacturing management approach recommended in this book meets this need while remaining consistent with a total quality strategy.

In one respect, this approach represents a point of arrival, insofar as more advanced systems may not yet have been examined. In another respect, it constitutes an obligatory transition to the indispensable high-tech management strategy for production systems. *Total Manufacturing Management** allows operational management that focuses upon maximum mobilization of human resources through top-down delegation of managerial functions.

The first operational phase in this process requires companywide participation in the improvement of operating processes (CWQC). It is oriented, on the one hand, toward establishment of an organizational framework of the group-dynamics type, and, on the other hand, toward high recovery of the firm's productivity, which is to be understood as total manufacturing costs (just-in-time).

Logic and Structure of the Model

The global revolution in industry organization has generated many new expressions. In addition to *companywide quality control, just-in-time,* and *stockless production,* there are now references to *total industrial engineering, quality improvement, process control, management by policy, quality deployment,* and *total productive maintenance.*

---

* The definition of *total manufacturing management* has been provided by Alberto Galgano & Associati of Milan.

Those who are not trained in this particular field may easily be disoriented by the proliferation of new terms. Moreover, managers who are already obliged to allow various approaches and techniques to coexist within their companies may be dismayed by the prospect of being called upon to introduce still more. Actually, however, the situation is simpler than it may first appear.

In fact, the new terminology as well as everything that underlies it comprises nothing more than various facets of a single organizational model; the different designations are merely correlated with the viewpoints from which the model is being examined. Thus, no precise boundaries exist between the concepts identified by the terms; there is significant overlapping, which promptly becomes clear to any persons whose management concepts are not excessively "Taylorized." It is obvious, for example, that extremely close interrelations exist among process control, stockless production, and total productive maintenance, inasmuch as it is not possible to produce with minimum inventories if processes are not reliable, whereby the respective processes must be controlled, and, for that reason, suitably maintained in addition. Accordingly, it is not logical to separate (in a Taylorist fashion) processes that occur simultaneously and must therefore also be managed simultaneously with an appropriate perspective.

The risk in Taylorist companies is that there may be only one person within the entire structure — namely, the general manager — who possesses an overview. He or she is the only person who oversees every "function" and who is therefore able to evaluate every aspect of the firm's operations in order to adopt decisions. The general manager is so remote from operational matters, however, that he or she cannot proceed knowledgeably in matters where a more hands-on perspective may be necessary for the adoption of decisions. Furthermore, this objective cannot be accomplished for various positions at the same time.

It is not the aim of this book to describe how organizational structure, independently from promotion of JIT, is evolving toward decentralization of managerial "totality." As indicated in Chapter 5, however, the trend is away from specialized and toward more entrepreneurial responsibilities. This trend is evident in the creation of *business units, divisions, product lines,* and *profit centers* (in contrast to cost centers). A similar trend is occurring in management control systems, where accounting according to total costs is becoming increasingly widespread.

The reference model is therefore becoming an *entrepreneurial* management model that descends toward the lowest levels of a firm. This model differs significantly from the prior model, which was based upon centrally managed mechanistic systems. It is in fact a transition from the *functional* model of a Taylorist-mechanistic system (in which companies were organized according to functions) to an *integrated* model (in which responsibility is shared within a matrix structure) or, even more frequently, to an *organic* system (in which small units, or "profit centers," maintain supplier-client relationships with one another). The organic system is the model adopted by Japanese firms, albeit with simpler forms of application than those which exist in the West.

Western management has not yet fully grasped the potential offered by total manufacturing management. Thus, in some instances, partial applications are attempted, with the result that the significant synergistic effects available through a unified action are forfeited. In this respect Westerners are victims of their own culture, which induces them through specialized publications or management schools, to approach problems from an overly specialized and academic viewpoint. The principal objective of this book is to provide the comprehensive view that is currently absent from the literature of management.

To that end, therefore, all the previously cited terms pertaining to production will henceforth be placed under the heading of *Total Manufacturing Management* (TMM). TMM consists of various subsystems, but it also establishes direct relations with the operating mechanisms of companywide quality control and with new management models.

A useful diagram for understanding this configuration is provided in Figure 8-1, where the term *Total Manufacturing Management* should be understood as encompassing the following subsystems:

- Just-in-time/stockless production (JIT/SP)
- Total industrial engineering (TIE)
- Total productive maintenance (TPM)
- In-process control (IPC)
- Quality improvement (QI)

As can be observed in the diagram, TMM also represents a direct expression of a CWQC strategy, because its objective is the eradication of all waste and defects ("waste" is equivalent to anything that

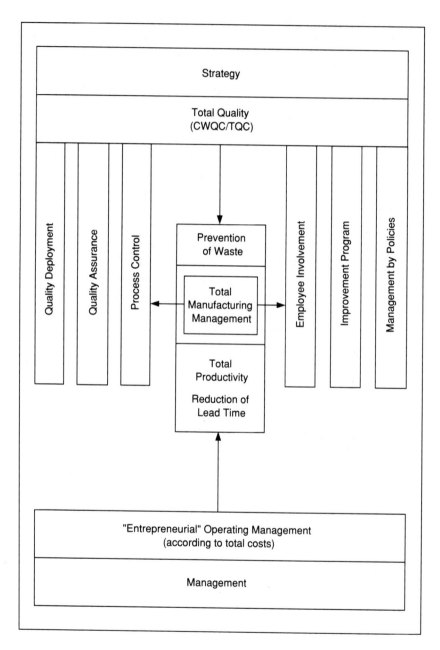

Figure 8-1. Total Manufacturing Management

does not add value to a product). Furthermore, it relies on the synergistic contributions of operating mechanisms that are inherent to CWQC. These same mechanisms constitute the necessary cultural basis for its functioning, and they include:

- Quality deployment
- Quality assurance
- Process control
- Participation
- Improvement program
- Management by policies

The entrepreneurial foundation for the TMM organization model consists of strategic factors, namely, lead time and overall productivity, which are developed to the fullest extent according to this model. These factors have entrepreneurial value only when considered according to accounting methods that have been developed on the basis of *comprehensive* accounting as opposed to traditional *analytical* "industrial" accounting.

When analytical accounting is applied, for example, a higher portion of overhead is recovered when the highest possible number of direct hours is attained. This means that it would be legitimate to expand a company's warehouses ("production" hours) in order to pay wages for indirect personnel and financial charges. It also means that outside processing would be preferable to internal processing when use of a given machine is infrequent on a yearly basis (producing high yearly and hourly costs and thus further discouraging use of the machine).

When comprehensive accounting is used, on the other hand, it can easily be observed that "an hour of inactivity is more beneficial than an hour of output that must be sent to the warehouse." This concept has produced what some people have called "a new economics of production."

TMM is closely related to CWQC in terms of three of the latter's operating mechanisms:

- Employee involvement
- Process control
- Improvement programs

The importance of these links is discussed further on. Insofar as the other mechanisms may be concerned, it should be observed that quality deployment is closely associated with TIE and TPM, that quality assurance is linked to QI and to SP, and that management by policies is linked to the management-control system.

The TMM organization model, which is partially derived from the Japanese model, is the reference model that has been developed in Western industry for competitively approaching the final decade of this century, during which the most industrialized Western nations and Japan will likely enter the post-industrial era.

Organizational Objectives

In keeping with its fundamental principles and its subsystems, TMM pursues the following organizational objective: *development of a highly flexible production system with zero defects and minimum throughput time.* The means to this goal is a production system characterized by:

- Organization according to flow (JIT-SP)
- Rapid setup (TIE-TPM)
- Small lots (TIE-SP)
- Highly reliable processes (TPM-PC)
- High flexibility (TIE-JIT)
- High product quality (QI-SP)

The abbreviations identify specific subsystems used to attain individual objectives.

Employee Participation

Essential to the success of TMM is *maximum involvement* of the company's human resources. *Management through people* (who must use systems and techniques), with the greatest possible decentralization, is a fundamental principle of TMM. This concept is counterposed to the principles of the mechanistic system, which requires centralized *management through systems.*

The distinction becomes extremely clear when the kanban system is compared with the MRP system (which was generated by the mechanistic approach). Kanban promotes sight management, which makes individual workers responsible for making decisions. In contrast, MRP obliges everyone to work on the operating outputs of the system, freeing executives and workers from concerns about the purpose of their work ("... so much is entirely taken care of").

The crucial importance of participation to development of effective and efficient JIT systems is too often overlooked by Western organization specialists, whose approach has accustomed them to favor the contributions of systems over those of people. Their diagnoses of the reasons that some JIT projects have failed are perhaps too facile.

One of the world's leading management experts, Ryuji Fukuda (who has been a consultant to Ford, Fiat, Philips, Motorola, Sony, Volvo, SKF, Mitsubishi, and Sumitomo, among others), regards creation of the stockless production system as merely an obvious consequence of adequate participation by employees who are appropriately prepared for improvement. According to Fukuda*, there are no precise operational reference models that must be applied. Instead, a company must internalize general organizational principles in order to arrive at its own optimal configuration (reference model). It does this by mobilizing the highest possible number of persons, because the results demonstrate that greater improvement is attained through a large number of small ideas than through large and far-reaching projects of a few individuals (or, in Japanese terms, through the principle of "many small steps", in contrast to Westerners' "few large steps").

Participation is probably not the only explanation for Japanese success, but it certainly constitutes a significant component. A study completed by the University of Kyoto in 1981 demonstrated that, in Western industry, knowledge of the problems associated with company processes was extremely limited below the highest levels of the hierarchy, in contrast to the situation in Japanese firms (Figure 8-2).

Obviously, employees' decision-making capabilities and their ability to contribute to a company's improvement are shaped by their levels of knowledge. Another aspect associated with the participation factor consists of required time for introducing changes.

As Figure 8-3 indicates, introduction of changes in Japanese companies takes place in a significantly different way than in Western companies. In the West, planning of changes and decisions concerning implementation occur extremely rapidly (in part because few

---

* Ryuji Fukuda, *Managerial Engineering*, Productivity Press, Cambridge, 1983.

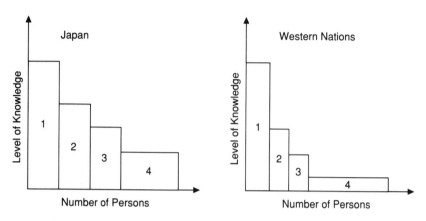

Source: University of Kyoto

Figure 8-2. Knowledge of Company Problems at Different Levels of the Hierarchy

people are consulted). On the other hand, actual implementation usually requires extremely long periods of time and often encounters significant resistance (imposed changes).

In Japanese firms, planning and decision making require longer periods of time (more persons are consulted, including those who will be affected by changes). On the other hand, implementation occurs more rapidly because planning and approval at all levels has already taken place.

The West	
Preparation	Implementation

Japan	
Preparation	Implementation

Source: University of Kyoto

Figure 8-3. Periods for Introducing Changes

According to the University of Kyoto, this phenomenon also explains the greater difficulty Western firms encounter in introducing management that relies on continuous improvement. The situation can be explained according to the siphon principle (Figure 8-4): in order to progress from (the less favorable) situation A to (the more favorable) situation B, one must surmount an initial phase of increased operational difficulty (the phase where change occurs). If this difficult phase is brief, it is easily surmountable. If it is protracted, however, efforts even cease in many instances, and one returns to the point of departure.

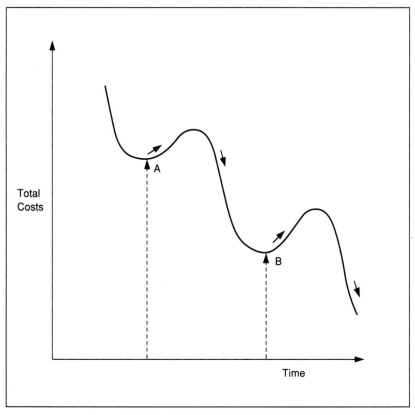

Source: Professor Hajime Yamashima, Koyoto University. Paper delivered at the First World Congress on Production and Inventory Control, Vienna, May 25-29, 1985.

Figure 8-4. An Interpretative Model for Change: The Siphon

According to this concept, the relatively long implementation periods typical in Western industry (on account of the lack of knowledge and approval of persons who will be affected) render the siphon process of improvement extremely difficult. It may be more worthwhile to spend more time planning and preparing for changes that can then be fully implemented, than to introduce changes hastily and ultimately fail to accomplish them.

9

The JIT
Organizing Approach

Basic Principles

Just-in-time organization of production finds its logical basis in certain fundamental premises. These premises can be stated in six principles, which are summarized in Figure 9-1.

From a cultural standpoint, it is revealing that the same model for organizing production has been identified by Western and Japanese managers with two different labels: just-in-time and stockless production.

The differing terms are not accidental. Instead, they embody differences between management perspectives. In the *market-oriented* approach of Western management, flow production is perceived as a series of events that must occur "just-in-time" within the framework of a process that begins with the market and proceeds in reverse toward raw materials. By contrast, in the *operations-oriented* approach adopted by Japanese management, flow production is regarded as a process that, when it is viewed from within or from a production standpoint, must occur with considerably smaller intermediate inventories at the outset ("stockless production"). Thus, two facets of the same phenomenon exist according to two different observation points.

The Value of the Production Flow

The six principles illustrate the importance of production flows to the just-in-time/stockless production model. The Japanese have created a special indicator termed *flow value* to compare flow levels in firms operating within the same market sector, or to analyze improvements within the same firm (flow value is a relative indicator). When

---

1st principle: Just-in-Time
Producing finished goods just in time to deliver them, producing semifinished items and subassemblies just in time to assemble them, resupplying oneself with purchased supplies just in time to use them

2d principle: Stockless Production
From *maximum energy* management (as much inventory as may be needed to cover problems) to *minimum energy* management (as much inventory as may be needed to identify problems)

3d principle: Preventing Waste
Nothing more than the quantities of materials, parts, space, and work time that are indispensable for adding value to products

4th principle: Flow Production
Comparable to a chemical process, which proceeds from raw materials to a finished product, without interruptions, unnecessary handling, or intermediate inventory

5th principle: Pull-system
From production that determines the flow of materials to a flow of materials that determines production

6th principle: Dynamic Responsibility
From static, unit-level responsibility to dynamic responsibility according to the flow

---

Figure 9-1. The Six Just-In-Time Principles

flow value is universally applied to all production processes, it is defined as the ratio between average production lead time and net required manufacturing time for producing a single unit of a given product. Using symbols from the field of work analysis, it is possible to express flow value as is shown in Figure 9-2.

The emphasis on production flow is operationally supported through use of indicators that have been developed for determining the efficiency of production flows. Their use is becoming increasingly widespread; in many instances, they are entirely or partially replacing traditional indicators, which are based solely upon efficiency in terms of resources. In fact, use of an operational model, wherein priorities are inverted in relation to those of the past, is becoming more common. Whereas it was customary, several years ago, to manage efficiency within individual units on a day-to-day basis, with periodic evaluation of logistical efficiency, the opposite is now becoming normal. In

$$F = \frac{L}{M} = \frac{\bigcirc + \Longrightarrow + \square + \triangle}{\bigcirc}$$

wherein

F = Flow

L = Average production lead time, from raw material to finished product (number of days, including days when there is no production — × 24 hours)

M = Net hours of production per unit of product, from raw material to finished product

Figure 9-2. Flow Value

other words, logistical efficiency is managed on a day-to-day basis, and production efficiency is evaluated periodically. The indicators employed are extremely varied, and they also depend significantly upon production categories. Moreover, no satisfactory "comprehensive" indicators are available, and it is therefore necessary to rely upon simultaneous use of multiple indicators that are intended for evaluating various logistical factors. Some of these indicators are cited in Figure 9-3.

Twenty Points for Organizational Transformation

A firm preparing to transform its own production structure according to total manufacturing management must, after it has assimilated the indispensable participation principle, decide where to begin.

Indeed, a model as comprehensive as TMM offers many possible access points, all of which are synergistically interrelated. However, different categories of production, different phases in the evolution of companies, and the critical nature or appropriateness of specific points in time call for extremely specific and carefully chosen inputs.

From a theoretical standpoint, it is possible to identify twenty possible inputs. These are TMM's *20 organizing points*, and they are listed in Figure 9-4.

The first 12 points pertain specifically to organization of production. The 13th and 14th pertain to the problem of quality, while the

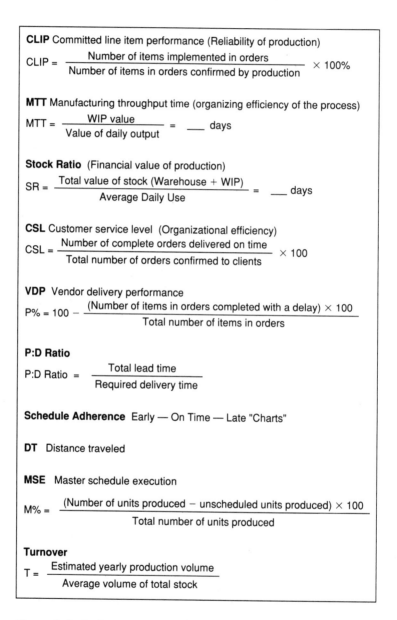

CLIP Committed line item performance (Reliability of production)

$$\text{CLIP} = \frac{\text{Number of items implemented in orders}}{\text{Number of items in orders confirmed by production}} \times 100\%$$

MTT Manufacturing throughput time (organizing efficiency of the process)

$$\text{MTT} = \frac{\text{WIP value}}{\text{Value of daily output}} = \underline{\quad} \text{ days}$$

Stock Ratio (Financial value of production)

$$\text{SR} = \frac{\text{Total value of stock (Warehouse + WIP)}}{\text{Average Daily Use}} = \underline{\quad} \text{ days}$$

CSL Customer service level (Organizational efficiency)

$$\text{CSL} = \frac{\text{Number of complete orders delivered on time}}{\text{Total number of orders confirmed to clients}} \times 100$$

VDP Vendor delivery performance

$$\text{P\%} = 100 - \frac{(\text{Number of items in orders completed with a delay}) \times 100}{\text{Total number of items in orders}}$$

P:D Ratio

$$\text{P:D Ratio} = \frac{\text{Total lead time}}{\text{Required delivery time}}$$

Schedule Adherence Early — On Time — Late "Charts"

DT Distance traveled

MSE Master schedule execution

$$\text{M\%} = \frac{(\text{Number of units produced} - \text{unscheduled units produced}) \times 100}{\text{Total number of units produced}}$$

Turnover

$$\text{T} = \frac{\text{Estimated yearly production volume}}{\text{Average volume of total stock}}$$

Figure 9-3. Indicators of Logistical and Production Efficiency

15th and 16th relate to manufacturing development. The 17th point addresses planning for products, the 18th addresses relationships with suppliers, and the 19th and 20th relate to organization of resources for operational management of production processes.

1. Reduction of Lead Time

2. Flow production

3. Short parallel lines/group technology

4. Leveling of production

5. Synchronized production

6. Overlapping/paralleling

7. Flexible/frequent/continuous scheduling

8. Pull control (kanban)

9. Visual control (VCS)

10. Stockless production

11. Jidoka

12. Reduction of setup time

13. In-process control

14. Quality improvement

15. Total cost cycles

16. Cost curves

17. Mushroom concept

18. Suppliers as comakers

19. Total industrial engineering

20. Total productive maintenance

Figure 9-4. The Twenty Organizing Points of Total Manufacturing Management

It is not possible to generalize models for an approach, because, as indicated previously, models are determined more by respective situations than by production categories. In terms of indicating the practicability and the priority of the preceding points on the basis of production categories alone, the following general framework is nevertheless valid.

Repetitive manufacturing production (distinct products)

All of the 20 points are applicable and relevant to repetitive manufacturing production. Nevertheless, it is advisable to choose from among the first 14 points for an approach to the first step, and to reserve TIE (19) and TPM (20) for subsequent periods.

Repetitive production by order (standard products, with only production by order)

Group technology (3), synchronized production (5), setup (12), and mushroom concept (17) are especially relevant to repetitive production by order; possibilities with "pull" control (today, kanban control is used for producing small numbers of items per year — for example, in machine tool production) may also be applicable.

"Batch" production (production by lots). Granting priority to stockless production (10), setup (12), mushroom concept (17), and suppliers (18) is recommended for batch production, but none of the other points should be discarded a priori.

Process production ("continuous" product). The best access points to process production are stockless production (10), setup (12), process control (13), TIE (19), and TPM (20), but mushroom concept (17) and comakers (18) are highly effective in some instances.

Pure production "by order" (specific products for specific clients). This category of production is usually inappropriately overlooked by JIT, precisely because the construction industry launched the JIT era in Japan. A significant transformation can be introduced, with exceptional gains in some instances, by using an approach based on total cost (15) in conjunction with setup (13), cost curves (16), the mush-room concept (17), and TIE (19). At the same time, synchronized production (5), VCS (9), quality (14), and comakers (18) should not be overlooked.

The principal points are examined more closely in the next chapter.

10

Organizing Production

Of the 20 points for organizational transformation that are required by the TMM model, the first 12 pertain directly to organizing and controlling production. These points are described in this chapter by means of a partially condensed format (with multiple points being discussed together) intended to offer a comprehensive managerial view of all pertinent techniques. Certain aspects, such as *jidoka*, have already been discussed (see Chapter 2). The remaining eight points, which pertain to process control, relationships with suppliers, industrial planning, and product development, are described in subsequent chapters.

Reducing Lead Time

The just-in-time approach strongly emphasizes throughput time (also referred to as lead time). Its purpose is to obtain drastic reductions. In repetitive production, it is possible to obtain reductions by as much as 90 percent. Usually, the point of departure in JIT is analysis of existing lead time, which often indicates a low flow level. Indeed, materials often remain in a plant for days, weeks, or even months, even though only a few minutes or a few hours of work may be needed. The diagnosis is obvious: plants often produce more waiting time (costs) than work (value). Indeed, one survey of metalworking firms indicated that active time (time during which value is added to the product) is often less than 5 percent of total throughput time (Figure 10-1). Such situations arise because the flow of materials — the vital factor with respect to costs and revenues — is not managed efficiently.

Analysis of lead time usually requires internal subdivision according to periods and categories, so as to determine the "weight" and importance of various phases. Nothing should be overlooked.

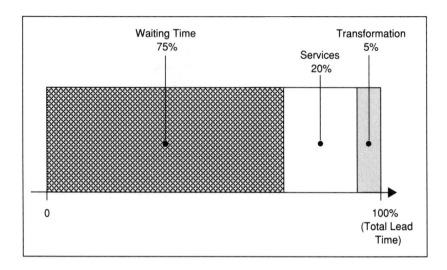

Figure 10-1. Composition of Production Time (in reference to material being processed)

Order-processing time and scheduling time, for example, are often among the principal culprits in extended periods for filling orders. Order processing alone often requires many days (whereas in some firms, even in the West, the filling of orders, including manufacturing and shipping, can be completed in only three days).

Another major factor in delays is regular scheduling, which, if it occurs every week, for example, involves average time losses of 2.5 business days for certain orders — namely, those which arrive one day after scheduling — because these orders may actually be ignored for an entire week. Restructuring projects that are intended to introduce flow production often require changes in this so-called bureaucratic area, where significant results are possible without intensive efforts.

Lead time analyses can be performed according to the diagram shown in Figure 10-2. The analytical objective is to identify all forms of waiting, along with the respective amounts of time. Then it is possible to proceed with analysis of specific causes and, subsequently, to planning of remedies and implementation. The following sequence of measures is most frequently adopted:

- Acceleration of order processing
- Technical standardization
- Leveling of production

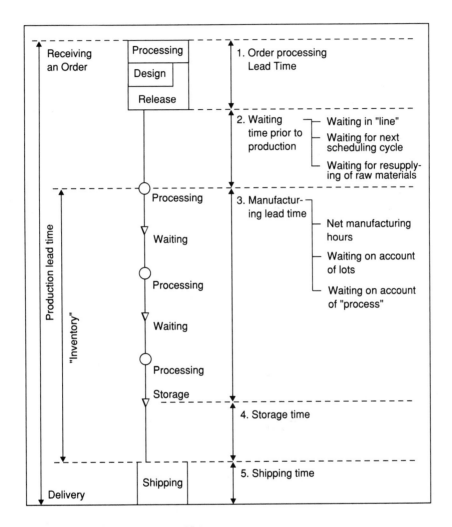

Figure 10-2. Lead Time Analysis

- Reducing the scheduling cycle, or sporadic scheduling
- Reducing bottlenecks
- Production in small lots (reduction of setup time)
- Single item flow
- Flow production
- Visual control

As previously observed, such a remedy includes the first 12 points of TMM.

Flow Production

Insofar as flow production may be concerned, the basic concept is to develop structures of the flow-shop type, in contrast to the job-shop category (Figure 10-3). The objective is to establish "smooth," or uninterrupted, flows, even at the expense of a certain degree of mechanization (Figure 10-4).

A comparison of the principal features of flow-shop organization with those of the job-shop system is given in Figure 10-5.

In terms of lead time, the advantages of flow production are revealed during training of operating personnel through the "overlapping" effects obtained with this particular layout. The significance of overlapping and its influence upon lead time are indicated in Figure 10-6.

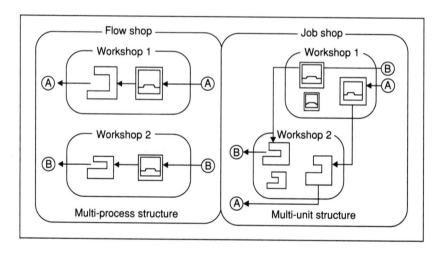

Figure 10-3. Flow Shops and Job Shops

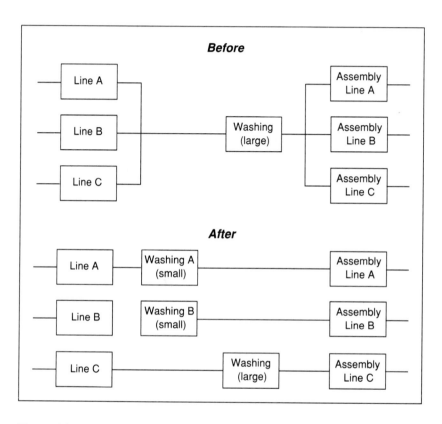

Figure 10-4. Uninterrupted Flow

Characteristics	Multi-process (Flow shop)	Multi-unit (Job shop)
Operating personnel	All skills	Specialized
Work-in-process	Almost none	Substantial
Lead time	Brief	Protracted
Type of production	Small lots, variety of products	Large lots, few types of products
Systems/machinery	Small, inexpensive, low speed, specialized according to products or categories	Large, expensive, not specialized according to products or categories
Space	Relatively small	Relatively large
Improvement of productivity	Companywide (according to flow)	Internal (according to units)
Handling operations	Unnecessary	Necessary
Quality	Item-by-item production	Risk of entire lots being defective
Setup	The need to reduce setup times is easily recognizable	The need to reduce setup times is not easily recognizable
Warehouses	No need to store semifinished items	Warehouses for semifinished items are needed

Figure 10-5. Flow Shop Organization and Job Shop Organization

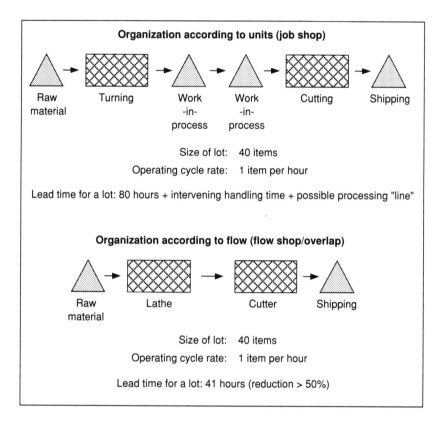

Figure 10-6. Overlapping

Cells and Group Technology

Another refinement in flow production is creation of multiple short parallel flows ("short" factories). The principle of *parallelism* often leads to the dismantling of extended flow lines with high output capabilities, in order to replace them with an equivalent number of short lines with low output capabilities. This step allows:

- Adherence to the "micro-mix = macro-mix" principle
- Acquisition of greater flexibility in terms of mixes and volumes
- Production of extremely small economical lots

Specific techniques for analysis and redesign have been developed for applying the paralleling concept. As soon as paralleling is implemented, it becomes necessary to decide how to organize individual production lines. When it is technologically possible to do so, it is advisable to create U-shaped lines (Figure 10-7) rather than straight lines. A U-shaped line is defined as a "cell" or as "group technology."

Flow production of the group-technology type offers the following advantages in relation to the traditional job-shop mode of organization:

- Shorter lead times
- Greater flexibility (response time)
- Less need to transport items
- Minimum work-in-process
- Elasticity with respect to volumes
- Less space
- No need for direct coordination

These advantages are accompanied by two possible disadvantages: (1) a possible need to increase the total number of required machines (sacrificing economy of scale) and (2) a need for versatile personnel. Another type of cell, depicted in Figure 10-8, illustrates how it might be possible to apply the principle of flow-controlled operations to achieve flexibility in terms of volume, and to automatically control absences and understaffing.

Usually, the advantages of this mode of organization decisively outweigh the disadvantages, no matter when it is introduced. Figure 10-9 portrays the outcome of a study undertaken by an automobile firm in designing a new transmissions plant. It should be observed that the need for two additional machines in the flow-shop configuration is largely offset by the smaller amount of required space (by one-half) and by the lower WIP level (by two-thirds). The difference in lead time seems truly exceptional (although in this context, it is normal): It has been reduced in the flow-shop configuration by 90 percent.

Differences in internal structure for the two types of configurations are clearly observable in Figure 10-10, which depicts the well-known example of Kawasaki-USA.

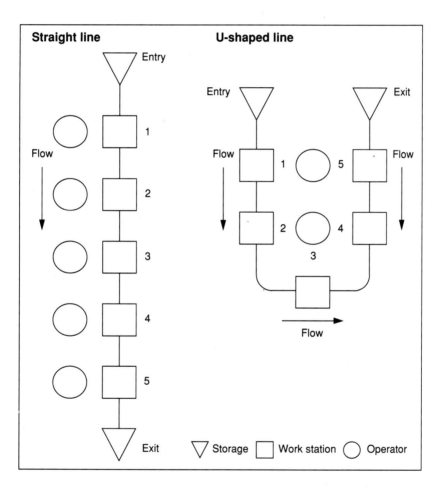

Figure 10-7. Comparison between a Straight Line and a U-Shaped Line

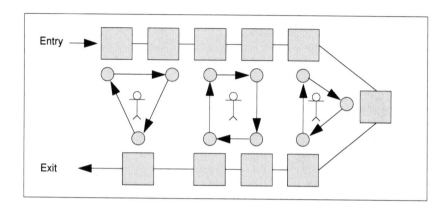

Figure 10-8. Organization of Work According to Cells

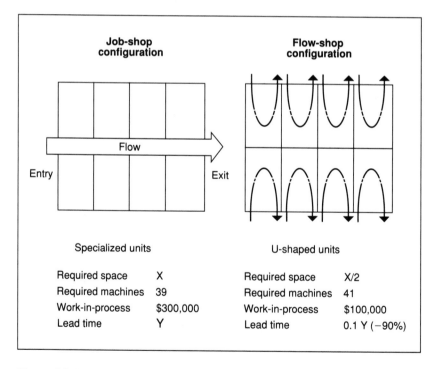

Figure 10-9. Ford Automobile Transmission Plant

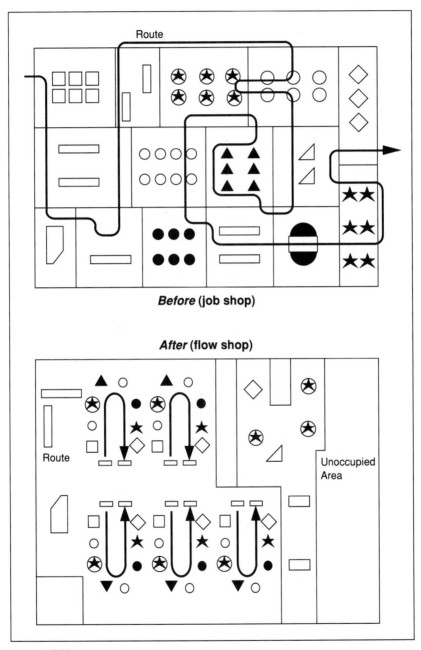

Route

Before (job shop)

After (flow shop)

Route

Unoccupied
Area

Source: APICS

Figure 10-10. Comparison between Flow Shop and Job Shop:
Kawasaki-USA

Scheduling and Controlling Production

In terms of scheduling and controlling production, the just-in-time/stockless production system inevitably requires changes in the mode of production. These changes include:

- Stabilization of production flows
- Leveling of production
- Balancing of production
- Control according to bottlenecks
- "Pull" control
- Synchronized production

For scheduling, too, total manufacturing management requires overturning of traditional principles. The conventional rationale was to *pursue optimal use of production resources through optimal development of the system's individual components*, whereas the TMM methodology affirms that *the sum of localized efforts to attain optimal levels does not equal total optimization*.

In order to achieve optimal development of the system, it is necessary to focus on the bottlenecks that determine overall flows.

A comparison of the scheduling rules derived from the two approaches is provided in Figure 10-11.

The next section contains an analysis of the structural changes that TMM calls for in terms of controlling and scheduling production.

Stabilization of Production Flows

One of the advantages of flow production is that it becomes more feasible to obtain "stable" production. This change allows extremely simplified control procedures, which are focused solely upon exceptions. An overview of the necessary steps for stabilizing production flow is provided in Figure 10-12.

Leveling Production

Leveling is a vital aspect of flow production. In order to produce according to a flow, it is necessary to establish permanent flows, even though volume may be variable. For example, instead of producing a product for which the required amount may be 60 units per year in one annual lot, the company produces the product in constant output

Efficiency-driven Approach	Comprehensive Approach—TMM
1. Balance capacity and then try to maintain flows.	1. Balance flows without being concerned about average total saturation.
2. Saturate each worker or machine as much as possible.	2. The level of saturation for each worker or machine is determined by clients' orders or by downstream bottlenecks.
3. An hour lost in a bottleneck has the same effect as an hour lost at any other location.	3. An hour lost in a bottleneck is an hour lost within the entire production system.
4. An extra hour of production at a position that is not a bottleneck is nevertheless regarded as an hour of "good" production.	4. An extra hour of production at a position that is not a bottleneck is regarded as wasted time (WIP).
5. Bottlenecks often obstruct the flow and increase WIP.	5. Bottlenecks control the flow and inventories.
6. Splitting of lots and overlapping of operations are regarded as uneconomical or risky.	6. It is possible that production lots may not coincide with flow lots.
7. Production lots coincide with flow lots.	7. (Flow) control lots should be variable instead of constant.

Figure 10-11. Rules for Scheduling Production

of five to six items per month. This feature of flow production offers a major advantage for a company, relieving it of the need to store lots that are equivalent to yearly or monthly needs and enabling it to produce on the basis of actual needs (rather than yearly projections).

Forming the basis of *leveling* is the availability of the entire required production mix within a brief period (micro mix = macro mix), with significant reduction of "mix turnover" time. Thus, leveling on a weekly basis means that each item so coded is produced within a period of one week, with weekly production runs; and leveling on a daily basis means that the items are produced in one day, with daily production runs, and so forth.

In addition to the obvious business advantages, leveling produces immediate and significant advantages in terms of lead time and WIP.

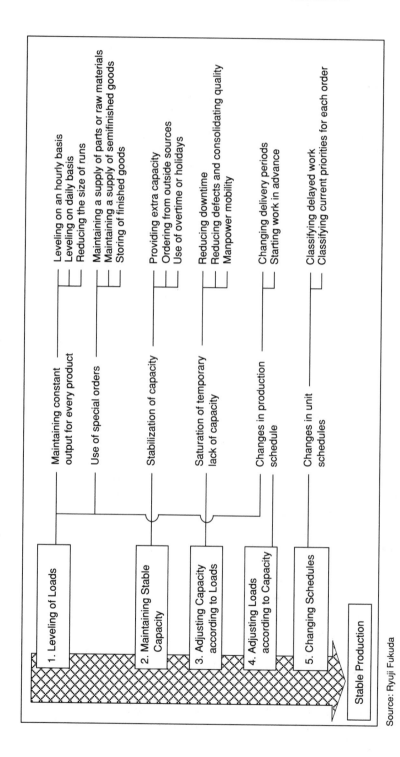

Source: Ryuji Fukuda

Figure 10-12. Measures for Stabilizing Production Flow

Consider the example given in Figure 10-13. Production is characterized by three sequential units: machining, painting, and assembly. Output requirements are 200 items per month for each product code.

Raw Materials Warehouse	Machining	Painting	Assembly	Shipping

	Machining	Painting	Assembly	Total
Monthly Leveling				
Work-in-process	200	200	200	600
Lead time (days)	20	20	20	60
Weekly Leveling				
Work-in-process	50	50	50	150 (-75%)
Lead time (days)	5	5	5	15 (-75%)
Daily Leveling				
Work-in-process	10	10	10	30 (-95%)
Lead time (days)	1	1	1	3 (-95%)

Figure 10-13. Monthly, Weekly, and Daily Leveling

It can be hypothetically assumed that production is possible according to three different types of leveling: monthly, weekly, and daily. In the case of monthly leveling, production lots should be 200 items. It can be observed that WIP with 600 items and a lead time of 60 days correspond to this type of leveling. For weekly lots, (50 items), WIP decreases to 150 items (− 75 percent), and lead time decreases to 15 days (− 75 percent). For daily leveling, with 10 item lots, WIP decreases to 30 items (− 95 percent), and lead time decreases to three days (− 95 percent). There are no lower limits for leveling, apart from those which are imposed by cycle length (sequence limit).

Figure 10-14 provides another example of sequential leveling, while Figure 10-15 depicts the type of leveling practiced by Toyota (economical lot = one item, micro mix = macro mix).

Model	Number of Items per:				
	Month	Week	Day	Hour	Mixed
A	6,400	1,600	320	40	
B	1,440	360	72	9	Sequence
C	960	240	48	6	based on
D	480	120	24	3	cycle length
E	320	80	16	2	

Figure 10-14. Sequential Leveling

Model	Monthly Quantity	Daily Quantity	Cycle Length
Sedan	5,000	250	2 min.
Hardtop	2,500	125	4 min.
Wagon	2,500	125	4 min.
Sequence: Sedan, Hardtop, Sedan, Wagon, Sedan, Hardtop, Sedan, etc.			

Figure 10-15. Toyota's Example of Leveling

Leveling of production also offers beneficial results in terms of controlling work loads. In firms that are still organized according to sequential units — where different items that generate different work loads are produced in separate departments (with the result that all of the problems associated with manpower saturation and mobility are present) — truly significant advantages can be obtained. Indeed, daily leveling considerably simplifies the unit supervisors' job of regulating work loads and scheduling production, because fluctuations are significantly reduced.

Balancing

Balancing of production has the same meaning in TMM that it does in traditional work analysis. The JIT approach emphasizes its role and scope, however. It is not the purpose here to offer an extended discussion of balancing techniques, which are already familiar. It is more relevant to emphasize the operational and managerial applicability of this concept, which can be understood when one recognizes the following principle: Any production flow is governed by the bottlenecks existing at a given moment, regardless of whether these are inherent or accidental bottlenecks.

This means that every machine or work station in the entire production process must operate at the same speed — the speed that bottlenecks impose upon the process. Hence, the efficiency of units or of the overall flow (billable flow, in JIT language) is more important than the efficiency of individual machines.

It also means that production must be managed according to bottlenecks, which therefore become a priority in production management, inasmuch as they determine the actual value of products. Management techniques must thus be oriented toward the following objective: An ability to adjust production flows when bottlenecks arise at a given moment.

This aim can be satisfied only through real-time management, which cannot be achieved with computer programming (on account of the numerous operational variables that must be controlled, if for no other reason). The kanban system, described in Chapter 2, specifically corresponds to this particular objective because it facilitates automatic production control according to bottlenecks existing at a given point. Visual control systems (which include kanban) are also intended to meet the need for prompt detection of production problems, such as bottlenecks. When chronic or easily predictable bottlenecks are present, a scheduling system of the OPT (optimized production technology) type may be extremely useful.

Scheduling and Pull Control

The technical importance of pull control has already been mentioned (Chapter 2). At this point, only certain conceptual aspects will be presented.

Pull systems are intended to prevent certain traditional production difficulties, such as:

- Idle time occurring between two scheduling points
- The need to maintain "aqualung" inventories in order to offset minor operational imbalances

- The need for rescheduling whenever imbalances exceeding the level of coverage offered by extra inventories occur
- The need to plan all of the target points within processes and to ensure that they are attained

Meanwhile, pull systems offer the following advantages:

- Implementation of automatic scheduling and dispatching.
- Maximum use of productive capacity according to possible flows.
- Visual control.
- Management of continuous improvement with the same tools that are used for routine management. This is possible because the system precludes functioning on the basis of pre-codified and unchanging standards, which would generate resistance to improvement.

The distinct approaches of push and pull systems are indicated within Figures 10-16 and 10-17.

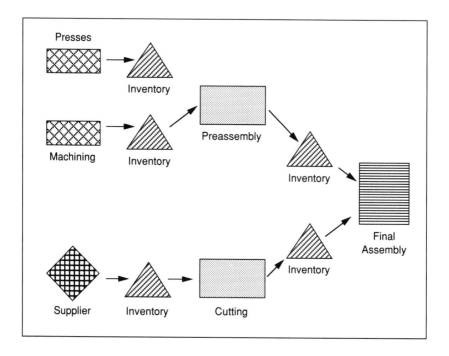

Figure 10-16. "Push" System: The Need for Anticipating Flows and Peak Levels

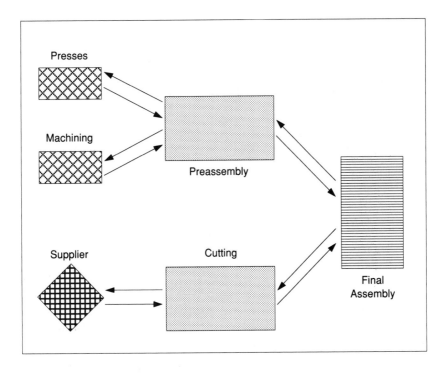

Figure 10-17. "Pull" System: Production and Resupplying "Pulled" by Actual Needs

A discussion of the operating techniques for kanban can be found in Chapter 2. It should be recalled, however, that the system offers different levels of sophistication that are essentially based upon two layers: *one-ticket* kanbans and *two-ticket* kanbans (Figure 10-18).

Apart from conventional kanbans, which are used in visual control systems, there are also kanban systems that can be combined with electronic data processing systems. This particular measure may be useful for three reasons:

- It controls the flow of materials from suppliers without restricting operating capabilities.
- It controls the flow of materials between large units or plants.
- It interconnects with MRP systems.

For these purposes, it is also possible to provide kanbans with a suitable bar code for any required "reading" (Figure 10-19).

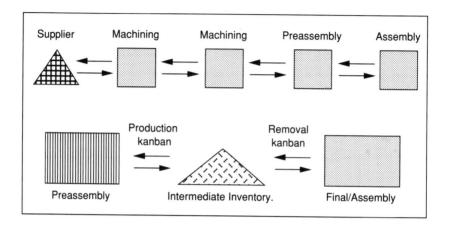

Figure 10-18. "One-Ticket" Kanban (operations directly associated with kanban) and "Two-Ticket" Kanban (intermediate inventories)

Scheduling production in a context that is controlled by kanbans with flow production is limited to performance of four tasks that are nevertheless extremely important:

- Regular presentation (every month, for example, with use of MRP systems) of order projections, so as to facilitate leveling for product lines, along with notification of suppliers (only approximate data are used)
- Screening of incoming orders and forwarding them to production units in accordance with planning for production capacity
- Control of confirmations for orders
- Performance of progress checks

So-called delivery times can be predicted with relative precision, and they can be computed without seeking information from the production division. In fact, it is sufficient to add the lead time for the final step in production — where orders are received (in flow production the lead time is a known quantity, which is constant) — to the amount of production time that is equivalent to the series of unfilled orders on a product line. Moreover, priorities can be directly managed by the firm's business departments, which can alter the sequence of pending orders, up to the final moment (with an advance period that is therefore equivalent to lead time for the final procedure).

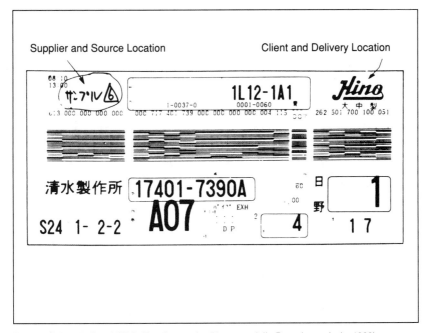

Source: Robert Hall — APICS, *Zero Inventories* (Homewood, IL; Dow, Jones, Irwin, 1983).

Figure 10-19. Supplier-Kanban Used by Hino Motors

As an example, one of the formulas used to determine the number of kanbans needed between two successive procedures situated in a pull relationship follows:

$$N = \frac{D(TA + TL)\,(1 + \alpha)}{C}$$

N = number of forms
D = daily production level
TA = waiting time for first card before machining begins
TL = machining time
C = number of items per transfer container
α = safety coefficient

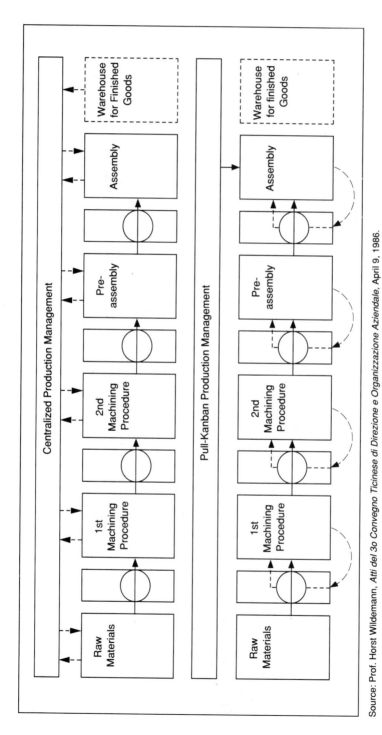

Source: Prof. Horst Wildemann, *Atti del 3o Convegno Ticinese di Direzione e Organizzazione Aziendale*, April 9, 1986.

Figure 10-20. Organization According to Self-regulating Circles

Pull systems can also be regarded as structures with *self-regulating circles*. This is a method by which automatic regulation of the production flow is performed by the circular routes being completed by kanbans (Figure 10-20), where centralized management is solely concerned with output.

Another characteristic of pull systems is their implementation of a continuous scheduling concept. With this system, scheduling on a regular basis does not actually occur; indeed, the scheduling function ceases to be useful.

MRP and Kanban

During the years before the Japanese organization model was fully understood, it was believed that JIT in Japan consisted solely of the kanban technique, and that Western JIT consisted solely of the MRP technique. For this reason, during the years from 1973 to 1978, there was extensive comparative discussion of MRP and kanban, with the result that there is now a substantial bibliography concerning this topic.

Such comparison was later understood to be fruitless, because it was based on superficial understanding of Japanese JIT. It is true, however, that as a scheduling tool, kanbans have the clear advantages of simplicity and efficiency. They are limited only in terms of applicability, being more feasible in production situations where visual control can be performed — that is, in repetitive production. For production to order, visual control is usually impossible, and kanbans are less effective.

For purposes of this discussion, *repetitive production* is to be understood as production of wholly or partially "precoded" products (through definition of a distinctive basis, along with distinctive relations and production flows) on a repetitive basis (at least ten items per year). Kanban control is feasible in such systems and is therefore oriented toward production of not only automobiles and televisions but also machine tools and automatic machinery.

Production to order, on the other hand, refers to one-time production of products tailored to individual clients (a system, a plant, a turboalternator, etc.) In such systems additional products with the same configuration are usually not required.

Visual control of production flows is to be understood as the ability to control production lead time through respective WIP levels. The curve in Figure 10-21 shows direct correlation between lead time and WIP within the context of production flow.

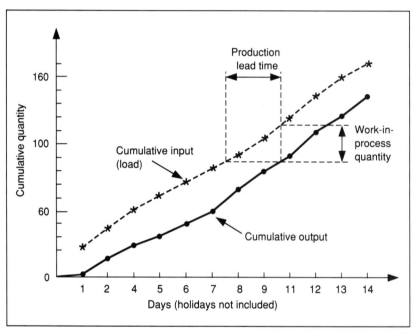

Source: Ryuji Fukuda.

Figure 10-21. Input/Output Graph

Controlling lead time through WIP is certainly the most immediate and effective method: *work-in-process can be seen, but time cannot*. In fact, kanbans also constitute a system for visually controlling work-in-process.

These aspects of kanban limit the benefits and appropriateness of any detailed comparison of the system with MRP, but, in the interest of thoroughness, some of the arguments invoked in the United States in 1977 — during the so-called JIT counterrevolution (whereby the myth that MRP was the most effective framework for introducing JIT systems collapsed), are cited in Figure 10-22.

27th APICS Conference, 1979
(American Production and Inventory Control Society)

"The principal error committed during the MRP crusade was that the strong need for operational production control was ignored."

"By means of computers, an effective and sophisticated model for controlling complex production situations with an adequate information system (MRP) was developed, although no attempts were made to reduce the complexity of these types of production."

International Management, March, 1984:
Study by Chalmers University, Sweden

"MRP is a 100-billion-dollar mistake, and 90 percent of the users are dissatisfied."

Harvard Business Review, September-October, 1985
Sumner C. Aggarval:

"The basic error is that MRP plans all resources according to infinite capacity, whereas certain points are inevitably bottlenecks. Moreover, it is rigid: it does not allow flexibility."

Richard J. Schonberger:

"Japanese JIT is strongly oriented toward reducing economical lots by compressing setup time. MRP regards a lot as a programming element."

"MRP response times are nearly a week, whereas kanban systems allow several hours (or minutes)."

"MRP plans according to 'infinite' capacity, and it requires a repetitive adjustment process. Kanban is controlled by the same production capacity but requires balanced processes."

"MRP allows better control of extremely diversified production, and kanban allows better control of more repetitive production."

"Kanban also allows lead time reductions and flexibility in production."

"MRP is not capable of halting production: whatever is programmed and set in motion shall be pushed downstream, independent of actual needs at the respective moment."

"Kanban can reproduce a limited number of components for the required marketing 'mix'."

"MRP is a push system; kanban is a pull system."

Figure 10-22.

With adoption of a pragmatic approach, the following conclusion emerges:

Wherever it is physically possible to do so, it is certainly appropriate to use production control systems of the pull-kanban type. MRP systems are used when it is not possible to control lead time by means of WIP.

The operational advantages of the JIT-kanban system in relation to MRP are indicated in Figure 10-23. It should be noted that kanban also possesses an additional dimension, namely, continuous improvement. Circumstances could not be otherwise, given its perspective. In contrast, however, MRP obstructs continual improvement: lot size and lead time — even planning standards — are rigidly defined elements that cannot be modified during day-to-day operation without plunging the system into a crisis.

On the other hand, although it is possible for scheduling and dispatching to take place with a kanban system, programming for projections cannot occur without a computer.

In the most advanced firms, production scheduling is now covered by combined MRP-kanban systems or similar methods. The examples of Hewlett-Packard and IBM are highly indicative. In these firms, which are obvious leaders in use of information systems, combined production control systems have been adopted (Hewlett-Packard) or are being tested (IBM) — with MRP systems being used for macro-scheduling, and kanban systems being used for micro-scheduling and operational production control. A counterpart in Japanese industry is Yamaha, which relies upon "Synchro-MRP."

Thus, various technical bridges between MRP and kanban, according to production categories and specific situations, are being developed. These bridges are illustrated in Figures 10-24 through 10-27.

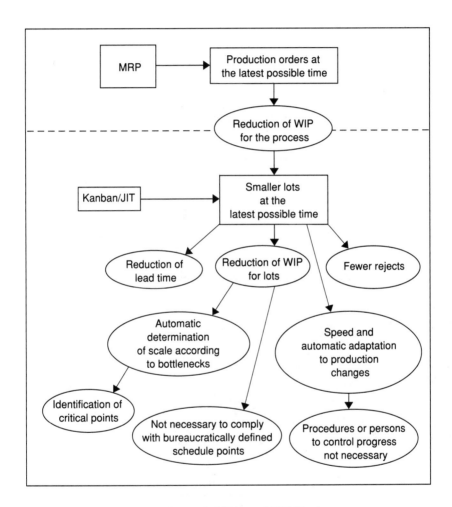

Figure 10-23. Inventory Control: MRP and JIT-Kanban

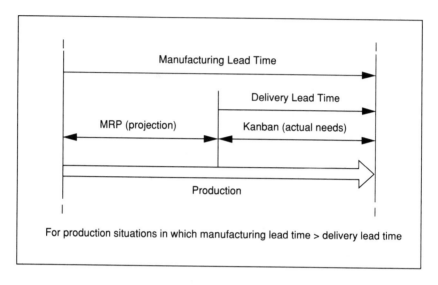

Figure 10-24. MRP-Kanban. "Lead Time" Bridge

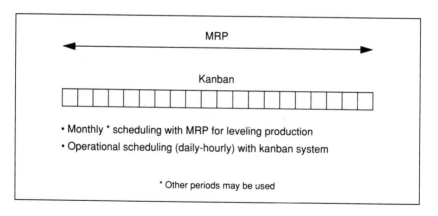

Figure 10-25. MRP-Kanban. "Period" Bridge

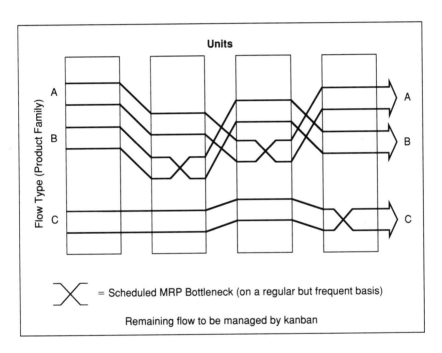

Figure 10-26. MRP-Kanban. "Flow Bottleneck" Bridge

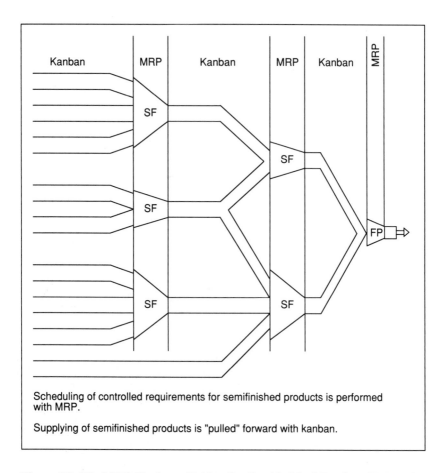

Figure 10-27. MRP-Kanban. Bridge for Semifinished Product (SF) and Finished Product (FP) "Funnels"

Synchronized Production

In situations where controlled production has not yet been introduced or where high numbers or diversification of subassemblies exist, a kanban inventory of even a few minutes would generate an unsupportable cost. Thus, it is necessary to rely upon synchronized production.

Synchronized production is actually an outgrowth of kanban systems. In more precise terms, there are two ways of evolving beyond or transcending kanbans:

- By developing comprehensive flows without disruption of continuity (pipelines, without a need for linkage through self-regulating circles or kanbans)
- By avoiding the need to wait for removal signals from a given location in order to start production upstream, whereby production must be activated by an advance requirements signal

The first objective can be pursued through complete flow production lines (also with CIM); the latter is accessible through introduction of synchronized systems.

Synchronized production is already extensively employed in the automobile industry, particularly in areas where it is physically impossible to maintain hourly inventories, because the components are either too large (seats, for example) or too expensive (engines, for example).

The system is based on rapid transmission of information originating at the beginning of an assembly line. The following example pertains to seats.

For seats, precise assembly requirements (types, colors, and sequence) become known only at the moment when automobile bodies are placed upon the line (after painting). At this point, a sensor reads a kanban/bar code and transmits the relevant information to the unit where seats are produced (in this instance, a supplier). The second unit is then given two hours to supply seats in the specified sequence, according to a predetermined rate and volume (for example, 12 sets of seats, which are equivalent to 12 minutes of production, or to 12 automobiles).

In this instance, two types of production (assembly of automobiles and seat production) are synchronized.

Use of such techniques for repetitive production in a job-shop milieu — where different situations generate different forms — is less extensive.

In Figure 10-26, for example, synchronization of bottlenecks occurs through scheduling with an MRP methodology, whereas operational synchronization of production flows (according to a sufficient capacity) is controlled by pull-kanban systems.

In complex job-shop environments, reliance upon OPT systems may be extremely useful.

OPT (optimized production technology) was developed by Creative Output of Milford, New York, for performing detailed computations for production schedules. This system, which is in a trial phase within many companies, may prove able to be more effectively combined with JIT systems than any system yet derived from MRP. Initial evaluations appear to confirm that OPT is more effective in job-shop environments with large volumes and few individual requirements.

The purpose of OPT is to achieve control of the work/flow rhythm by means of bottlenecks within processes, with application of the following principles:

- Scheduling of work in relation to bottlenecks is based upon market demand.
- The schedule for subsequent operations is determined by bottleneck output.
- The schedule for prior operations is determined on a pull basis, by the inventory that supplies the respective bottleneck.
- Operations involving flows where no bottlenecks exist are likewise controlled by orders obtained from the market.

The following consequences emerge:

- Maximum productive output is ensured by optimizing the schedule for bottlenecks in relation to clients' orders.
- The reference sequence is provided by the sequence of clients' orders, but it may also be partially modified according to operational problems.

Visual Control

The visual control system (VCS) occupies an extremely important role in terms of the operational aspects of just-in-time. Reliance upon such systems is becoming increasingly extensive. Once they surmounted the psychological barrier against a system that does not require advanced EDP support, is easy to use, and is non-technological, leading American and European multinational firms began to promote extensive use of visual control in their own production units.

The kanban system, which was soon followed by andon and jidoka, was the ice-breaker. Visual control is more an approach than an organizing technique, and it is justified through the following principle: For effective and timely operational control, all required information must be disseminated among the appropriate persons.

Every situation, especially anomalous ones, must be promptly and automatically identified. Only with visual control can this step occur easily.

When visual control is applied to the continuous improvement strategy of Japanese origin, it acquires even greater importance, because it offers two advantages considered indispensable:

- "In order to solve problems, one must see them. Hence, it is necessary to pursue efforts to render every production activity visible" (andon system).
- "Identification of non-optimal situations by means of light signals is an effective means of promoting everyone's participation in improvement of activities." (Fukuda)

Within a "zero defects" context, visual control can be defined as an information dissemination system that:

- Identifies abnormalities
- Promotes prevention
- Facilitates prompt corrective measures

thereby allowing:

- Prevention of waste
- Continuous improvement of processes
- Workers' autonomy

The practical approach for establishing visual control is summarized by the *Five S's* rule, which is provided in Figure 10-28.

THE FIVE S'S

1. *Seiri*	Sort through and sort out.	
2. *Seiton*	Set things in order.	
	Set limits; standardize.	
3. *Seiso*	Shine equipment, tools, and workplace.	
4. *Seiketsu*	Share information.	
	No searching.	
5. *Shitsuke*	Stick to the rules scrupulously.	

Figure 10-28. The Five S's

When this rule is applied to the materials area, for example, it can be expressed in the following form:

1. Eliminate anything that is not strictly necessary.
2. Decide where and how to place each material, along with necessary quantities.
3. Standardize containers and determine the required number.
4. Confirm whether products are accompanied by all necessary production information.
5. Follow the preceding rules strictly.

Figure 10-29 provides an example of a checklist used for establishing a visual control system at Volvo (at the recommendation of Ryuji Fukuda). The points cited constitute a general list for an initial approach, and it is necessary for all of them to be expressed by visual indicators that are readily understood by everyone. Use of the following visual communication signs is recommended:

- Lines on the floor to define areas where containers are to be placed under normal production conditions; lines of different colors can be used to indicate dangerous situations in terms of excesses or shortages.
- Lines or pennants on the walls for similar purposes.
- Andon panels to express point-by-point production status. Lights of various color can be used to indicate the status of different processes (this system is highly useful in managing with "water at the same level as the reefs," as described previously).
- Lights of different colors on machinery in order to indicate operating situations such as:
  — normal operating conditions
  — stopping when a load is not present
  — accidental and unexpected stopping
  — stopping for maintenance
  — lower than normal speed

- Containers with specific colors (associated with a kanban system in appropriate instances) for indicating abnormal flow or problems, or for allowing availability of specific semifinished items to be evaluated from a distance.

Category	Aspect	Control Points
Material	What How much When Which	1. Content of warehouses or containers 2. Quantity (size of lot) 3. Date for completion of process 4. Delivery date for product 5. Production priorities
Process	Quality Report	6. Frequency, methods, and results of quality inspection 7. Various indications for products according to specifications, defective products, or products for which decisions are pending 8. Person in charge, and date for decisions concerning defective material or material on waiting status 9. Daily report on quality defects 10. Daily production report 11. Actual production compared with monthly production schedule
Machines/ Systems	Processing Maintenance	12. Proper functioning 13. Scheduled stopping or stopping on account of damage 14. Work load for most important machines for the next period 15. Routine maintenance procedures for machinery 16. Positions of most frequently used tools 17. Maintenance procedures: tools, accessories, measuring instruments 18. Frequency of inspections/person in charge
Inventory	How much When How	19. Work-in-process quantity 20. Maximum allowable inventory 21. Area intended for "good" material and defective material 22. Storage system (front section, width, weight for each area) 23. Standard containers 24. First-in, first-out system
Personnel	Allocation	25. Distribution and responsibilities

Figure 10-29. List of Suggestions for Visual Control

In some companies, VCS is even used for upgrading actual visual control of machinery or systems. For example, the level of visual control can be expressed through symbols placed upon machines, so that the machine seems to say: "You hardly have time to look for a way to make me function better." Usually, five levels of visual control are applied, and the final level is "autonomous control of defects," or "autonomation," which is the level preceding complete automation.

It is also possible for visual control to be applied to kanban systems in order to control bottlenecks. Indeed, the presence of anomalies and, hence, bottlenecks within a process is indicated by abnormal accumulations of empty or full containers. This phenomenon occurs as a direct result of the number of containers that are present, or by means of the corresponding kanbans, namely, the tickets accumulating on the kanban board.

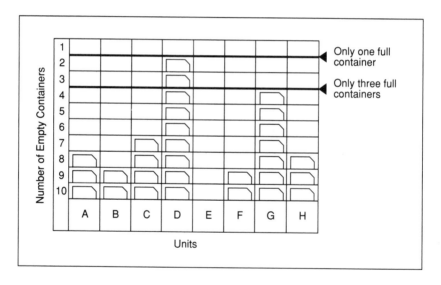

Figure 10-30. Kanban Board for Visual Control

As it is possible to observe in Figure 10-30, the flow can be controlled with WIP in each kanban station. The tickets placed in rows of card slots represent empty containers located at stations A, B, C..., H, which are sequentially arranged according to production flow. If the tickets at a given location exceed the precautionary level (only one or three full containers, for example), it means that difficulties have arisen at an upstream unit (unit D in the illustration), because it is not keeping pace with removals occurring at a downstream unit. If tickets are wholly absent, it means that a downstream unit is encountering difficulties, because materials are not being removed (in the illustration, unit F is not removing from unit E, for example). This situation enables the production manager to determine where bottlenecks may exist within the production flow and to intervene promptly, without waiting an extended period for computations to be available (which would be comparable to looking at the speedometer of an automobile on the day following a drive). Because visual control relies more upon application techniques and examples than upon a reference model, it is best explained through its applications. Readers wishing for further technical explanation should consult Hall's *Zero Inventories* and other manuals pertaining to applications.

Stockless Production

As an introductory operational step to the TMM model, stockless production requires an "attack" on WIP. In conceptual terms, stockless production represents a building block in the minimum energy organization model that was described in Chapter 2. Indeed, it constitutes a highly pragmatic approach that seeks significant economic advantages (reduction of financial charges) in the shortest possible period of time, along with a significant reduction in lead time.

The most recent experiences suggest that this simple approach should be used as a point of departure when it is urgently necessary to obtain results. In practice, the situation involves vigorous efforts to lower the "water level" so as to observe any "reefs" (problems) that may be present, and later approach them systematically.

Considerable expertise is required to manage this approach, since sudden and significant inventory reductions must be balanced with the effort to maintain a stable "water level." The first step often consists of an outright reduction of WIP by 30 percent, followed by smaller systematic reductions totaling ten percent.

In *Managerial Engineering*, Ryuji Fukuda provides an effective reference model for confronting inventories. Reflecting the logic that is characteristic of Fukuda's methods, this approach is based on active participation by the entire company structure.

Basic training, with stockless production as the ultimate aim, is required for the entire intermediate management layer and for at least 10 percent of the other personnel. Such training imparts knowledge about the causes of work-in-process, along with concepts for reducing it ("removal of causes"). After being trained, employees become systematically involved in inventory reduction projects, where the mode of organization parallels that described in Chapter 3 ("Organizing Improvement"). The primary objective of training is to motivate executives to seek inventory reductions.

Training relies upon transmission of the 13 principles of stockless production, which are cited in Figure 10-31. Each principle is demonstrated during training through specific drills.

These principles are oriented toward providing cognitive and therapeutic "prescriptions" for causes of work-in-process. There are seven principal causes:

1. Appropriate WIP level is not determined
2. Imbalances in production (including differences among shifts)
3. Excessive size of the lots in use (setup problem)
4. Excessive subdivision of processes for allowing optimal development of efficiency for individual operations
5. Processes are not under control (quality, products, and reliability of processing)
6. Lack of sufficiently qualified workers
7. Production control system is not effective (significant production in advance)

Figure 10-32 provides a general diagram explaining Ryuji Fukuda's approach to stockless production.

1. There are two dimensions of production, which exist in contrast to one another: *processes* and *operations*.

2. Waiting is a consequence of the division of labor. Handling procedures are required when processes are divided into subprocesses.

3. There are two types of waiting: *waiting on account of lots* (delaying all items in a given lot while work is performed on a single item) and *waiting on account of processes* (delaying an entire lot between two processes).

4. The majority of production lead time consists of waiting.

5. Waiting on account of processes is reduced significantly by balancing the line and by decreasing bottlenecks.

6. Waiting on account of lots is reduced when the size of lots is reduced.

7. Reducing work-in-process is an effective means of shortening production lead time.

8. Balancing the line is an effective method for reducing production lead time and increasing efficiency at the same time.

9. Whether a line is well-balanced or not, efficiency decreases significantly if WIP is eliminated. For this reason, the optimal WIP quantity should be determined for the purpose of balancing efficiency and lead time.

10. Capacity should be immediately adjusted in relation to loads so as to avoid increasing lead time (as well as waiting on account of processes).

11. Waiting time prior to the start of production should be regulated by controlling backlogs.

12. Shortening the scheduling cycle leads to reduced waiting time.

13. Maintaining inventories of semifinished items is an effective means of shortening production lead time for products that must be made to order. Nevertheless, these inventories must be reduced to the indispensable minimum.

Figure 10-31. The 13 Principles of Stockless Production

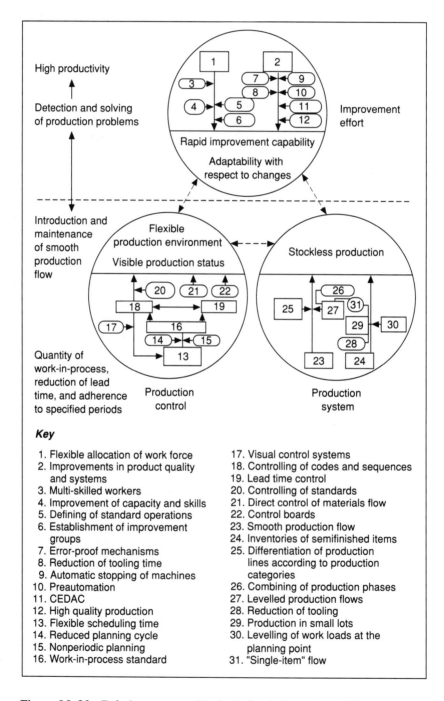

Figure 10-32. Relations among Methods for Achieving Stockless Production (according to Ryuji Fukuda)

Reducing Setup Time

Reduction of setup time is another unavoidable priority of JIT/ stockless production. Indeed, this aspect produces multiple effects:

- Direct determination of the size of economical lots, while affecting inventories and mix-turnover
- Strong influence upon production turnover
- Effects upon consequences of "non-quality"

The Problem of Economical Lots

It is not true that production according to economical lots is sufficient to eliminate the problem of setup time. Time lost on account of production changes can never be recovered. The process of producing exceedingly numerous lots does not remedy the situation. Instead, it makes matters worse by generating other costs, such as costs for the inventories of finished or semifinished goods generated. As the Japanese say, setup time is one of the worst forms of waste in production; the entire firm continues to incur costs, while no value is produced.

Reducing setup time does not necessarily directly reduce unit costs for products. In many instances, it merely corresponds to a changing of cost categories. Nevertheless, this step allows production with considerably smaller lots (faster mix-turnover), with significantly greater flexibility (greater sales opportunities), and with less impact from processing defects (smaller quantities to be rejected). Thus, there is a significant improvement in terms of general operating costs and entrepreneurial categories.

The change in costs often consists of a reduction in inventory costs (financial charges, warehousing, and handling) in favor of fixed product costs (initial outlays). This happens because, in order to obtain faster setup times, it is often necessary to make an initial outlay for specific machinery in order to obtain smaller economical lots. Indeed, initial outlays do not influence the determination of economical production lots because they are amortized according to total planned output — independently of how it will be divided into lots. Figures 10-33 and 10-34 contain graphs illustrating this particular concept.

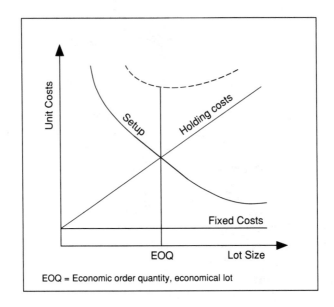

Figure 10-33. Economical Lot with High Setup Time

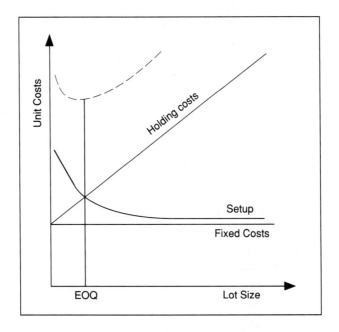

Figure 10-34. Economic Lot with Reduced Setup Time

Technical Approach

As Shigeo Shingo has indicated in his book *Toyota Production System*, "reducing setup time essentially depends more strongly upon conceptual changes than upon specific techniques." Indeed, Western Tayloristic perspectives were so profoundly concentrated on direct labor that indirect procedures were often shortchanged or overlooked. At best, there was nothing more than upgrading of certain remedies (economical lots merely represent a remedy for the problem of setup).

The problem of setup also generated extremely important techniques that gave confirmation to Shingo's observation. These techniques are explained more adequately by Fukuda and Shingo, but some of the principles behind them can be indicated here. The first point falls within the domain of statistics: In forms of production where setup time has just become a priority, it is legitimate to expect reductions by as much as 90 percent.

The reductions are distributed accordingly:

- 50 percent by converting internal setup to external setup. This type of conversion often requires extremely limited modifications that are relatively inexpensive, and it nearly always constitutes an initial step for reducing setup.
- 25 percent by changing positioning methods and accessories.
- 15 percent by eliminating adjustments.

In Japan during the 1970s, reduction of setup time was promoted by means of specific campaigns. These campaigns referred to two successive phases, each of which was identified by an acronym:

- First phase: SMED = Single Minute Exchange of Dies (changing of dies should be completed in less than 9 minutes)
- Second phase: OTED = One Touch Exchange of Dies (changing of dies should be completed in a single step: that is, within less than 100 seconds)

As was explained in Chapter 2, Toyota was one of the first to join this campaign. A checklist for approaching setup reductions follows:

1. Clear separation of internal setup (procedures that can occur only when a machine is shut off) from external setup (procedures that can occur when a machine is operating)

2. Eliminating loss of time during both internal and external setup (loss of time due to unnecessary motion, searching for tools, accessories, etc.)
3. Converting internal setup to external setup
4. Completing positioning and disassembly procedures with a single movement
5. Eliminating adjustments
6. Identifying possibilities for parallel work by two or three persons

All of these measures must be supported by techniques learned through specific training.

11

Process Control

Process control is significant at two levels. On the one hand, it constitutes a pillar of companywide quality control, and it is the fulcrum of Japanese organizing strategy. On the other hand, it represents an essential condition for proper functioning of just-in-time systems.

In fact, stockless production is unimaginable in the presence of uncontrolled processes for which contingency inventories are required at every point. It is not accidental that process control is said to represent one of the two operating keys to JIT, along with "housekeeping" (another confirmation of the importance of visual control, where housekeeping is the basis).

For a process control structure to be effective, it must be based on an extremely comprehensive approach that incorporates coverage of three general categories of problems:

- Approach
- Organization
- Technical aspects

Approach

A "logical" approach to developing an effective process control system is outlined in Figure 11-1.

As is shown, the approach consists of anticipating rather than inspecting, and standardizing processes instead of controlling their consequences. The Japanese have demonstrated that this approach is significantly more cost-effective.

A. Processes are the highest priority in production, and the entire mode of organization should be oriented toward maintaining process control in the most effective and economical manner.

B. This goal requires continuous activity, which must take place at every point where a process is occurring.

C. Process control can be carried out through two forms of regulation:
  • Regulation based upon errors
  • Direct or conscious regulation

D. Direct or conscious regulation corresponds to the situation in which maximum efficiency and cost effectiveness can be attained.

E. Direct regulation can be provided through sharp awareness of essential variables for processes, in order to be able to anticipate uncontrolled situations.

F. The purpose of process control is to obtain the greatest possible number of directly regulated situations.

Figure 11-1. The Approach to Process Control

Organization

The reference model for organizing process control takes its cue from the system's objectives. To satisfy these, the requirements set forth in Figure 11-2 must be fulfilled.

Technical Aspects

A reference model for a technical approach to process control is given in Figure 11-3.

Certain clarifications are necessary in terms of the technical meaning of this approach, which was developed by Shewhart and Deming.

Typical Factors

In every system there are certain typical factors — traits that are a product of the system's design, production, raw materials, operators, and so on. These factors can be removed only by modifying the system.

Premise: Regulating processes is performed by operating units referred to as regulators. In a production unit, numerous regulators are necessary, and planning them is the most important element of organizing process control.

A. Line supervisors must be fully involved in the functioning of regulators.

B. To pursue maximum quality and productivity, operating personnel also become fundamental resources for regulators.

C. It is therefore necessary to entrust operating personnel with all or some of the duties promoting functioning of various regulators.

D. The quality control department must essentially function as a "regulators' regulator." In other words, it is not directly involved in regulating processes, but it does regulate the system that performs regulation. Thus, process control gains reliability through confirmation that the process regulator, which is to be provided directly by supervisors and operating personnel, shall maintain required performance levels.

Figure 11-2. Organizing Process Control

A. In order to perform process control efficiently, full comprehension of the functioning of the respective process is required.

B. Hence, the fundamental point is the designing of memories (in a cybernetic sense) and use of quality techniques for diagnosing control problems.

C. Implementation of the initial level of process control consists of two phases:
- Identification of *special factors* and elimination of conditions that are not under control.
- Removal of *typical factors* and continuous improvement of the process.

D. After identifying various factors, it is necessary to develop remedies and to standardize operating procedures.

E. Process control should operate so as to allow continuous improvement of process capability.

Figure 11-3. Technical Approach to Process Control

In situations where only typical factors are present, the amplitudes of data distributions are predictable and constant. Within the framework of these intervals, variability is entirely accidental. In other words, the way in which individual data elements may emerge over time is governed solely by chance. If a system is affected solely by typical factors, it is not logical to intervene on the basis of a single variation in data, in order to change a specific aspect of the system. If data variability exceeds requirements, however, it is only possible to reduce variability by modifying the system.

Special Factors

Special factors are specific aspects (irregularity of operating parameters for a process, unacceptable batches of raw materials, errors in use of equipment, etc.) that disrupt a system. In the presence of special factors, amplitudes of data distributions are not predictable, and decisive variations are generated. In such a case, it is necessary to change specific features of the system so as to eliminate the special factors and thus, the resulting variations.

Distinction Between Typical Factors and Special Factors

Effective process control measures require clear differentiation between typical factors and special factors. It is also essential to understand the different effects of each type of factor on the functioning of the system. Ignorance on these points invites the risks of either not taking action at the necessary time or taking improper action. Without an objective means of distinguishing one situation from the other, any attempts to interpret or regulate the functioning of a process become wholly subjective endeavors.

Statistics and statistical techniques offer one such objective tool. Control graphs are the simplest and most effective method. They are characterized by an upper control limit and a lower control limit ("natural" limits). So long as the various points remain within the limits, it can be assumed that only typical factors are at work; deviations from the control limits indicate the presence of special factors. Another indicator of special factors are specific patterns affecting points situated within the limits.

Process Capability

The process capability is the level of capability of a process for satisfying indicated output specifications. In practical terms, the concept involves the ratio that exists, for example, between the Gauss curve representing the level of dispersion for a process and the indicated specifications (Figure 11-4). The ratio between the distance between two specified limits and six times the average quadratic deviation from Gauss curves is defined as the *process capability index*.

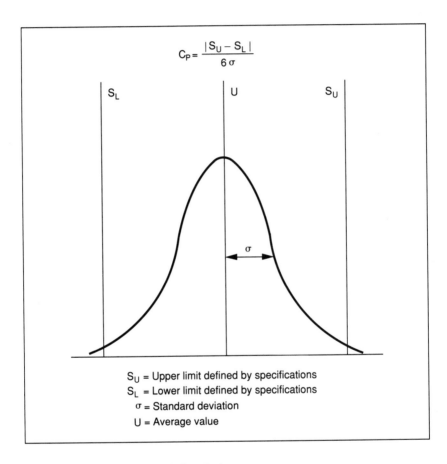

$$C_P = \frac{|S_U - S_L|}{6\sigma}$$

S_L U S_U

σ

S_U = Upper limit defined by specifications
S_L = Lower limit defined by specifications
σ = Standard deviation
U = Average value

Figure 11-4. Process Capability Index

12

Product Development
and Industrial Engineering

Organization

The application of TMM to product development and industrial engineering produces truly significant results. The TMM model allows extremely brief periods for developing and designing products, low start-up costs, and high reliability of production processes. It bears obvious links to research and development, concepts pertaining to the "structuring" of products, quality deployment, and with other CWQC mechanisms. Accordingly, it can only be described in the comprehensive terms befitting the TMM approach.

Figure 12-1 indicates results obtained by Toyota through application of quality deployment. Note that start-up costs and the start-up period were reduced by approximately 90 percent.

The contrast between product and/or process modification requirements at two firms — another Japanese automobile firm that adopted quality deployment and a Western firm operating with traditional methods — provided in Figure 12-2.

Significant results have also been obtained in amounts of time needed for developing new products.

Application of JIT-QD techniques has allowed these operating configurations to be obtained:

- From 5 years to 3 years at Toyota and Honda
- From 2 years to 1 year at AT&T (telephone equipment)
- From 4.5 years to 22 months at Hewlett-Packard

The TMM model allows for changes at both a structural and a technical level. In terms of *organization*, it ensures that R&D and industrial engineering shall not be separate activities. In keeping with current trends in general organizational concepts, it becomes fundamentally necessary to dismantle Taylorist perspectives whereby every activity

217

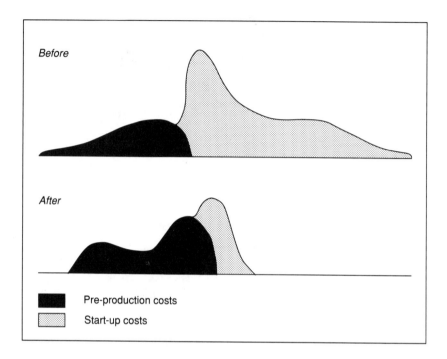

Figure 12-1. Reduction of Start-Up Costs at Toyota

within the process-marketing, R&D, IE, and production — is regarded as being structurally separate. TMM allows for reunification of all activities and disciplines related to product development. After all, a product cannot be developed unless production problems are taken into account from the outset; neither can a product enter the preproduction phase without initial input from the marketing division.

The reunification of company functions has paved the way for application of the strategic concept that brought success to the Japanese during the 1970s — the concept that products and processes should originate in conjunction with one another. Structures based upon functions are replaced by structures based upon working groups (*product teams*). These include all of the previously cited functions, although the importance of these functions may vary according to progress in developing particular products.

This approach ensures that the interests (or, more precisely, the viewpoints) of various positions are always upheld during product development. It also prevents products from "ping-ponging" between

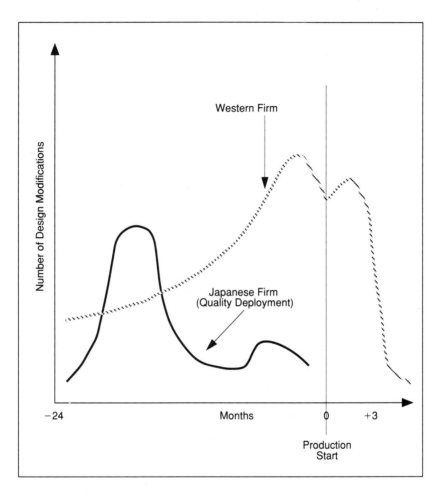

Figure 12-2. Number of Modifications over Time

functions, where the only result is that planning periods lengthen while costs increase, and products do not necessarily correspond to opportunities identified by the marketing division or opportunities generated by R&D. Figure 12-3 provides an illustration of this type of transformation.

The recommended approach allows:

- Significant reduction of lead time for planning
- Continuous and instantaneous removal of any technical obstacles that may arise

- Automatic approval from downstream divisions
- Real-time calibration of necessary categories and quantities of resources
- Avoidance of "shock" effects
- Reduced risks of failure

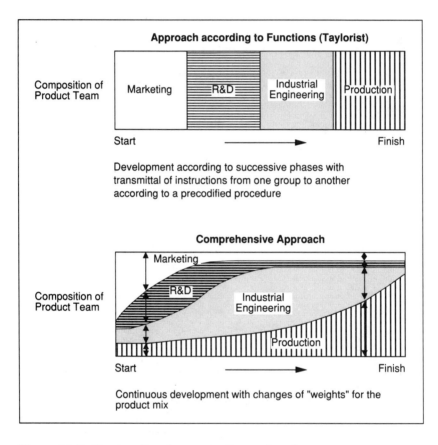

Figure 12-3. Product Development: Comparison between Taylorist Approach Based upon Functions and Comprehensive Approach

Techniques

So that products may be designed rapidly without loss of quality or reliability, various engineering techniques and tools have been developed (by both Japanese and Western companies). These include:

- CAD (computer-aided design)
- CAE (computer-aided engineering)
- Design review
- Quality function deployment (developed by Professor Akao)
- FMEA (failure mode effect analysis) for products and processes
- FMEI (failure mode effect improvement)
- PERT-CEDAC (Fukuda's Cause-and-Effect Diagram with the Addition of Cards applied to Program & Evaluation and Review Technique critical paths)
- DOE (Design of Experiments according to the Taguchi, Shainin, Kobayashi approaches)
- SPC (Shewhart, Deming, Shainin, Langevin, Kobayashi, and other Statistical Production Control methods)

Nevertheless, the true problem lies in the use and organization of these techniques during development of new products.

Figure 12-4 contains a reference model now being developed in Europe. The author is conducting trials with this same model at Fiat.

Of the techniques that have been cited, only the most innovative and significant, namely, quality deployment — which also constitutes the basic support for all of the other techniques — shall be described here.

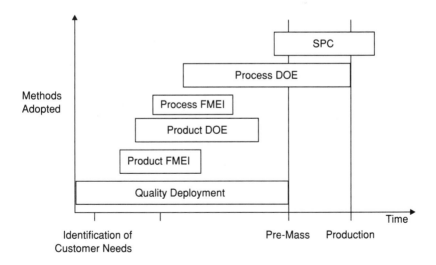

Figure 12-4. Use of Quality Engineering Methods in Developing New Products

Quality Function Deployment

Quality function deployment (QFD) was developed to ensure that products entering production would fully satisfy the needs of their customers by building in the necessary quality levels as well as maximum economic suitability at every stage of product development.

This technique, which was developed in Japan, is now being introduced in Western firms. A summary prepared with the assistance of Franco Zucchelli* follows.

History of QFD

Quality function deployment plays a key role in the implementation of CWQC. It represents an integrated model for the development and the planning of new products and for the implementation of total quality in preproduction phases. The term *deployment* was first used in this context in 1969, by the Japanese company Shimpo. The first ideas on how to implement companywide quality control early in the development of new products came at around the same time. Not until 1975, however, did full-scale development and application of QFD begin. In the Western world, QFD has been known since 1983, the year Professor Y. Akao (awarded the Deming Prize for quality function deployment in 1978) of the University of Tamagawa presented a paper on this subject at a conference in Chicago. At present, Japanese companies in various commercial sectors — in particular, the mechanical, electronmechanical, electronic, chemical, pharmaceutical, foodstuffs, textile, and building-construction sectors — are applying QFD. Each of these, starting from a common base model, has tailored the approach to its own needs. Applications in the Western world, however, are limited to a few American and European companies, predominantly in the mechanical, chemical, and electronic sectors.

QFD As a Tool for Customer Satisfaction

The main element in CWQC strategy is customer satisfaction. It is on this element that the attention of the entire company is concentrated. The entire company, then, becomes customer-oriented. To

---

* Franco Zucchelli is a senior consultant with Alberto Galgano & Associati, and he is introducing this important technique in leading European firms, including Olivetti, Volkswagen, Fiat, Philips, and IRE/Whirlpool.

satisfy customers, however, the company must listen to what the customer is saying. QFD is the means by which the customer's voice is not only heard throughout all product-development activities but constitutes the reference for every decision relating to the development of new products. Until the fifties, *quality* was associated with *inspection*; therefore, all activities associated with quality were located downstream from production, in the inspection phase. The revolutionary idea of the sixties (represented by Deming, Juran, and CWQC) was that *greater quality* at *less cost* could be had by attending to quality during the *production* phase. In other words, it was understood that better quality and greater productivity go hand in hand. Considering quality at the production phase meant that specifications had to be defined in advance and that inspections had to be made to verify that products and processes conformed to those specifications.

Eventually, however, it was realized that even when all specifications were met, success could not be guaranteed. In the seventies, consequently, quality became a consideration even before the specifications were determined, as early as the planning and design phases. The technique that gave concrete form to such early consideration of quality was QFD. QFD ensures that quality is built into the product in the development and planning phases.

Negative and Positive Quality

Negative quality, or reactive quality, refers to any part of the production process where a problem exists: delays in delivery, product defects, machine downtime, or excessive costs. An area of negative quality is easily quantifiable, making an analytical approach (based on mathematics and statistics) indispensable. Nevertheless, even when negative quality has been eliminated (problems reduced to zero) success is still not guaranteed. The absence of negative quality does not by itself guarantee that the products are actually those desired by the customer. Rather the focus must be on *positive* (or *active) quality.* This area is more difficult to quantify because it is not expressed in figures that measure discrepancies but by the customer's wishes — which tend to be vague, variable, and difficult to codify.

QFD is the technique that companies use to operate in the area of positive quality so as to produce real customer satisfaction, which is not just the elimination of reasons for complaint (negative quality) but is also an active response to customer wishes and expectations.

Coherence in the Various Development Stages

At any stage in product development there is a risk of finding oneself with a telephone but no wires. Every person involved in the process can introduce errors through misinterpretations, distortions, misunderstandings, and personal biases. Communication problems are also often at fault: Marketing people often don't understand technical language, while technicians generally turn a deaf ear to customers, regarding customer requirements as almost an interference with their work. All this distances the company from the customer and renders its response to customer demand inadequate. QFD helps to guarantee coherence between the various phases, ensuring that the finished product truly responds to the market's expectations. It ensures that the customer's wishes are the thread running through all phases. QFD also carries secondary organizational benefits; it promotes the comprehensive structure that keeps the customer's wishes in high profile and discourages the system of watertight compartments that alienate the company from the customers.

Total Quality

Quality in the development phases refers not just to the product but also to the service. Indeed, *Quality Equals Customer Satisfaction* is intended to underline the notion that it is not sufficient to simply respond to the customer's requests. In addition to that type of quality (*expressed quality*) there is also *implicit quality* (quality that is not specifically asked for but is assumed to be there), and *attractive quality* (quality that is not asked for because the customer does not even imagine that it can exist; this is the area of dormant needs).

QFD gives the fullest possible depth to the quality concept and ensures performance capable of satisfying the customer in the most complete sense.

Do It Right the First Time

This slogan reflects the idea that reductions in the time and cost of product development can be brought about only through reduction of the need for modifications and corrections during the course of development. The only way to do this is to set off "on the right foot." QFD introduces from the start all the conditions necessary to "do it right the first time."

Quality in Planning and Design

In short, QFD makes it possible to:

- Define product specifications meeting customer requirements while attending to the competition
- Ensure consistency between customer requirements and the product's measurable characteristics, assemblies, components, and materials
- Instill in all company members an understanding of the relation between their individual contribution and characteristics of the finished product, and between the product and the market
- Ensure consistency between the planning and the capability of the production process
- Speed up the production process because planning takes place at an early stage, thus minimizing mistaken interpretations of priorities and objectives

Quality Deployment as Part of QFD

In the field of QFD a distinction is made between *quality deployment* and *quality function deployment*. Quality deployment refers to the final quality and service that a product offers. Quality function deployment refers to the company functions involved in product development. Figure 12-5 indicates that by building quality into the development stages — from planning and design through manufacturing and service — the measureable features of quality in the final product will be improved.

Quality Process in New-Product Development

Seven phases in logical and temporal sequence can be distinguished:

1. Complete and correct perception of the needs and requirements of the customer, *customer* here meaning primarily the end user but also all internal or external handlers situated between the development phases and the end user
2. Complete and competent translation of customer requirements into product specifications
3. Planning, design, and assignment of specifications for the product's individual details

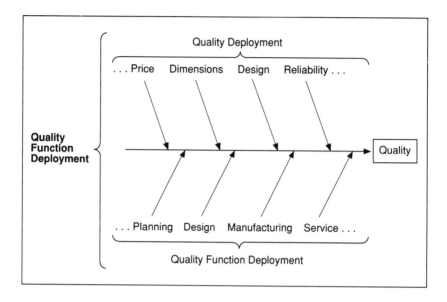

Figure 12-5. Quality Deployment as Part of QFD

4. Upgrading and development of technologies and processes to obtain the product thus planned — that is, the translation of product characteristics to process characteristics
5. Definition of the specific operational conditions (SOP) and procedures that must be constantly applied in the production phase
6. Production
7. Definition of the performances and functions of the product and instructions for its use

The management of these processes has traditionally focused on the conformity of the finished product to predefined specifications. This orientation produces a slew of quantitative data aimed toward defining quality characteristics and production criteria. In a process that requires competence and precision at every stage, however, there are areas in which the quality-codification forms are insufficient and ill-defined.

Problems in New-Product Development

Difficulties in new-product development can be traced to the following causes:

- Lack of comprehension of customer needs and wishes. This happens because customers generally express their desires in an unclear, fragmentary manner. Additionally, they often have vague, unexpressed, or unformulated wishes.
- Faulty translation of verbally expressed needs into numerical expressions that make up a product.
- Incomplete transfer of information from the beginning of the chain (marketing, etc.) to the end (production, etc.).
- Other problems. These include problems of quantitative translation, of identification of criticality and priority, and of comparison with products of the competition.

All this results in:

- Insufficient understanding of the quality required by the customer
- Emphasis on quality characteristics that are wrongly considered important
- Sampling and other conditions of testing for incorrect qualitative appraisals
- Delegation to planning technicians of important decisions relating to the product
- Little understanding by the planner of the critical production engineering issues
- Insufficient time to perform quality checks throughout product development

QFD provides the technique for avoiding and overcoming these problems.

The Ten Zones of QFD

The framework of QFD consists of certain basic activities, techniques, and instruments. This framework has undergone expansion in the course of time; furthermore, every company that has introduced QFD has tailored the system to its own specific demands.

The role of QFD in new-product development is shown schematically in Figure 12-6. The "quality table" is a kind of meeting place for customer requirements, production capacity, and all the comparisons and parameters needed to develop new products successfully.

These parameters are classified into 10 zones, which are described as follows.

Zone 1: Deployment of quality needs

In zone 1 of the quality table are customer requirements (the primary purpose), always broken down into elementary needs in accordance with a process that branches out from the general to the particular. That means that the necessary procedures for implementation are specified for the primary purpose identified. These procedures, in turn, constitute the second-level purposes, for which the relative procedures are specified, and so on down to the fourth or fifth level of purposes/needs. Implementation of zone 1 is completed by identifying the priority needs among all the elementary needs listed — for example, by means of soundings taken among potential users of the product. Then, for each elementary need, a comparison is effected between the company's position and that of the competition, so as to identify points of superiority or inferiority.

Zone 2: Deployment of quality characteristics

In zone 2 are shown the technical requisites to a correspondence between the final product and the originating needs and wishes. These are the product of the translation of the quality required into quality characteristics that can be measured and represented with precision. Starting from the quality requirements at a lower level, the corresponding quality characteristics are identified; these in turn are regrouped, and the process continues through subsequent levels in the branching fashion followed by deployment of quality needs in zone 1.

Zone 3: Quality and characteristics correlation

Once zones 1 and 2 have been completed, the relation between the required quality and the resulting quality characteristics must be defined.

The relation between each elementary need and each quality characteristic must therefore be determined, along with the "intensity" of that relation (great, normal, doubtful); this is done by constructing a matrix in zone 3 showing the intersection of needs with

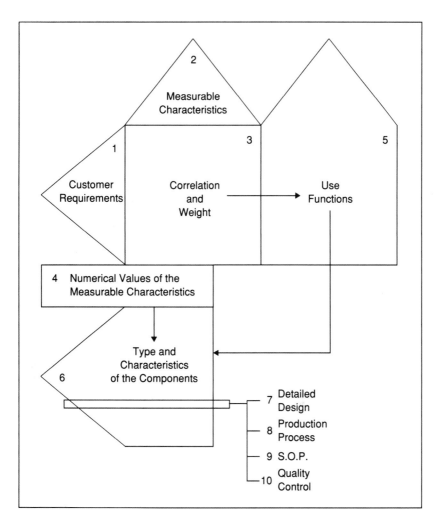

Figure 12-6. Quality Table

characteristics (a sample matrix is provided in Figure 12-7). Such a matrix makes it possible to identify strategies demanding priority in the development of the new product.

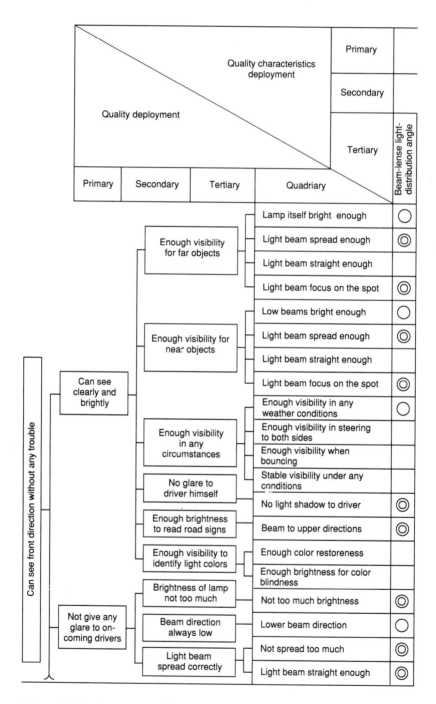

Figure 12-7. Quality Table (Car's Headlight)

| | Light distribution | | | | | | | | | Longevity | | | | | | Safety | |
| | Light distribution angle | | | Light beam | | | | | | Efficiency | | | | | | | |
	Beam-lense size	Filament-changing angle	Beam-changing angle	Light intensity	Transmission factor	Reflectivity	Color temperature	Electric power	Voltage	Air tightness	Filament strength	Sealed gas properly	Bulb size (volume)	Consumed electricity		Redundancy	Recovery angle
	○	△	△	○	◎	◎	○	◎	○					◎			
	○	△		△	△	△		△						△			
		△	◎														
	○	◎	△	△	△	◎	◎	○	◎	○				◎			
	○	△		△	△	△	△							△			
		△	◎														
		△															
	△	○	○	△													
				○			◎	○						○			
							○	○						○			
	△	○	○	○				○	△					○			
		○	◎														

Zone 4: Numerical values

Zone 4 consists of the numerical values assigned to each quality characteristic. These values must not only correspond to the measurable characteristics but must also derive from comparisons with products previously manufactured and with those of the competition.

Zone 5: Deployment of quality functions

Once customer requirements and the corresponding quality characteristics have been identified and quantified, the next step is to identify the technologies necessary to transfer the programmed characteristics and to integrate them into the product. This zone is devoted to linking individual needs to the functioning of the product, by means of an analysis of the process in which the product will be used.

Zone 6: Deployment of the subsystems

The purpose of zone 6 is to promote the integral development of quality specifications for the individual components. In other words, once the functioning of the product has been identified and described, it is the task of zone 6 to ensure that the development of the individual components, subsystems, and constituent systems is carried out in a coordinated and integrated fashion. The completion of this zone consists of the detailing of the individual subsystems and components as identified in the preceding phases.

When the filling-in of zone 6 has been completed, it is possible to proceed, in greater detail for every component, with the activities described in the last four zones.

Zones 7-10

Zone 7 — Detailed Design is concerned with the detail and planning of every component. Zone 8 — Production Process is concerned with the definition of the production processes. Zone 9 — SOP has to do with the definition of the Standard Operating Procedure

(SOP). Zone 10 — Quality Control relates to quality-inspection activities.

As Figure 12-6 shows, the last four zones derive directly from the preceding ones and are also linked to them. This logical flow of activities ensures that the customer's voice is heard equally and coherently in all development activities and thus that every detail is consistent with the market expectations.

Quality tables can be extremely complex, with truly impressive dimensions. Some tables, for example, measure as much as 22×2 meters. Furthermore, development of quality deployment varies greatly from one firm to another, depending on the various types of products being manufactured.

At first it may seem that new-product development is more time-consuming with QFD than with traditional planning methods. When conventional development processes are completed, however, the results usually require retouching and modification, whereas QFD — with its adherence to the well-known slogan of CWQC, "Do It Right the First Time" — offers a practical demonstration that a precise and detailed beginning allows substantial savings in both time and effort later on. Indeed, upon completion of the development and design phases, production can proceed in a linear manner.

It should not be forgotten that QFD is the only method that promotes close consistency of products with the market's actual needs. Moreover, it addresses every company function that may influence product quality. Achieving quality deployment requires definition of procedures and responsibilities on the one hand and definition and measurement of quality for the upstream portion of the production process on the other hand. This is to ensure that attention to quality extends to marketing, planning, and design activities. Figure 12-8 indicates the steps that quality deployment requires for the initial process of product development.

The total flow of the quality function deployment process can be represented in a diagram, as shown in Figure 12-9.

The initial fundamental phases are summarized within Figure 12-11, while Figure 12-10 shows a more general conceptual and practical presentation of quality deployment.

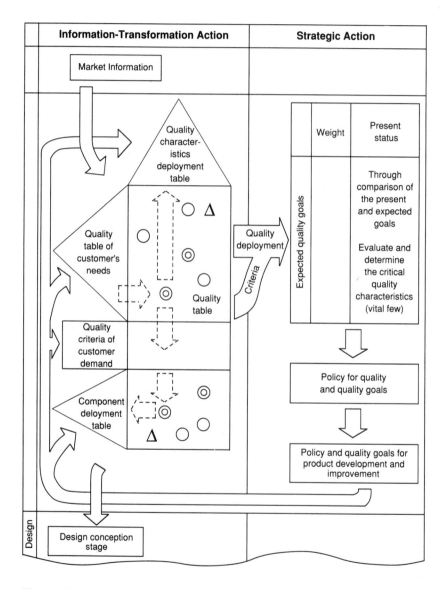

Figure 12-8. Quality Deployment at Marketing and Design Stages

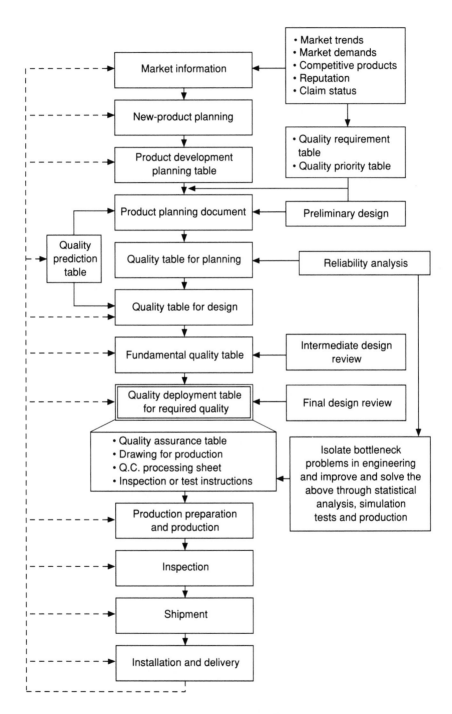

Figure 12-9. Quality Function Deployment (flow)

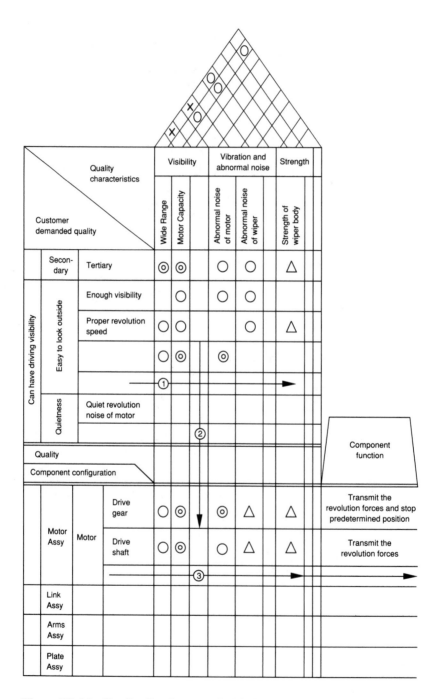

Figure 12-10. Quality Deployment Table (Quality, Cost and Weight Relation Table)

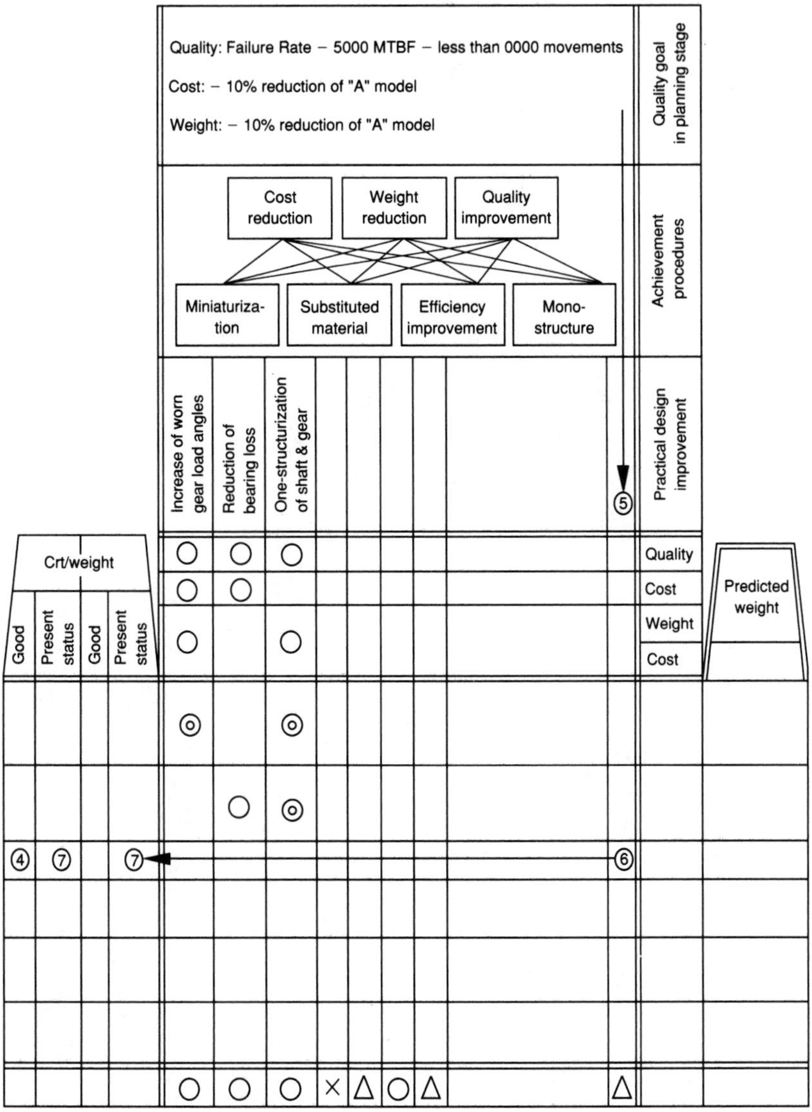

Quality: Failure Rate — 5000 MTBF — less than 0000 movements

Cost: — 10% reduction of "A" model

Weight: — 10% reduction of "A" model

Quality goal in planning stage

| Cost reduction | Weight reduction | Quality improvement |

| Miniaturiza-tion | Substituted material | Efficiency improvement | Mono-structure |

Achievement procedures

Practical design improvement

Increase of worn gear load angles | Reduction of bearing loss | One-structurization of shaft & gear

⑤

Crt/weight

Good | Present status | Good | Present status

Quality
Cost
Weight
Cost

Predicted weight

④ ⑦ ⑦ ⑥

○ : means acceptable

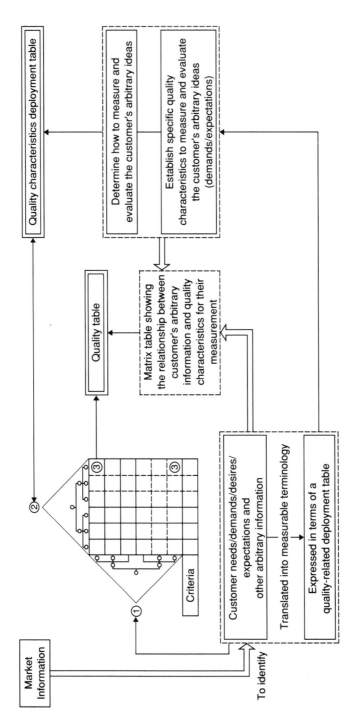

Figure 12-11. Fundamental Quality Deployment Flow

The "Mushroom" Concept

As previously indicated, the TMM model allows for evaluation in terms of total costs. Application of the total costs concept to product development presupposes a development outlook that differs sharply from traditional concepts.

In planning processes and products, there are not only costs of the *hard* type (direct labor and materials), but those of the *soft* type, such as costs for services (preparation and handling), funds invested in inventories, lead time, and lack of production flexibility.

The "soft" costs cannot be overlooked; indeed, they may actually exceed direct costs. For example, specific subassemblies for similar products may require inventory costs that are often higher than those for subassemblies that are "expanded" so as to permit their use in a larger number of finished products. Nevertheless, many specific processes are often justified solely on the basis of direct costs, without consideration of total costs. Moreover, many business opportunities are forfeited when a firm fails to produce a specific product during the required amount of time solely because it lacks "all-purpose" semi-finished items that can be used for more than one product.

The process of generating specific coded items involves service costs that are not insignificant. It is said that inventory costs (physical and accounting control of coded items) increase in geometric proportion to the number of codes that must be managed.

By using a total costs approach, a certain Italian electrical equipment firm has decided that it is more advantageous to approach a given subassembly in the most expensive manner — that is, to adapt it to numerous functions rather than maintaining specific inventories for limited purposes. The result is that, during the penultimate phase of work, the respective item is still an all-purpose item, so that lead time for any given product can be reduced to the amount of time necessary for completing final procedures. Today, this firm is able to avail itself of many business opportunities it was formerly obliged to forfeit. The concept of keeping processes standardized for as long as possible and creating a product structure that is diversified only at the final levels is known as the *mushroom concept*.

The structure of products and of the respective processes (technological layout) actually resembles a mushroom, as shown in Figure 12-12.

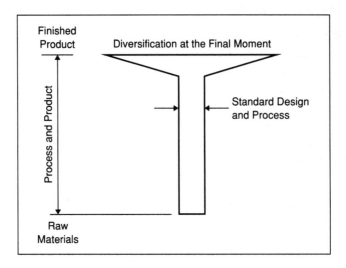

Figure 12-12. Structure of the Mushroom Concept

Production Cycles Based upon Total Costs

The total costs concept has also produced a significant impact upon industrial engineering, at a juncture where planning of optimal production cycles has become important.

Here a true cultural revolution must occur, however, because the persons who plan production cycles — namely, "time and methods specialists" — are those who have been most deeply indoctrinated with Taylorism, a perspective based upon direct costs. This outlook has induced Western companies to adopt cycles on the basis of "direct" efficiency, in other words on the basis of 10 to 15 percent of the firm's costs (real costs for direct manpower, which is managed according to "assigned" time). With two cycles as possible alternatives, the cycle with the lowest level of direct hours is always chosen, while overall indirect costs, which are treated as the same percentage for both alternatives, are overlooked. Yet, it is well known that needs in terms of preparation, handling, lot size, and intermediate storage differ greatly from one cycle to the next. If one only considers direct costs, one risks unknowingly increasing indirect costs, which have not been analyzed.

The following categories should be considered in planning cycles based upon total costs (or, indeed, "total direct costs"):

- Material
- Direct time
- Indirect time
- WIP cost

It is likewise important to determine economical lots and lead time in relation to every cycle, since these are significant business factors. Although they may not be directly quantifiable in economic terms, knowledge of these factors is essential to any decision regarding operating configuration.

Determining the importance of the first four categories is relatively easy. When man-hours, instead of machine-hours, are used as a standard, it is advisable to adopt a single hourly rate ("unit man-hours," instead of "direct time"). It is no accident that many multinational firms (the JIT "wind" is originating more from the United States and northern Europe than from Italy) have abandoned classification of departmental manpower as "direct" and "indirect," while affirming that, however manpower may be defined, real costs are increasingly similar. Comparison of these four categories can lead to some interesting discoveries about the cost effectiveness of different cycles. Figure 12-13 provides an example of a cycle based upon total costs: the difference between the results obtained from an analysis according to direct costs and an analysis according to total costs becomes obvious.

	Cycle A	Cycle B
Material ($)	12.00	11.00
Direct time ($)	50.00	52.00
Total direct costs ($)	62.00	63.00
Indirect time ($)	5.00	2.00
WIP cost ($)	1.00	0.50
(Unit effect)		
Total costs ($)	68.00	65.50
Lead time (days)	12	4
Economical lot (number)	100	20

Figure 12-13. Cycles Based on Total Cost

Another significant influence on WIP is the "shape" of the manufacturing costs curve generated by a given cycle. This topic is examined in more detail in Chapter 13.

13

Just-In-Time
in Production to Order

Production to order can absorb many advantages from the TMM model. This chapter focuses on "pure" production to order (specific products for specific clients), which has been covered somewhat less extensively heretofore, but the concepts discussed are applicable to all categories of production.

As the preceding chapters have demonstrated, TMM offers advantages to various aspects of production, including:

- Short or parallel lines (group technology)
- Control according to bottlenecks/synchronized production
- Reduction of setup times
- Mushroom concept
- Pull control
- In-process control
- Visual control
- Suppliers as comakers

Nevertheless, the greatest advantage consists of better control of curves for manufacturing costs. The term *control* is the key to this approach, which has already been explained from a technical standpoint.

Technically, a manufacturing costs curve is defined as a graphic presentation of the time-based process whereby manufacturing costs accumulate in relation to billing, which takes place only upon completion of the respective order. These costs belong to two categories: costs for purchasing of materials (M), and transformation costs (L). Accumulation of these costs over time is a function of the operating cycle that is being used.

Conceptually, the manufacturing costs diagram is of the type appearing in Figure 13-1. The shape of the resulting curve is of fundamental importance in terms of the WIP costs generated. Indeed, these costs are proportional to the integral of the curve itself, or the area subtended by the curve. If the curve assumes the shape of a straight line and generates a triangular area, average investment (WIP) will be equivalent to 50 percent of the final cost of the order (Figure 13-2).

If the curve is concave, average investment will exceed 50 percent (Figure 13-3). If the curve is convex, average investment will be less than 50 percent (Figure 13-4). Hence, the shape of the curve is extremely significant in terms of economical management of orders.

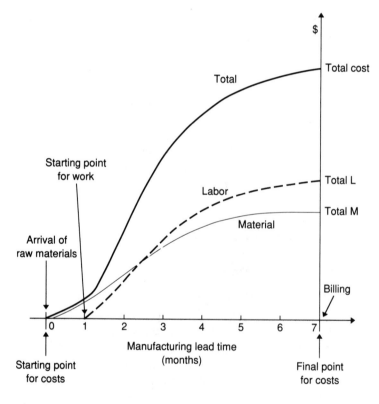

Figure 13-1. Manufacturing Costs Diagram

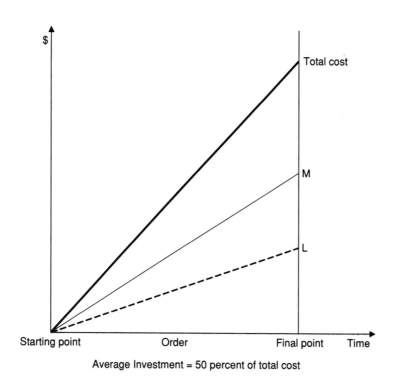

Average Investment = 50 percent of total cost

Figure 13-2. Manufacturing Costs Diagram (Situation A)

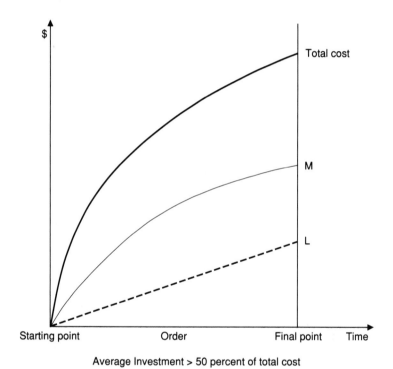

Average Investment > 50 percent of total cost

Figure 13-3. Manufacturing Costs Diagram (Situation B)

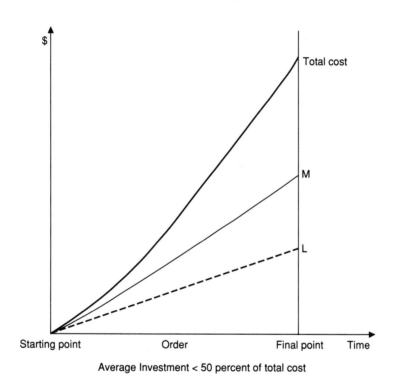

Figure 13-4. **Manufacturing Costs Diagram (Situation C)**

Figure 13-5 shows the costs curve obtained at a particular Italian company. The product, here referred to as "a system," is characterized by the costs curve appearing in the diagram, according to current production cycles. As it is possible to observe, this particular system involves a high level of costs for purchasing parts (73 percent), with a sharp rise during the fourth month, at which point the firm buys the most expensive part for the system. The cost of the system is nearly $10 million. The area subtended by the curve represents 78 percent of the total cost, so that the average investment will be $7.8 million. Thus, the accompanying financial charges will be nearly $1.0 million.

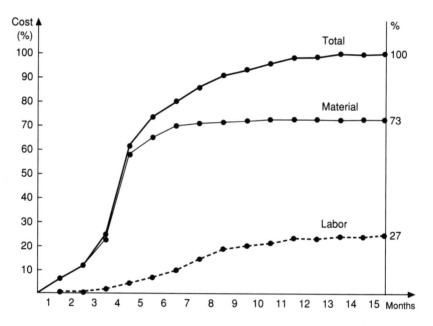

Figure 13-5. Costs Curve for a System Produced by an Italian Company

How was this curve established? It is nothing more than the result of the production cycles then in use, and those cycles had been developed on the basis of efficiency in terms of direct costs (and, as a result, direct labor). Thus, a decision had been adopted to seek optimal efficiency in terms of direct labor (12 percent of total costs for this company), where a 5 percent difference between one cycle and the other represents only 0.6 percent of total costs for a given order (approximately $60,000). Thus, a decision based upon less than $100,000 is the source of a problem costing more than $1,000,000.

With optimal efficiency being sought in regard to direct manpower, it became necessary for the core of the system to be available at the plant from the earliest phases, so that the rest of the system (the "frame") could then be built around it. Another type of cycle that had required completion of the frame as an initial procedure, with subsequent reopening of it to install the expensive core, was rejected because a greater quantity of labor was required. The additional cost would have consisted of nearly 100 hours of labor (approximately $5,000 at hourly rates, but much less in terms of real costs), in contrast to a reduction to the integral for the curve of almost 30 percent (− 50 percent), as Figure 13.6 indicates. This reduction would have led to a WIP reduction from $7.8 million to $3 million, with financial charges being reduced by more than $0.5 million; in other words, $0.5 million; versus $5,000.

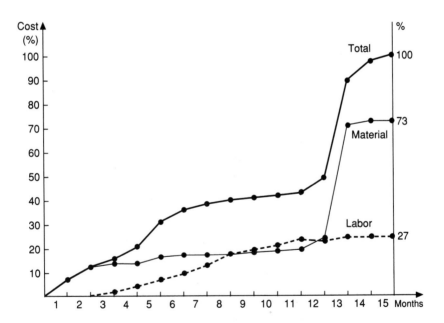

Figure 13-6. Costs Curve for a Different Production Cycle

Choosing $5,000 instead of $1 million is the inevitable consequence of a direct costs approach, where financial management is regarded as an isolated entity that cannot be technically controlled from one day to another.

A similar mode of reasoning could be adopted for the resulting lead time. In the same example, the lead time of 15 months is a consequence of the cycles being adopted. It was discovered that it would be possible to reduce lead time by 4 months with a different production cycle, although this cycle would generate a need for 80 additional hours of labor (in other words, $4,000). On the other hand, 4 months less lead time provides a 25 percent reduction of financial charges (several hundred thousand dollars), and, more important, it provides far greater marketing power, namely, an ability to deliver in 11 months instead of 15 (it suffices to consider frequent penalties, or orders that are not obtained on account of problems with delivery periods). This example demonstrates the impact that a JIT approach may produce on total costs within the context of production to order.

14

Relationships with Suppliers (Comakership)

The supplier-client relationship is undergoing rapid and substantial changes. The direction of these changes and the operational model that is emerging are becoming clearly defined. Current strategic developments in manufacturing firms are beginning to affect "vendor-vendee" (supplier-client) relationships according to their own guiding principles. Thus, the total quality approach and just-in-time organizing principles are transforming procedures in the domain of procurement. A trend among some companies toward "whittling down" the number of suppliers can be observed.

Of course, the most advanced applications exist in Japanese industry, but indications of current changes in supplier-client relationships are already a cultural reality for Western companies. Heard with increasing frequency in these companies are statements such as: "Prices are only one component of total purchasing costs, and the best prices often become the worst costs," "The transformation process begins at the supplier's facilities and ends at the facilities of the ultimate client," and "Quality and reliability in a final product are the result of contributions from the entire chain of suppliers and clients for a given business." Indeed, the last of these statements is receiving de facto reinforcement from legislative changes in the United States and in Common Market nations.

In a similar vein, those among us who are suppliers are now hearing requests for goods of better quality, more reliability in terms of deliveries, greater flexibility and promptness in our responses, more subdivided and more frequent deliveries, approval procedures, self-certification, guaranteed improvements, and, of course, reduction of prices.

Why are these changes strategically legitimate? How must companies organize their activities for allowing supplier-client relationships to develop along these lines? Which techniques should be adopted? These are the themes that will be examined in this chapter.

Comakership and Current Strategic Changes

The need to rely upon a comakership approach is intrinsic to all of the strategic changes occurring in business management. The following new strategic concepts can be cited:

- Groupwide quality control (Japanese strategy)
- Value chains (new strategy in American business)
- Time-based company (new manufacturing strategy)
- Product-process development (emerging R&D strategy)

The most significant implications of these concepts are described below.

Groupwide Quality Control

Whereas approaches inspired by a total quality (companywide quality control) strategy already emphasize close linkage between companies and their suppliers, especially for quality assurance, more recent changes in this strategy, in the direction of *groupwide quality control,* have established supplier-client relationships as a focal point in terms of policies, management, and expansion of business within a customer satisfaction framework.

Value Chains*

The most widely accepted strategic models now strongly link a company's ability to pursue business activities with the business chain in which the company is situated.

Such a model reflects the outlook that even a "perfect" company will fail if it is situated in a business chain with low value added, and has suppliers and clients with limited capabilities, whereas mediocre companies in appropriate chains are destined to succeed, especially if there are capable suppliers and clients.

---

* Michael Porter, *Competitive Advantage: Creating and Sustaining Superior Performance*, New York, The Free Press, 1985.

Within this context, supplier-client relationships, from strategies to operating relations, have become priority factors in determining the "value" of a business chain.

Time-based Company

In time-based just-in-time systems, relationships with suppliers are a fundamental operating factor in terms of obtaining significant results, a fact that has already been incorporated into many firms' methods.

Changes in management control and industrial accounting systems, with an orientation toward total cost analyses, have introduced significant modifications in vendor rating systems and are based on partnership approaches to operating costs.

Product-process Development

The most recent and innovative approaches to research and development, as well as to industrial engineering for new products, depend upon closely interrelated forms of development for products and processes (planning products and technology according to contexts, or at least according to existing technology), with client needs as a point of origin (quality deployment process).

Because suppliers' technologies constitute a significant portion of the technological content of a product, this approach necessarily involves suppliers in product development.

The implications of this approach in terms of strategy, policies, and operations produce a need for development of new rules, namely, those which can be derived from the comakership model.

Policies for Transforming the Relationship

The changes that are occurring provide a basis for the following policies concerning vendor-vendee relations:

- Develop stable, long-term relations.
- Limit the number of active suppliers.
- Stay with the same suppliers.
- Engage in procurement marketing to a greater extent, and bargaining to a lesser extent.
- Institute a "comprehensive" selection system.

- Evaluate suppliers according to total costs, as well as prices.
- Cooperate with suppliers in order to render their processes more reliable and less costly.

The Reference Model

Operating Relations

The principles governing operating relations according to the new vendor-vendee model are derived from concepts representing the total quality and just-in-time approaches.

The first attempt to codify these principles occurred in Japanese industry. Then the Western managerial milieu drew on this source for a slightly modified version, based upon one premise and ten principles. This version is described below.

- *Premise:* Preconditions for suitable supplier-client relationships are mutual trust and cooperation within the framework of responsibility to the final clients.
- *First Principle:* Suppliers and clients must remain independent, and they must respect one another's independence, in order to maintain a relationship of trust grounded in open market rules.
- *Second Principle:* Suppliers and clients are both responsible for applying quality control with mutual knowledge and cooperation in regard to the control systems that are in use.
- *Third Principle:* The client is responsible for accuracy and adequacy of information and specifications intended for the supplier, so that the supplier understands required procedures.
- *Fourth Principle:* Before suppliers and clients enter into relationships, they should adopt a suitable contract concerning quality, quantities, prices, delivery terms, and payment methods.
- *Fifth Principle:* Upon becoming aware of the nature of the products or services to be supplied, the supplier is responsible for providing a level of quality that fully satisfies the client.
- *Sixth Principle:* Methods and resources for determining specifications that are satisfactory to both parties must be chosen beforehand.
- *Seventh Principle:* The contract governing the relationship should allow for preliminary agreement on the system and

procedures to be used in the event of disagreements, so as to permit amicable resolution.

- *Eighth Principle:* The parties are obliged to exchange information necessary for obtaining the best level of quality control, in keeping with their respective situations.
- *Ninth Principle:* Both the supplier and the client must be able to ensure control of each phase of their own processes (from issuing of orders to production, scheduling, employees, and systems) in keeping with approved policies, so as to allow amicable cooperation.
- *Tenth Principle:* In their dealings with one another, the supplier and the client must always keep the needs of the ultimate consumer firmly in mind.

In addition, three reference levels are emerging in operational relations between supplier and client. These are:

- Level 3: normal supplier
- Level 2: associated supplier
- Level 1: comaker supplier

Every supplier enters into a comakership at level 3; it then becomes necessary to decide which suppliers shall advance to level 2 and ultimately to level 1.

In advanced situations, obviously, suppliers from levels 1 and 2 are always present; this condition depends either upon a company's ability to influence its own group of suppliers or upon considerations of expediency (including economic aspects) in conjunction with A-B-C analysis of the entire group.

A brief description of supplier relationships at each level follows.

Level 3 (normal supplier). The level 3 relationship is characterized by minimum quality specifications, and it is centered upon prices. Supplying is based upon individual short-term orders, and the goods being supplied are systematically inspected ("acceptance").

Level 2 (associated supplier). The level 2 relationship is long-term, with periodic reviews. Price fluctuations on the basis of approved criteria are allowed, while quality is guaranteed and self-certified by the supplier, who is fully responsible for the goods being supplied. Moreover, acceptance procedures are waived for goods directly supplied to company units operating without contingency inventories. Supplying is frequent and in small lots, in keeping with open-ended orders.

The contract specifies systematic improvement of product quality, enabling the client company to provide consulting services and training for its suppliers.

Level 1 (comaker supplier). The level 1 relationship is the same as that for level 2, but cooperation also exists for developing new products and technologies, with mutual investments in R&D and in technological improvements. In addition, information concerning processes and products is exchanged on a continuous basis.

Operating levels are determined according to appropriate vendor ratings.

Vendor Ratings

The vendor rating system that is created during implementation of comakership policies is obviously intended to facilitate company selection of suppliers and define the operating relations between them. The system is also characterized by evaluations according to total costs and evaluations on a strategic level.

The evaluation factors can be summarized in the following manner:

Level 3 (normal supplier). This is a "technical" evaluation in terms of a supplier's output. The factors examined usually include:

- Prices
- Product quality
- Delivery periods
- Reliability of deliveries

Level 2 (associated supplier). The supplier's performance is evaluated more comprehensively (according to total costs). Factors taken into account include:

- Level 3 factors
- Process capability
- Quality assurance system

- Technological level
- Flexibility/elasticity
- Improvement capability and improvement trend

Level 1 (comaker supplier). "Strategic evaluation" of a level 1 supplier occurs on the basis of:

- Level 2 factors
- Technological development capabilities
- Coherence with the client's strategies

It should be noted that, in Japanese industry, considerable emphasis is given to the "improvement capability" factor, in the belief that, for "marriages," firms must choose not only the best suppliers but those with the best trends.

For example, Toyota grants two levels of rewards — namely, "excellence" rewards and "superiority" rewards — according to the following forms of evaluation:

"Excellence" reward. Evaluation of quality control and quality improvement activities in relation to production is required.

"Superiority" reward. Evaluation of the entire control and management system (including management policies and long-term policies) is required. Recognition is granted only if the firm being examined can guarantee systematic yearly improvement in quality costs with a value exceeding 1 percent of sales volume.

Total costs evaluation. In terms of economic aspects, suppliers are selected and compared on the basis of *total costs* for the client company rather than on the basis of prices for the products being purchased. This practice acknowledges the possibility that the most favorable prices will lead to the most unfavorable costs.

A checklist of factors in total costs evaluation follows:

- Quality costs
- Costs for reliability of deliveries
- Costs for response time
- Costs for resupply lots
- Costs for lack of improvement

- Costs for technological obsolescence
- Purchase price

Each of these points corresponds to a series of subcategories that facilitate comparisons of total costs among competing suppliers.

Logistics

The logistics aspect of the comakers model pertains to improvement objectives and capabilities, as well as to techniques derived from just-in-time. The principal objectives consist of:

- Reduction of lead time
- Reduction of operating costs
- "Pull" or synchronized resupplying
- Information network

In terms of lead time for supplying, JIT techniques establish the possibility of dramatic reduction (75 to 90 percent) of the total amount of time through elimination of some components and reduction of others. Therefore, every phase must undergo improvement, as is indicated in Figure 14-1.

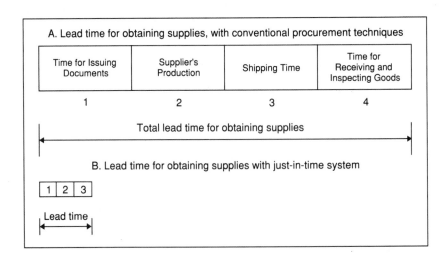

Figure 14-1. Lead Time for Obtaining Supplies

Likewise in terms of costs for being resupplied, a JIT/TQC model allows significant reductions in every category, as shown in Figure 14-2. As a result:

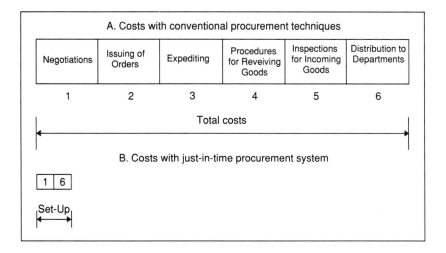

Figure 14-2. Costs for Resupplying

- Costs for bargaining with suppliers are reduced, because negotiations occur far less frequently and because the number of suppliers has been reduced.
- Costs for issuing orders are reduced nearly to zero, inasmuch as supplying takes place according to an open-order arrangement, while resupplying occurs only in relation to actual needs, through kanban systems or other automatic pull systems.
- Expediting costs are included in pull procedures, and they are significantly curtailed as a result of the JIT relationship. Procedures are kept extremely simple and efficient by the visual control systems in use.
- Costs for controlling incoming goods are reduced, because the need to compare delivery notices with order documents (replacement by kanbans) is reduced. Furthermore, it is no longer necessary to maintain intermediate supplies in raw materials warehouses, nor to provide intermediate transportation, inasmuch as materials are unloaded at the locations where they are to be used.

- Inspection costs for receiving goods are eliminated, because inspections are no longer required.

It may be possible, however, to observe increases in more "strategic" costs (as a result of the need for improved procurement marketing), and in costs for training and assistance provided to suppliers.

For pull resupplying, essentially innovative concepts should be applied: resupplying according to kanbans (physical or electronic), synchronized resupplying, projections according to periods of one month and six months, and daily confirmation (or confirmation several hours in advance).

Information networks offer additional operating possibilities that range from scheduling to management of operating flows and administrative and fiscal functions. Some possibilities include:

- Abandoning orders on paper
- Real time transactions
- Automatic billing
- Elimination of transmittal documents (only identification labels)
- A shared comprehensive planning and scheduling system

In regard to the problem of shipping, the objection often arises that a JIT configuration — on account of the need for frequent, small-scale shipments — is uneconomical, because it is not possible to establish optimal loads. In non-JIT approaches, however, shipping costs may significantly influence procurement lots, which must often coincide with the capacity of the particular type of transportation.

Actually, experience thus far appears to support the opposite conclusions, namely, that optimal shipping results are more likely obtained *with* a JIT approach. Whereas the traditional system usually allowed individual shipments for individual supply orders, optimizing each shipment according to each supply order (Figure 14-3), the JIT shipping system is based upon the "routes" concept (Figure 14-4), which specifies that vehicles must complete rounds among suppliers or clients instead of delivering individual shipments (Figure 14-5).

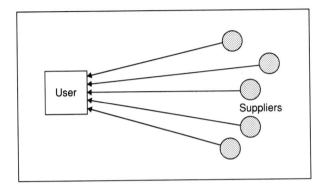

Figure 14-3. Shipping for Individual Supply Items

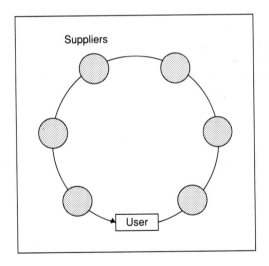

**Figure 14-4. Shipping by means of a
Suppliers' Route**

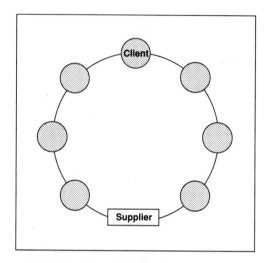

Figure 14-5. Clients' Route

Under this system, whereby it is possible to make use of small quantities, optimal use of shipping is statistically easier than it is with individual supply orders. Nevertheless, it is often more economical to rely upon a more specialized fleet of vehicles, with smaller unit capacities. When a supplier's route is not feasible on account of excessive distance to the user (a 100- to 200-kilometer radius is considered to be the maximum limit), a compromise system can be used. This might be a model that allows for suppliers in distant locations but requires that they be concentrated within a specific area and be organized according to the pick-up center model (Figure 14-6). A model allowing for suppliers distributed along a straight line (sequential route, Figure 14-7) is also possible.

Efficient use of the "geography" of the entire group of suppliers is a typical problem for firms pursuing JIT programs. In order for this type of program to be suitably upgraded, it must be evaluated according to a total costs approach.

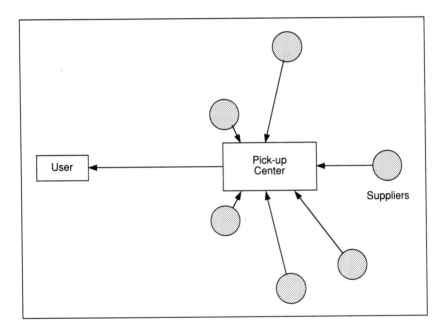

Figure 14-6. Shipping Organized according to a Pick-up Center

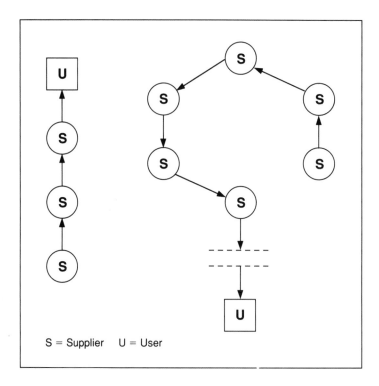

Figure 14-7. Sequential Supplying

Quality and Reliability

As indicated previously, quality constitutes the strategic entry point for a companywide quality control or groupwide quality control model. It also nearly always represents the first operational hurdle for improvement of vendor-vendee relations.

The time requirements and costs of an acceptance system are significant obstacles to the desired operational model, for example — ones that cannot be eliminated by merely adopting a decision. Assuring quality products being supplied is considered so important for the system (in terms of time and simplification) that some firms, when suppliers can offer suitable products in suitable periods of time, are prepared to allow price increases equivalent to potential savings through elimination of the acceptance phase.

The ability to achieve this goal, however, does not depend upon the adoption of different procedures. Instead, upgrading the process capability of the supplier-client system is required.

This kind of improvement can occur only in a step-by-step form, with "seating" at every step.

A useful diagram for visualizing this process (in eight steps) appears in Figure 14-8, which indicates various possible vendor-vendee relationships in regard to quality.

The optimal level is 8, but 7 is an adequate level for suitable relations within a JIT/TQC context.

Self-Certification

As shown in Figure 14-8, a key point in the development of the supplier-client relationship occurs in phase 5, at which point "acceptance inspections" of products are eliminated, thereby permitting suppliers to obtain direct access (free pass) to production lines. This happens when the client has obtained full assurance concerning self-inspection procedures conducted by the supplier, so that certification by the supplier is sufficient to confirm the quality of the goods being supplied. In other words, the supplier has attained a *self-certification* status, which is one of the basic requirements for being classified as an *associated* supplier.

How can suppliers and clients develop a self-certification program that allows attainment of this important step toward comakership?

Self-certification programs intended to promote a "free-pass" situation vary according to the particular conditions of the supplier-client relationship — conditions relating to market categories, intended functions of products, relevant standards, suppliers' levels of knowledge, and so on. Some typical, and even obligatory, features can be identified, however. Self- certification programs generally proceed according to three principal phases:

- Phase 1: *Commitment* consisting of preparation for the project, that is, everything from evaluating a supplier to developing an operating plan.
- Phase 2: The *operational* phase, consisting of implementation of the improvement program.
- Phase 3: *Maintenance,* consisting of routine activities that are to be initiated after self-certification by the supplier.

Relationship Level	Supplier		Client	
	Production	Inspection	Inspection	Production
1	No inspection	No inspection	No inspection	100% inspection
2	No inspection	No inspection	100% inspection	—
3	No inspection	100% inspection	100% inspection	—
4	No inspection	100% inspection	Inspection of samples	—
5	100% inspection	Inspection of samples under client's supervision	No inspection Limited inspection of samples	—
6	Process control and 100% inspection	Inspection of samples under client's supervision	No inspection Limited inspection of samples	—
7	Process control	Limited inspection of samples	No inspection	—
8	Process control	No inspection	No inspection	—

Figure 14-8. Levels of Quality Assurance in a Supplier-Client Relationship

The Commitment Phase. Self-certification programs require an average time outlay of approximately one to two years, and they initially require an investment of resources and capital whose returns are identifiable only at subsequent points.

For this reason, three essential elements are necessary for the success of a program:

- A joint strategy for the client and the supplier. On the basis of knowledge of possible mutual advantages from the program, a new procurement policy must emerge
- Basic operating principles for establishing the vendor- vendee relationship
- An information system capable of creating suitable indicators for evaluating the timeliness of the program and for measuring its benefits over time

Insofar as strategy and basic operating principles may be concerned, the aspects cited heretofore continue to be relevant.

In sum, supplier-client associations must evolve from predominantly adversarial relationships based upon self-interested economic considerations into relationships molded by cooperation and mutual trust within the context of shared objectives of growth and development.

Figure 14-9 provides a list of some of the principal advantages for clients and suppliers when a self-certification system exists.

The Operating Phase. Once the three basic premises of the commitment phase have been established, the conditions under which free-pass status is granted must be defined clearly and objectively.

Naturally, this decision is influenced by many factors, including the nature of the product and the market, the price of the purchased component relative to the general economic characteristics of the product, and so on. Nevertheless, it is possible to identify seven operating criteria that can be applied to nearly every program and/or contract for supplies:

1. Absence of unacceptable production lots for a significant period of time
2. Absence of lots that are unacceptable because of problems unrelated to the product itself, during a specified period of time

Advantages of Self-Certification	
Client	**Supplier**
A. Being sure that goods are supplied according to specifications	A. Reducing quality costs
B. Reducing quality costs	B. Organizing a quality system
C. Eliminating acceptance inspections	C. Increasing flexibility
D. Eliminating reserve inventories	D. Acquiring the capability to improve the products being supplied
E. Obtaining adherence to delivery schedules	E. Obtaining information in advance
F. Obtaining smaller but more frequent deliveries	F. Obtaining guarantees of a long-term supplier
G. Reducing procurement lead time	G. Increasing the volume of goods supplied
H. Eliminating contingency inventories	H. Obtaining economic benefits
I. Obtaining suppliers' know-how for developing new products	I. Access to potential new markets
J. Receiving information promptly	

Figure 14-9. Advantages of Self-Certification

3. Absence of difficulties or serious production problems attributable to the product being purchased, during a specified period of time

4. Successful completion of an evaluation according to the quality system developed by the client (or by a representative of the client), at the supplier's facilities

5. Agreement in regard to purchasing specifications and review of these specifications in close cooperation, whenever the need may arise

6. Availability of full documentation on the quality system that has been approved and on the processes that are to be in use

7. Consent for prompt transmittal of results from tests and inspections performed by the supplier upon its own processes and products

After defining the final goals of the program, it is useful to establish certain intermediate goals in order to verify progress. For this reason, regular "commitment meetings" should be planned so that supplier and client can evaluate the results being obtained and identify any corrective measures required. As a minimum, the following aspects should be examined:

- Program progress through analysis of established indicators
- Obstacles to progress and measures to overcome them
- Required time and resources for achieving subsequent goals

The maintenance phase. As previously indicated, the free-pass and self-certification represent important milestones in the development of comakership.

For this reason, the awarding of such status should be properly emphasized, as should the procedures for the awards (joint meetings for key personnel from the client company and the supplier, signing of agreements, etc.).

As in any improvement program, however, attaining the desired level does not mean achievement of the entire set of tasks, because that is the point when the maintenance and continuous improvement phase must begin.

Furthermore, it is possible that some self-certified suppliers will not reach the level of comakership, which also depends upon other types of strategic decisions for both parties. Nevertheless, it is clearly necessary for every supplier to not only maintain the standards that have been established but to pursue efforts for continually improving products in relation to growing market demand.

It is therefore necessary to initiate and maintain a system that ensures continuous supervision of suppliers, along with a rapid and constant exchange of information for the purpose of preventing or correcting any impediments to quality.

The maintenance program, which should be adopted on a yearly basis by supplier and client, should specify:

- Objectives, areas of improvement, and reference parameters and/or indicators
- Procedures permitting the client to intervene in the supplier's processes, along with types of information that are to be exchanged and procedures for making such exchanges

- Times for contact, or for commitment meetings, for the purpose of examining progress

Reference Standards. Self-certification programs are usually individualized programs developed by clients and suppliers. Thus, the rules for implementing these programs are developed and negotiated in relation to many different parameters (such as the type of product and its importance).

Nevertheless, there are certain standards available that may guide attempts to define a quality assurance system, which, as has been explained, is one of the requisites to self-certification.

The ISO 9000 series on quality management and quality assurance standards represents the most advanced formulation of quality assurance specifications. That it has international validity is evident through its adoption by the principal European and non-European nations (it has been translated as the UNI-29000 standards in Italy, the B-S standards in Great Britain, the DIN standards in West Germany, etc.).

The ISO 9000 series classifies requirements according to the nature of work entrusted to suppliers. Specifically, it contains the following standards:

- ISO 9001: "Quality System — Model for Quality Assurance in Design/Development, Production, Installation, and Servicing." This standard is applicable when compliance with standards indicated by the client must be assured through various activities, such as:
  — planning/development
  — production
  — installation/operation

- ISO 9002: "Quality System — Model for Quality Assurance in Production and Installation." This standard applies when quality must be guaranteed for production or installation/operation phases.
- ISO 9003: "Quality System — Model for Quality Assurance in Final Inspection and Test." This standard applies when quality must only be assured through final inspections.
- ISO 9004: "Quality Management and Quality System Elements Guidelines." This standard provides indications concerning:

— technical factors
— human factors
— management factors

These factors influence the quality of products or services throughout the cycle from identification of needs to customer satisfaction.

Information Systems. For every improvement program, an information system, which is to be understood as a structured system for controlling data and/or information, offers a fundamental form of support. An information system allows:

- Analysis of the initial situation for the purpose of identifying improvement opportunities and the advantages to be derived from the program
- Introduction of a data acquisition and control program in order to create suitable indicators for measuring improvement and progress

In regard to the supplier-client relationship the information system should reflect the viewpoint that *price* is only one element of a product's *cost*, and that overall business advantages do not always correspond to price reductions. More important is the *total purchasing cost,* which is composed of multiple aspects:

- Quality costs
- Costs for reliability in terms of deliveries
- Shipping costs/periods
- Costs for resupply lots
- Costs for lack of improvement
- Costs for technological obsolescence
- Prices for purchased components

Also to be considered are the components of quality costs:

- Costs for internal failures (e.g., rejected items, repetition of work, selection of unsuitable lots, disputes with the supplier, production losses)
- Costs for external failures (e.g., damage to finished products that may be caused by purchased materials)
- Assurance costs (e.g., acceptance tests and inspections, delays on account of quality assurance inspections, inspections performed at suppliers' facilities)

- Prevention costs (e.g., issuing purchasing specifications, evaluating suppliers, periodic audits)
- Costs for additional lots in order to surmount inefficiency in supply procedures

Strategic Guidelines for Promoting Transformation

Transformation of the supplier-client relationship according to comakership concepts is already occurring in many companies, even though the objectives and the reference model may not yet be precisely defined.

The practical guidelines that companies are following offer an idea of the issues that should be confronted at the outset as well as of the procedure for change. The following measures are most frequently adopted:

- Reduction of the number of suppliers to a maximum of two or three for each specific market category
- Selection of suppliers on the basis of process capability evaluations, quality assurance systems, and possible quality improvement trends
- Establishment of long-term relationships with close technological cooperation
- Limitation of frequency of negotiations, although optimal knowledge of the market for supplied goods (procurement marketing) is a required basis, with price fluctuations accepted according to a predetermined range in relation to the market average
- Relationships based upon open orders and ordering schedules that are maintained through automatic pull supplying, guarantees on delivery times and quality, and significant penalties for transgressions
- Possibility of special payment methods and/or terms for suppliers who are "wedded" to a company

15

Total Industrial Engineering

The expression *total industrial engineering* (TIE), coined by Professor Ryuji Fukuda, constitutes an interesting dichotomy for the TMM model. TIE offers proof of how organizational, technical, and industrial relations elements are so interrelated that any attempt to separate them applies duress to the company system. Indeed, the operational capabilities of companies depend on the equilibrium of these three aspects.

On the one hand, TIE incorporates some of the elements previously discussed in this book, such as organizing improvement, mobilization of resources, and industrial engineering techniques. On the other hand, it represents a vantage point from which the TMM model can be viewed as a whole.

Although Ryuji Fukuda's *Managerial Engineering* should be consulted for a more detailed explanation, the following basic definition of TIE, offered by Marco Diotalevi* is sufficient here:

> Total Industrial Engineering constitutes an integrated approach to production problems, whereby continuous improvement of production processes is sought through involving the entire work force and through use of specific techniques.

In relation to approaches derived from traditional analysis of work, TIE possesses the following characteristics:

- It is oriented toward efficiency in a system instead of efficiency in individuals.

---

* Marco Diotalevi is a partner of Alberto Galgano & Associati.

- It requires participation by all employees, instead of by a privileged few, in examining and implementing measures intended to improve organization of production.
- It is based on knowledge and continuous use of IE techniques (either basic techniques or advanced techniques such as the CEDAC system) by everyone.
- It tends to motivate employees through activities for improving organization of production, especially by means of small autonomous groups.

Thus, TIE is significantly compatible with TMM. A fuller comprehension of its operational aspects can be gained through closer examination of certain significant elements.

Employee involvement requires creation of working groups with an interhierarchical composition whenever necessary. Their composition should be based upon the organizational structure of the small groups for improvement of activities (SGIAs), which were cited earlier. Analysis and improvement encompass every aspect of production, such as structure of work (employees, machinery, and procedures), work methods, layout, technological processes, and production cycles. In particular, these groups pursue so-called prevention of waste (in regard to setup time, for example). The techniques to be used include methods of Taylorist origin, as well as more specific methods oriented toward a process of diagnosis and improvement. These include:

- The seven tools
- The seven new tools
- Window analysis
- CEDAC (cause and effect diagram with addition of cards)
- OET (on error training)
- WD (window development)
- HEA (human error analysis)
- Skill analysis
- Day-to-day management
- VCS (visual control system)

All of the work analysis techniques of the Taylorist school are extensively used in TIE, although there is a major difference in approach. These techniques are used by operating personnel specifically to improve their own work, and to prevent waste, instead of being used to increase the pace of work. Hence, videotapes prepared by the workers themselves are often used to facilitate analysis of their own activities.

The TIE approach, in a general or partial form, is being rapidly adopted by American companies (several hundred already), and is beginning to make headway in Italian companies as well. Figure 15-1 contains a TIE operating diagram that can be applied to problem finding and solving.

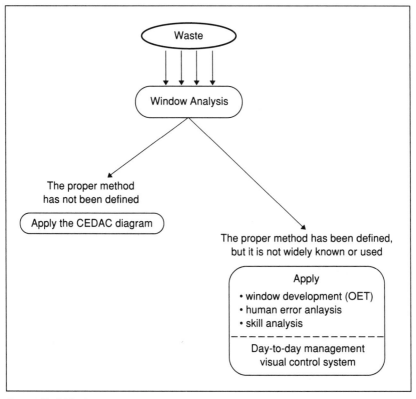

Source: Ryuji Fikuda

Figure 15-1. TIE Diagram for Detecting Waste

16

Total Productive Maintenance

The TMM model includes a *total productive maintenance* component that despite its different purpose is similar to TIE. In fact, TPM also encompasses organizational, participatory, and technical aspects, which makes it similar to TMM.

TPM is one of the most recent approaches to emerge from Japanese industry; in keeping with Japanese customs, it is accompanied by a prize (the Distinguished Plant Prize). This approach is also being introduced in the West. In Finland, for example, TPM is being applied in 400 companies and is being promoted on a nationwide basis. General training was provided for 1,400 top managers from 718 firms; then, more specialized training was provided for 2,000 middle managers from the 400 firms where experimentation is occurring. The results obtained so far are promising:

Accidental stoppages per month	From 1,000 to 20
Efficiency of systems	+ 50%
Quality defects	From 1% to 0.1%
Customers' claims	From 100 to 25
Maintenance costs	− 30%
Required inventories	− 50%
Value added per employee	+ 50%
Accidents	None

TPM is consistent with general objectives (TMM) and also with specific JIT operational objectives. In general terms, the observations made about TIE hold true for TPM, although the following definition is also important in terms of the systems synergy with JIT:

Systems and machines must ensure maximum reliability of processes to avoid the need for safety inventories and to obtain efficient, smooth flows. For maintenance to be effective, it must be performed *continuously and promptly.* TPM meets this need.

The operational links between just-in-time (in reference to the Toyota Production System) and TPM are clearly indicated within Figure 16-1.

The six types of losses identified on the right side of the diagram are points of concentration for TPM as *the six big losses.* These losses include:

1. Shutdowns resulting from unexpected damage (breakdowns)
2. Setup and adjustment time
3. Unused time and brief shutdowns
4. Speeds below specified levels
5. Losses on account of defects
6. Production losses during starting procedures

The first two losses are caused by *stoppages,* the next two pertain to *speed,* and the final two are caused by *defects* (quality). "Total" efficiency of systems can be improved by surmounting these losses. The Japanese employ an *overall equipment effectiveness* index, which can be defined in the following form:

OEE = Level of Availability of System × Efficiency ×
Percentage of Acceptable Products

To be eligible for the Distinguished Plant Prize, a firm cannot score lower on this index than 85 percent. Hence, the six big losses should not surpass 15 percent of "installed" time (in other words, total availability of systems) in terms of total frequency. This objective can be pursued by means of the following secondary reference objectives:

1. *Stoppages:* Downtime exceeding 10 minutes for each unit (or system) should occur no more than once per month.
2. *Setup and Adjustment Time:* Setup and adjustment procedures should require no more than 10 minutes.
3. *Brief Shutdowns and Minor Losses:* These situations should not exceed 10 minutes, and they should not occur more than three times per month.
4. *Speed:* Full speed should be attained for 115 percent or more of the technical cycle length.

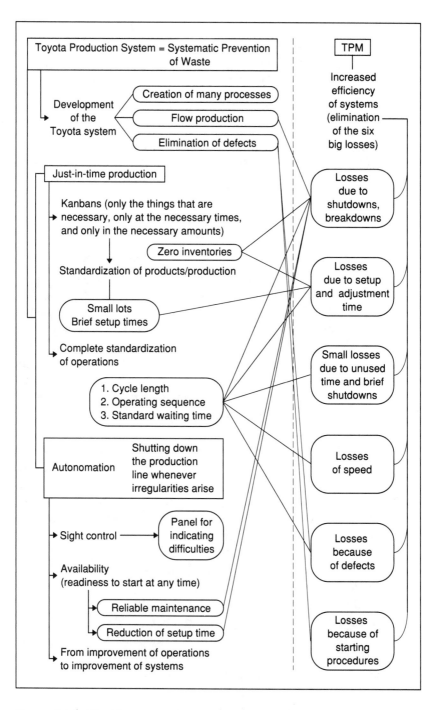

Figure 16-1. The Toyota Production System and TPM

5. *Defects in Processes*: The percentage of defects for each process (including repeat work) should be less than 0.1 percent.
6. *Yield from Starting Procedures*: The yield from starting procedures should allow 99 percent or more of the lot size.

The *five basic activities* for achieving TPM follow:

1. Improve the efficiency of all components of machines.
2. Introduce "autonomous" maintenance.
3. Have the maintenance department define a maintenance program.
4. Train maintenance personnel.
5. Create a situation of reliability and maintainability from the point when equipment is designed.

Although these five points provide a concept of the organizational aspects of TPM, it should be remembered that TPM also includes significant technical components, such as operational use of Weibull curves. It should also be observed that, from a technical standpoint, there is significant overlapping between TPM and CDP (process control), especially in regard to managing and improving process capability.

In terms of human resources, TPM requires changes in structuring of work and positions, in contrast to TIE, which merely produces a direct impact with respect to involvement. Indeed, autonomous maintenance even calls for performance of maintenance tasks by operating personnel.

Maintenance functions entrusted to operating personnel are developed gradually, until contact with the maintenance department is necessary only in terms of requests for special procedures, consulting services, support, and scheduling (an analogy can be made to the relationship that process control is expected to create between operating personnel and the quality department, whereby the latter department becomes the "regulators' regulator").

The TPM model was developed by Professor Nakajima, who also provided the definition. TPM programs are now being introduced in Italy with assistance from Alberto Galgano & Associati.

To summarize, total productive maintenance (TPM) accomplishes "productive maintenance" through involvement of all employees in participating company units (design, production, maintenance, etc.). Specifically, the following measures are carried out:

- The overall efficiency of systems and machinery is maximized through prevention of waste and losses caused by machines (the *six big losses*).
- The reliability of systems is increased to improve product quality and machine productivity.
- Economical systems are developed and controlled throughout their useful life.
- All employees, from top management to workers, are mobilized.
- The traditional division of activities between production personnel and maintenance personnel is overcome.
- Operating personnel are trained to use and maintain systems and machinery.
- Workers are motivated through autonomous maintenance activities, which can also be carried out in small groups.

17

How to Initiate TMM Structural Changes

Approach and Examples

The managerial approach necessary for applying TMM has already been described in Chapter 8. The ways in which companies approach these structural changes from a technical standpoint is the subject of this chapter. Figure 17-1 provides data obtained in the United States.

In relation to examples in Europe, it may be useful to cite certain projects receiving consulting services or training support from Alberto Galgano & Associati (100 JIT projects in progress). Companies have been chosen so as to represent various sectors and scales (Figure 17-2).

The Implementation Schedule

A model schedule for implementing a TMM project follows. This schedule was developed by Alberto Galgano & Associati on the basis of experiences in American and European (including Italian) companies, a thorough knowledge of the Japanese model and of CWQC, and advice from Ryuji Fukuda — who has systematically provided assistance since 1985.

Objectives and Methods

Implementation of the total manufacturing management model should begin with testing in a pilot area within the firm's production section. Operational objectives for testing the pilot area may involve:

- Reduction of production flow time (lead time)
- Reduction of "flow components" (raw materials, work-in-process, finished products)

Company	Product	Starting Point for Conversion	Reasons	Methods	Results
Deere & Company	Machinery	1982	Survival	• Pilot areas • Training • Flow production	• Productivity: +25% • Handling: −40% • Setup: −45% • Inventory: −31% • Quality: 40% of processes "under control"
Black & Decker	Electrical equipment	1982	Financial charges	• Education • Balancing • Weekly leveling • Comakers	• Productivity: +60% • Setup: presses from 1 hour to 1 minute • Inventory: rotation from 16 to 30 • Quality: claims = −98%, CSL = 100% • Weekly lots • Number of suppliers: −40%
3M	Audio-visual cassettes	1983	Improvement of production organization	• JIT committee • Education • Project groups • MRP 2	• Inventory: rotation from 26 to 60 • Quality: from 30,000 to 1,500 p.p.m. • Repeat work: 1/8 • Space: −50% • Lead time: −90%
Motorola	Instrument-ation, automobile alternators	1983	Corporate program Customer's requirement	• Flow analyses • MGT commitment • Education • Training of workers • Pilot area • Dedicated lines	• Productivity: +8% • Inventory: from 5.6 to 2.6 weeks = +$70,000 per year • Promptness: +15% • Lead time: significant reduction
FMC	Items for military use and for the automobile industry	1982	Survival	• TQC/JIT • Pilot areas • Education • Reducing"water" levels • Setup	• Productivity: +13% • Setup: −75% • Inventory: rotation from 1.1 to 4 • CSL: from 88% to 98% • Quality costs: from 3.5% to 2.1% • Space: −25% • Lead time: from 1 month to 1 week • Suppliers: from monthly deliveries to daily deliveries: 50% reduction

Company	Product	Starting Point for Conversion	Reasons	Methods	Results
General Electric (Housewares)	Electrical appliances	1982	Results obtained by Toyota, Toshiba, Hitachi	• Pilot area • Quality improvement • Flow line • VCS • Leveling (mixed production) • Group technology • Kanbans	• Productivity: +20% • Setup: from hours to minutes • WIP: −40% • Quality costs:−30% • Space: − 4,830 sq. meters • Lead time: from weeks to days
General Electric (Switch gears)	Electrical components	1982	Results obtained by Toyota, Toshiba, Hitachi	• Training • Pilot area • Setup • Day-to-day leveling • Andon • Poka-yoke • Continuous improvement • Kanbans	• Productivity:+11% • Setup: from 56 to 1.5 minutes • WIP: from 10 to 1.5 weeks • Space (no warehouse for finished products = + $130,000 per year
Franklin Electric (Siloam Springs)	Electric motors	1980	Need to improve productivity and quality	• Training • Bottom-up • Leveling • Daily schedule • MRP-Kanbans • SQC	• Overhead: −27% • Structure: from 24 to 13 middle managers • Inventory: rotation from 7 to 16 • WIP: −30% • Defects: from 5% to 2% • Rejects: from 2.6% to 0.9% • Space: − 30% • Lead time: from 15 to 5 days
Omark Industries	Athletic and leisure products	1980	Management decision (TQC/JIT)	• TQC/JIT • 5 pilot plants • Project teams • Pilot areas • Decisionmaking by workers	• Productivity:+30% • Setup: from 165 to 5 minutes • Inventory:−92% • Quality costs:− 20% • Handling:− 68% • Lead time: from 3 weeks to 3 days
Hewlett Packard (Computer Systems Division)	Computers	1980-TQC 1983-JIT	Quality of Japanese products	• Flow production • TQC • SQC • Participation • Leveling • Kanbans	• Productivty:+55% • Inventory:−72% • Quality:+98% • Quality costs:− 94% • Space:+33% • Lead time: from 15 to 1.5 days

Source: APICS, First World Congress of Production and Inventory Control *Presentations*, Vienna, 1985.

Figure 17-1. Methods of Introducing TMM-JIT in the United States

Company	Product	Initial Year	Methods	Examples of Results
Michelin Italiana (11,000 employees)	Tires	1987	Pilot factory Setup Kanban Flow manufacturing	Setup: −90% WIP: −70%
Olivetti (DSIC Division) (9000 employees)	Typewriters	1982-TQC 1985-JIT	CWQC/JIT JIT/CIM Flow production Setup VCS Kanban	Setup: from 3 hours to 18 minutes
Pietro Fiorentini (250 employees)	Components for gas distribution	1985	Pilot area Flow production Group technology Setup Pull-kanban	Lead time: from 6 to 1 week WIP: −69%
Uno A Erre (Gold Division) (650 employees)	Jewelry Gold chains	1985-CWQC 1986-TMM	CWQC/TMM Flow production Group technology Kanban Setup Mushroom concept	Lead time: −90% WIP: −75% Economical lot: −50%/90%
Wegaplast (80 employees)	Molding plastic products	1985	CWQC/TMM Setup	Setup: 1st step: −20% Improvement of process quality: +20%

Company	Product	Initial Year	Methods	Examples of Results
Farmitalia Carlo Erba (4000 employees)	Pharmaceuticals	1988	Flow manufacturing Pilot area Setup	Lead time: −30% WIP: −60% Productivity: +18% Setup: from 19 to 10 hours
Firestone Italy (1000 employees)	Tires	1988	Kanban Setup SPC Pilot area	WIP: −55% Setup: −45% Waste rework: −50%
Alu-Suisse (900 employees)	Plastics	1988	SPC	Productivity: +50% Quality in process: +21%
Lever Ind. (200 employees)	Detergents	1988	Flow manufacturing Setup Work organization	WIP: −50% Lead time: −50%
Gruppo Ind. Le Ercole Marelli (1000 employees)	Electric motors	1987	Flow manufacturing Work organization	Throughput time: from 12 to 2 days
Innocenti Sant'Eustachio (1400 employees)	Iron working equipment	1988	Flow manufacturing Work organization	Lead time for orders: −20% Design lead time: −20%
Sipe Nobel	Explosives	1988	Setup Planning	Finished products warehouse: −50% Raw materials warehouse: −50%

Source: Alberto Galgano & Associati.

Figure 17-2. Italian Examples

Company	Product	Initial Year	Methods	Examples of Results
Italora (150 employees)	Timers	1987	Flow manufacturing Setup Kanbans Self-certification	Setup: −90% Lead time: −90% WIP: −70% Quality: +30%
SAFTA (600 employees)	Flexible packaging	1987	Setup SPC	Setup: from 6 to 1.5 hours Process quality: +60%
BBB (350 employees)	Wool yarn	1988	Flow manufacturing Stockless production Pilot area	Lead time: −30% WIP: −30%
IREM (200 employees)	Electronics	1989	Flow manufacturing New planning system	Lead time: from 5 to 2 weeks
SCM International (350 employees)	Woodworking equipment	1987	Flow manufacturing Kanban Planning	Lead time: from 10 to 5 weeks
BELFE (420 employees)	Sports apparel	1988	Flow manufacturing Planning	Lead time: from 6 to 3 weeks
Europa Metalli (10,000 employees)	Non-ferrous metals	1984	SPC Quality Setup	Setup: −60% Quality: +4% in process productivity

Company	Product	Initial Year	Methods	Examples of Results
Arcotronics (1200 employees)	Condensers	1985	Intensive training JIT/TQC (TMM) Pilot areas Flow production Kanbans TPM	70% reduction in production lead time Lead time for confirming clients' orders: -66%
Agie (Switzerland) (1100 employees)	Electrical welding machinery	1984	JIT Flow production Group technology Setup Kanbans/Self-regulating units	Lead time: -80% WIP: -55% Productivity: +20%
Elettroconduttore (1000 employees)	Electrical components	1982	CWQC/JIT 15 secondary projects Flow production Group technology Comakers Quality circles	Defects: from 1% to 0.1% Total lead time: 3 days Factory lead time: 1 day Economical lot: from 10,000 to 30 items 30 partner-suppliers Production according to orders: no warehouse for finished products
Fiat Aviazione (5000 employees)	Components for aircraft engines	1988	JIT Pilot area Flow manufacturing Setup VCS Self-certification	(Objectives) Total lead time: -30% Production lead time: -70% Setup: -70%

Figure 17-2. (cont.)

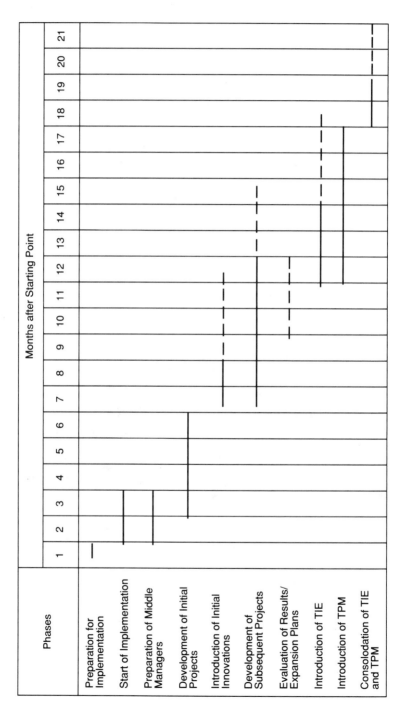

Figure 17-3. Schedule for Experimental Application of TMM Model

- Increasing of production flexibility (reduction of production lots and time required for production changeovers)
- Introduction of a production control system of the pull type
- Improved control of production processes and introduction of a mechanism to allow continuous improvement of production processes
- Restructuring of methods for designing and manufacturing products

The project requires direct mobilization of the structure of respective sectors (executives and, ultimately, operating personnel) at both the planning and implementation levels.

Phases in Developing the Program

The model program is structured according to 10 phases that follow one another in terms of logic and time. The Gantt diagram appearing in Figure 17-3 provides a summary.

About the Author

Giorgio Merli is a senior partner in Galgano & Associati, one of Italy's largest management consulting firms.

A Graduate Engineer with a Master's Degree in Manufacturing Management, Merli started his career in Philips, where he held several positions in the manufacturing area, including Industrial Manager. After working as Central Technical Director of an Italian company, he became a management consultant in 1978.

He has carried out several reorganizational projects in Italian and multinational companies and is particularly involved in the implementation of Total Quality and Just-in-Time strategies in Western companies. At present he is in charge of managing strategic programs for important companies, such as Fiat, Michelin, Alitalia, Ericsson, Unilever, Pirelli, Roche, Philips. He is also a consultant to the European Foundation for Quality Management (EFQM) and holds conferences and seminars in the USA.

Merli has published numerous articles and is the author of several books: *ICircoli della Qualita* (Edizioni Lavoro, 1985), *Il management nella cooperazione* (Edizioni Lavoro, 1986), *Total Manufacturing Management* (Productivity Press, 1990), and *Comakership* (Productivity Press, in press).

Bibliography

Abegglen James C. & Stalk George Jr, *Kaisha: The Japanese Corporation*, Basic Books, New York 1985.

Aggarwal Sumer C., "MRP, JIT, OPT, FMS?", in *Harvard Business Review*, September-October 1985.

APICS, *Proceedings*, Orlando Seminar, 1983.

APICS, *Presentations*, First World Congress of Production and Inventory Control, Vienna 1985.

ASQC, *I costi della qualita: definizione, controllo e riduzione*, ISEDI, Torino 1986.

Athos A. G. & Pascal R. T., *Le 7 S, ovvero l'arte giapponese di gestire con successo l'azienda*, Mondadori, Milano 1982.

Comai R., Merli G. & Studer A., *Il management nella cooperazione*, Edizioni Lavoro, Roma 1986.

Crosby Philip B., *Quality is Free: The Art of Making Certain*, McGraw-Hill, New York 1979.

De Vio Sergio, *Dagli Stati Uniti al Giappone: andata e ritorno*, ISEDI, Torino 1985.

Feigenbaum A. V., *Total Quality Control*, McGraw-Hill, New York 1982.

Fukuda Ryuji, *Managerial Engineering: Technique for Improving Quality and Productivity in the Workplace*, Productivity Press, Cambridge 1983.

Gay Sergio, *Flessibilita strategica dei sistemi di produzione*, Franco Angeli, Milano 1986.

Hall Robert W. & APICS, *Zero Inventories*, Dow Jones – Irwin, Homewood, Illinois 1983.

Imai Masaaki, *Kaizen*, Random House, New York 1986.

Ishikawa Kaoru, *Guida al controllo di qualita*, 3a ed., Franco Angeli, Milano 1986.

Jacobs Robert F., "The OPT Scheduling System: A Review of a New Production Scheduling System" in *Production and Inventory Management*, Volume 3, 1983.

Juran J. M., *Quality Control Handbook*, McGraw-Hill, New York 1974.

Marchisio Oscar & Mariucci Luigi, *Progetto Saturno: Una rivoluzione nel modo di produrre*, Costa & Nolan, Genova 1986.

Merli Giorgio, *I Circoli della Qualita*, Edizioni Lavoro, Roma 1985.

Merlino Massimo, editor, *La fabbrica competitiva: I processi gestionali*, ISEDI, Torino 1987.

Monden Yasuhiro, *Produzione just-in-time: Come si progetta e si realizza*, ISEDI, Torino 1987.

Naisbitt John, *Megatrends*, Warner Books, New York 1984.

Ohmae Kenichi, *The Mind of the Strategist: The Art of Japanese Business*, McGraw-Hill, New York 1982.

Orlicky Joseph, *Materials Requirements Planning*, McGraw-Hill, New York 1975.

Ouchi William G., *Theory "Z": How American Business Can Meet the Japanese Challenge*, Addison-Wesley, Reading, Mass 1985.

Peters T.J. & Waterman R. H., *In Search of Excellence*, Harper & Row, New York 1982.

Porter Michael E., *Competitive Advantage: Creating and Sustaining Superior Performance*, The Free Press, New York 1985.

Shingo Shigeo, *A Study of the Toyota Production System from an Industrial Engineering Viewpoint*, Revised Edition, Productivity Press, Cambridge 1989.

Schonberger Richard J., *Japanese Management Techniques*, The Free Press, New York 1983.

Vogel E. F., *Japan as Number 1: Lessons for America*, Harper & Row, New York 1979.

Index

Other Books on Manufacturing Improvement

JIT Factory Revolution
A Pictorial Guide to Factory Design of the Future
by Hiroyuki Hirano/JIT Management Library

Here is the first-ever encyclopedic picture book of JIT. With 240 pages of photos, cartoons, and diagrams, this unprecedented behind-the-scenes look at actual production and assembly plants shows you exactly how JIT looks and functions. It shows you how to set up each area of a JIT plant and provides hundreds of useful ideas you can implement. If you've made the crucial decision to run production using JIT and want to show your employees what it's all about, this book is a must. The photographs, from Japanese production and assembly plants, provide vivid depictions of what work is like in a JIT environment. And the text, simple and easy to read, makes all the essentials crystal clear.
ISBN 0-915299-44-5 / 227 pages / $49.95 / Order code JITFAC-BK

The Visual Factory
Building Participation Through Shared Information
by Michel Greif

If you're aware of the tremendous improvements achieved in productivity and quality as a result of employee involvement, then you'll appreciate the great value of creating a visual factory. This book shows how visual management can be used to make the factory a place where workers and supervisors freely communicate and take improvement action. It details how to develop meeting and communication areas, communicate work standards and instructions, use visual production controls such as kanban, and make goals and progress visible. Over 200 diagrams and photos illustrate the numerous visual techniques discussed.
ISBN 0-915299-67-4 / 256 pages / $49.95 / Order Code VFAC-BK

Achieving Total Quality Management
A Program for Action
by Michel Perigord

This is an outstanding book on total quality management (TQM) — a compact guide to the concepts, methods, and techniques involved in achieving total quality. It shows you how to make TQM a company-wide strategy, not just in technical areas, but in marketing and administration as well. Written in an accessible, instructive style by a top European quality expert, it is methodical, logical, and thorough. A historical outline and discussion of the quality-price relationship is followed by an investigation of the five quality imperatives (conformity, prevention, excellence, measurement, and responsibility). Major methods and tools for total quality are spelled out and implementation strategies are reviewed.
ISBN 0-915299-60-7 / 384 pages / $39.95 / Order Code ACHTQM- BK

Productivity Press, Inc., Dept. BK, P.O. Box 3007, Cambridge, MA 02140 1-800-274-9911

Introduction to TPM
Total Productive Maintenance
by Seiichi Nakajima

Total Productive Maintenance (TPM) combines the American practice of pre-ventive maintenance with the Japanese concepts of total quality control (TQC) and total employee involvement (TEI). The result is an innovative system for equipment maintenance that optimizes effectiveness, eliminates breakdowns, and promotes autonomous operator maintenance through day-to-day activities. This book summarizes the steps involved in TPM and provides case examples from several top Japanese plants.
ISBN 0-915299-23-2 / 149 pages / $39.95 / Order code ITPM-BK

Variety Reduction Program (VRP)
A Production Strategy for Product Diversification
by Toshio Suzue and Akira Kohdate

Here's the first book in English on a powerful way to increase manufacturing flexibility without increasing costs. How? By reducing the number of parts within each product type and by simplifying and standardizing parts between models. VRP is an integral feature of advanced manufacturing systems. This book is both an introduction to and a handbook for VRP implementation, featuring over 100 illus-trations, for top manufacturing executives, middle managers, and R&D personnel.
ISBN 0-915299-32-1 / 164 pages / $59.95 / Order code VRP-BK

Kanban and Just-In-Time at Toyota
Management Begins at the Workplace (rev.)
Japan Management Association (ed.), David J. Lu (translator)

Based on seminars developed by Taiichi Ohno and others at Toyota for their major suppliers, this book is the best practical introduction to Just-In-Time availa-ble. Now in a newly expanded edition, it explains every aspect of a "pull" system in clear and simple terms — the underlying rationale, how to set up the system and get everyone involved, and how to refine it once it's in place. A groundbreak-ing and essential tool for companies beginning JIT implementation.
ISBN 0-915299-48-8 / 224 pages / $36.50 / Order code KAN-BK

Canon Production System
Creative Involvement of the Total Workforce
Japan Management Association (ed.)

A fantastic success story! Canon set a goal to increase productivity by three percent per month — and achieved it! The first book-length case study to show how to combine the most effective Japanese management principles and quality improvement techniques into one overall strategy that improves every area of the company on a continual basis. Shows how the major QC tools are applied in a matrix management model.
ISBN 0-915299-06-2 / 251 pages / $36.95 / Order code CAN-BK

Productivity Press, Inc., Dept. BK, P.O. Box 3007, Cambridge, MA 02140 1-800-274-9911

20 Keys to Workplace Improvement

Iwao Kobayashi

This easy-to-read introduction to the "20 keys" system presents an integrated approach to assessing and improving your company's competitive level. The book focuses on systematic improvement through five levels of achievement in such primary areas as industrial housekeeping, small group activities, quick changeover techniques, equipment maintenance, and computerization. A scoring guide is included, along with information to help plan a strategy for your company's world class improvement effort.
ISBN 0-915299-61-5 / 264 pages / $34.95 / Order code 20KEYS-BK

Japanese Management Accounting
A World Class Approach to Profit Management

Yasuhiro Monden (ed.)

Just as the Japanese redefined manufacturing excellence, so they have transformed management accounting in world class companies. Here is a comprehensive overview of the Japanese approach to management accounting, especially helpful for companies that have adopted Just-In-Time manufacturing. More than thirty chapters discuss how to account for, and reduce, costs in every area of a company, from the plant and warehouse to design and planning. This unprecedented inside view reveals different strategic approaches to profit planning in Japan and shows how they can be adapted to American needs.
ISBN 0-915299-50-X / 568 pages / $59.95 / Order code JMACT-BK

The Eternal Venture Spirit
An Executive's Practical Philosophy

by Kazuma Tateisi

Like human health, organizational health depends on discovering the causes of symptoms that indicate an imbalance in the system. Tateisi, founder and CEO of Omron Industries, one of Japan's leading electronics companies, analyzes the signals of "big business disease" and how to respond to them so that technological innovation and entrepreneurial spirit can thrive as the organization grows and the market changes. An outstanding book on long-term strategic management.
ISBN 0-915299-55-0 / 208 pages / $19.95 / Order code EVS-BK

Productivity Newsletter

Productivity Newsletter has been helping America's most effective companies improve quality, lower costs, and increase their competitive power since 1979. Each monthly issue contains detailed case studies, articles on important innovations and world trends, book reviews, and much more. Subscribers save money on Productivity conferences and seminars. To subscribe, or for more information, call 1-800-888-6485. Please state order code "BA" when ordering.

Productivity Press, Inc., Dept. BK, P.O. Box 3007, Cambridge, MA 02140 1-800-274-9911

COMPLETE LIST OF TITLES FROM PRODUCTIVITY PRESS

Akao, Yoji (ed.). **Quality Function Deployment: Integrating Customer Requirements into Product Design**
ISBN 0-915299-41-0 / 1990 / 320 pages / $75.00 / order code QFD

Asaka, Tetsuichi and Kazuo Ozeki (eds.). **Handbook of Quality Tools: The Japanese Approach**
ISBN 0-915299-45-3 / 1990 / 336 pages / $59.95 / order code HQT

Belohlav, James A. **Championship Management: An Action Model for High Performance**
ISBN 0-915299-76-3 / 1990 / 272 pages / $29.95 / order code CHAMPS

Christopher, William F. **Productivity Measurement Handbook**
ISBN 0-915299-05-4 / 1985 / 680 pages / $137.95 / order code PMH

D'Egidio, Franco. **The Service Era: Leadership in a Global Environment**
ISBN 0- 915299-68-2 / 1990 / 194 pages / $29.95 / order code SERA

Ford, Henry. **Today and Tomorrow**
ISBN 0-915299-36-4 / 1988 / 286 pages / $24.95 / order code FORD

Fukuda, Ryuji. **CEDAC: A Tool for Continuous Systematic Improvement**
ISBN 0- 915299-26-7 / 1990 / 144 pages / $49.95 / order code CEDAC

Fukuda, Ryuji. **Managerial Engineering: Techniques for Improving Quality and Productivity in the Workplace** (rev.)
ISBN 0-915299-09-7 / 1986 / 208 pages / $39.95 / order code ME

Hatakeyama, Yoshio. **Manager Revolution! A Guide to Survival in Today's Changing Workplace**
ISBN 0-915299-10-0 / 1986 / 208 pages / $24.95 / order code MREV

Hirano, Hiroyuki. **JIT Factory Revolution: A Pictorial Guide to Factory Design of the Future**
ISBN 0-915299-44-5 / 1989 / 227 pages / $49.95 / order code JITFAC

Hirano, Hiroyuki. **JIT Implementation Manual: The Complete Guide to Just-In-Time Manufacturing**
ISBN 0-915299-66-6 / 1990 / 1000 + pages / $3500.00 / order code HIRANO

Horovitz, Jacques. **Winning Ways: Achieving Zero-Defect Service**
ISBN 0-915299-78-X / 1990 / 176 pages / $24.95 / order code WWAYS

Japan Human Relations Association (ed.). **The Idea Book: Improvement Through TEI (Total Employee Involvement)**
ISBN 0-915299-22-4 / 1988 / 232 pages / $49.95 / order code IDEA

Japan Human Relations Association (ed.). **The Service Industry Idea Book: Involvement in Retail and Office Improvement**
ISBN 0-915299-65-8 / 1990 / 272 pages / $49.95 / order code SIDEA

Japan Management Association (ed.). **Kanban and Just-In-Time at Toyota: Management Begins at the Workplace** (rev.), Translated by David J. Lu
ISBN 0-915299-48-8 / 1989 / 224 pages / $36.50 / order code KAN

Japan Management Association and Constance E. Dyer. **The Canon Production System: Creative Involvement of the Total Workforce**
ISBN 0-915299-06-2 / 1987 / 251 pages / $36.95 / order code CAN

Productivity Press, Inc., Dept. BK, P.O. Box 3007, Cambridge, MA 02140 1-800-274-9911

Jones, Karen (ed.). **The Best of TEI: Current Perspectives on Total Employee Involvement**
ISBN 0-915299-63-1 / 1989 / 502 pages / $175.00 / order code TEI

Karatsu, Hajime. **Tough Words For American Industry**
ISBN 0-915299-25-9 / 1988 / 178 pages / $24.95 / order code TOUGH

Karatsu, Hajime. **TQC Wisdom of Japan: Managing for Total Quality Control**, Translated by David J. Lu
ISBN 0-915299-18-6 / 1988 / 136 pages / $34.95 / order code WISD

Kobayashi, Iwao. **20 Keys to Workplace Improvement**
ISBN 0-915299-61-5 / 1990 / 264 pages / $34.95 / order code 20KEYS

Lu, David J. **Inside Corporate Japan: The Art of Fumble-Free Management**
ISBN 0-915299-16-X / 1987 / 278 pages / $24.95 / order code ICJ

Merli, Giorgio. **Total Manufacturing Management: Production Organization for the 1990s**
ISBN 0-915299-58-5 / 1990 / 224 pages / $39.95 / order code TMM

Mizuno, Shigeru (ed.). **Management for Quality Improvement: The 7 New QC Tools**
ISBN 0-915299-29-1 / 1988 / 324 pages / $59.95 / order code 7QC

Monden, Yasuhiro and Michiharu Sakurai (eds.). **Japanese Management Accounting: A World Class Approach to Profit Management**
ISBN 0-915299-50-X / 1990 / 568 pages / $59.95 / order code JMACT

Nachi-Fujikoshi (ed.). **Training for TPM: A Manufacturing Success Story**
ISBN 0-915299-34-8 / 1990 / 320 pages / $59.95 / order code CTPM

Nakajima, Seiichi. **Introduction to TPM: Total Productive Maintenance**
ISBN 0-915299-23-2 / 1988 / 149 pages / $39.95 / order code ITPM

Nakajima, Seiichi. **TPM Development Program: Implementing Total Productive Maintenance**
ISBN 0-915299-37-2 / 1989 / 428 pages / $85.00 / order code DTPM

Nikkan Kogyo Shimbun, Ltd./Factory Magazine (ed.). **Poka-yoke: Improving Product Quality by Preventing Defects**
ISBN 0-915299-31-3 / 1989 / 288 pages / $59.95 / order code IPOKA

Ohno, Taiichi. **Toyota Production System: Beyond Large-Scale Production**
ISBN 0-915299-14-3 / 1988 / 162 pages / $39.95 / order code OTPS

Ohno, Taiichi. **Workplace Management**
ISBN 0-915299-19-4 / 1988 / 165 pages / $34.95 / order code WPM

Ohno, Taiichi and Setsuo Mito. **Just-In-Time for Today and Tomorrow**
ISBN 0-915299-20-8 / 1988 / 208 pages / $34.95 / order code OMJIT

Perigord, Michel. **Achieving Total Quality Management: A Program for Action**
ISBN 0-915299-60-7 / 1991 / 384 pages / $39.95 / order code ACHTQM

Psarouthakis, John. **Better Makes Us Best**
ISBN 0-915299-56-9 / 1989 / 112 pages / $16.95 / order code BMUB

Robson, Ross (ed.). **The Quality and Productivity Equation: American Corporate Strategies for the 1990s**
ISBN 0-915299-71-2 / 1990 / 558 pages / $29.95 / order code QPE

Productivity Press, Inc., Dept. BK, P.O. Box 3007, Cambridge, MA 02140 1-800-274-9911

Shetty, Y.K and Vernon M. Buehler (eds.). **Competing Through Productivity and Quality**
ISBN 0-915299-43-7 / 1989 / 576 pages / $39.95 / order code COMP

Shingo, Shigeo. **Non-Stock Production: The Shingo System for Continuous Improvement**
ISBN 0-915299-30-5 / 1988 / 480 pages / $75.00 / order code NON

Shingo, Shigeo. **A Revolution In Manufacturing: The SMED System**, Translated by Andrew P. Dillon
ISBN 0-915299-03-8 / 1985 / 383 pages / $70.00 / order code SMED

Shingo, Shigeo. **The Sayings of Shigeo Shingo: Key Strategies for Plant Improvement**, Translated by Andrew P. Dillon
ISBN 0-915299-15-1 / 1987 / 208 pages / $39.95 / order code SAY

Shingo, Shigeo. **A Study of the Toyota Production System from an Industrial Engineering Viewpoint** (rev.)
ISBN 0-915299-17-8 / 1989 / 293 pages / $39.95 / order code STREV

Shingo, Shigeo. **Zero Quality Control: Source Inspection and the Poka-yoke System**, Translated by Andrew P. Dillon
ISBN 0-915299-07-0 / 1986 / 328 pages / $70.00 / order code ZQC

Shinohara, Isao (ed.). **New Production System: JIT Crossing Industry Boundaries**
ISBN 0-915299-21-6 / 1988 / 224 pages / $34.95 / order code NPS

Sugiyama, Tomo. **The Improvement Book: Creating the Problem-Free Workplace**
ISBN 0-915299-47-X / 1989 / 236 pages / $49.95 / order code IB

Suzue, Toshio and Akira Kohdate. **Variety Reduction Program (VRP): A Production Strategy for Product Diversification**
ISBN 0-915299-32-1 / 1990 / 164 pages / $59.95 / order code VRP

Tateisi, Kazuma. **The Eternal Venture Spirit: An Executive's Practical Philosophy**
ISBN 0-915299-55-0 / 1989 / 208 pages / $19.95 / order code EVS

AUDIO-VISUAL PROGRAMS

Japan Management Association. **Total Productive Maintenance: Maximizing Productivity and Quality**
ISBN 0-915299-46-1 / 167 slides / 1989 / $749.00 / order code STPM
ISBN 0-915299-49-6 / 2 videos / 1989 / $749.00 / order code VTPM

Shingo, Shigeo. **The SMED System**, Translated by Andrew P. Dillon
ISBN 0-915299-11-9 / 181 slides / 1986 / $749.00 / order code S5
ISBN 0-915299-27-5 / 2 videos / 1987 / $749.00 / order code V5

Shingo, Shigeo. **The Poka-yoke System**, Translated by Andrew P. Dillon
ISBN 0-915299-13-5 / 235 slides / 1987 / $749.00 / order code S6
ISBN 0-915299-28-3 / 2 videos / 1987 / $749.00 / order code V6

Productivity Press, Inc., Dept. BK, P.O. Box 3007, Cambridge, MA 02140 1-800-274-9911

TO ORDER: Write, phone, or fax Productivity Press, Dept. BK, P.O. Box 3007, Cambridge, MA 02140, phone 1-800-274-9911, fax 617-868-3524. Send check or charge to your credit card (American Express, Visa, MasterCard accepted).

U.S. ORDERS: Add $4 shipping for first book, $2 each additional for UPS surface delivery. CT residents add 8% and MA residents 5% sales tax.

INTERNATIONAL ORDERS: Write, phone, or fax for quote and indicate shipping method desired. Pre-payment in U.S. dollars must accompany your order (checks must be drawn on U.S. banks). When quote is returned with payment, your order will be shipped promptly by the method requested.

NOTE: Prices subject to change without notice.